Short-changed

Current books in Women's Studies

Accommodating Inequality Women and Housing
Sophie Watson

Basis of the Bargain Gender, Schooling and Jobs
Carol O'Donnell

Crossing Boundaries Feminisms & the Critique of Knowledges
Edited by Barbara Caine, E.A. Grosz & Marie de Lepervanche

Demanding Skill Women and Technical Education
Barbara Pocock

Female Crime The Construction of Women in Criminology
Ngaire Naffine

Feminist Challenges Social & Political Theory
Edited by Carole Pateman & Elizabeth Gross

Getting Equal Carol O'Donnell & Philippa Hall

Subordination Feminism & Social Theory
Claire Burton

Teaching Gender? Sex Education & Sexual Stereotypes
Tricia Szirom

Where it Hurts An Introduction to Sociology for Health Workers
Cherry Russell & Toni Schofield

Women, Social Science and Public Policy
Edited by Jacqueline Goodnow & Carole Pateman

Short-changed

Women and economic policies

Rhonda Sharp
and
Ray Broomhill

Sydney
Allen & Unwin
Wellington   London   Boston

© Rhonda Sharp and Ray Broomhill 1988
This book is copyright under the Berne Convention. No
reproduction without permission. All rights reserved.

First published in 1988
Allen & Unwin Australia Pty Ltd
An Unwin Hyman company
8 Napier Street, North Sydney NSW 2059 Australia

Allen & Unwin New Zealand Limited
60 Cambridge Terrace, Wellington, New Zealand

Unwin Hyman Limited
15-17 Broadwick Street, London W1V 1FP England

Unwin Hyman Inc
8 Winchester Place, Winchester, Mass 01890 USA

National Library of Australia
Cataloguing-in-Publication entry:
Sharp, Rhonda (1953-)
    Short-changed: women & economic policies.

    Bibliography.
    Includes index.
    ISBN 0 04 320219 5.

    1. Women – Australia – Economic conditions. 2. Women
    – Government policy – Australia. 3. Women – Employment
    – Australia. 4. Sex discrimination against women
    – Australia. 5. Australia – Social policy. 6. Australia
    – Economic policy. I. Broomhill, Ray, 1948– .
    II. Title.

305.4'2'0994

Library of Congress Catalog Card No: 88–71847

Set in 10/11pt Aster by Graphicraft Typesetters Ltd., Hong Kong
Printed by Kim Hup Lee Printing, Singapore

Contents

Tables vii
Acknowledgements viii
Introduction ix

PART I THEORETICAL PERSPECTIVES
1 Women and the capitalist state 3
   Feminist views of the state
   Neo-Marxist theories of the state
   Theories of the family and the welfare state
   Theories of the state and women's paid work
   Extending feminist theory
2 Women and economics 33
   Mainstream economic theory and policy
   Feminists and economics
   Towards a feminist critique
   The economics of the New Right

PART II CASE STUDIES
3 Women and the Hawke Labor government 61
   Labor's macroeconomic strategy
   Budgetary policy
   The Prices and Incomes Accord
   The social wage
   Labour market policy
   Trade and industry policy
   Lessons from the Labor government
4 Women and taxation 96
   Why taxation is an important issue for women
   Women and the Australian taxation system
   The taxation crisis and its impact on women
   Policy responses to the taxation crisis
   Tax reforms under Labor
   Feminist critiques
   A feminist taxation strategy
5 Women and superannuation 130
   Why superannuation is an important issue for
      women
   Women's unequal access to superannuation

        Why women do not join superannuation schemes
        How superannuation schemes discriminate against women members
        The role of the state
        The Hawke Labor government
        A feminist strategy on superannuation

PART III   CONCLUSION

6 From theory to strategy   161
    Expanding the progressive role of the state
    Challenging mainstream economics
    Towards an alternative economic strategy
    Implementing a feminist economic strategy

Notes   170
Bibliography   178
Subject index   189
Author index   196

Tables

3.1	Social wage outlays 1972/73–87/88	77
3.2	Social wage outlays as a percentage of total outlays 1972/73–87/88	78
4.1	Reform of the personal income tax rates 1986–87	116
4.2	Net gains and changes in disposable income for single-income earners from Labor's 1985 tax reforms	117
4.3	Tax reforms under Labor 1985–87	118
4.4	Tax paid as a percentage of pre-tax profits by 16 Australian companies 1987/88	121

Figures

3.1	The impact of devaluation on budgetary policy	93
4.1	Federal government tax mix 1986/87	103
4.2	Shares of personal and company taxes in total federal government taxation revenue	109

Acknowledgements

Although we have identified our sources of information and ideas throughout the book, we would like to acknowledge in a more general way the published work of the many Australian feminist writers whose intellectual labours have provided us with enormous inspiration in our own work. Writing this book has provided us with a greatly enhanced appreciation of the skill, discipline and political commitment involved in the difficult task of attempting to build a feminist strategy for change. While a complete list would be extremely lengthy, we feel particularly indebted to the following writers whose analyses have stimulated and clarified our thinking: Lois Bryson, Eva Cox, Ann Curthoys, Sara Dowse, Meredith Edwards, Barbara Pocock, Margaret Power, Elizabeth Savage, Sheila Shaver and Kim Windsor.

On a more personal note we would like to express our appreciation for the contribution of the following people. Sandra Ball, Lesley Dormer, Suzanne Franzway, Barbara Pocock, Elizabeth Savage, Ross Shanahan and Kim Windsor read and made valuable comments on various drafts of the book. Judy Barlow patiently and efficiently typed the manuscript and Jenny Taylor assisted with the index and proof reading. Catherine Baker skillfully edited the text and greatly improved its 'readability'. John Iremonger was a supportive and encouraging publisher. His occasional early morning phone calls also helped us meet our deadlines. Our friends provided us with much emotional and social support. The members of our blended family, Denise, Donna and Daniel, provided love and (mostly) tolerated our bizarre decision to spend the past 18 months upstairs in our study.

Finally, our employer, the South Australian College of Advanced Education, provided us with a period of 'professional experience leave', which was an invaluable contribution to the project.

Introduction

This book is intended to provide a framework and guide as to how women and men committed to a more sexually equal society might think about economic strategies for change.

The project began as an attempt to develop a feminist analysis of a wide range of economic issues affecting women in Australia. In retrospect, we were probably thinking along the lines of a book titled something like 'All the feminist arguments you need to win any economic debate'. Gradually, we found that in looking at any specific issue our attention was constantly being drawn back to two more general theoretical issues—the ambivalent role of the state in relation to women and the cast-iron grip that conservative economic theory seems to hold over every economic issue. It became clear to us that our 'activist's manual' had to provide a systematic critique of the theories of the state and economics themselves.

Consequently, the book has emerged in two parts. Firstly, we have developed theoretical analyses of the roles of the capitalist state and economics in relation to women's economic position. Here we have attempted to analyse the basic principles that influence the role of each. Secondly, we have applied these principles in the analyses of three case studies. In each of the case studies, therefore, we have tried to develop a feminist critique of current Australian economic policies that incorporates an understanding of the role of the capitalist state and economics.

Throughout the book, and more explicitly in the first chapter, we have raised questions about the role of the capitalist state, through its economic policies and strategies, in influencing the economic position of women in society. We explore the ways in which the state has historically reinforced the economic subordination of women and ask why the state should act in this way. We have also asked what role the state, through its economic policies, can play in women's struggle for equality.

Similarly, in Chapter 2, we have sought to raise broad questions about the role of mainstream economic theories and policies in influencing women's economic position. Economics has played an important part in reinforcing the subordinate position of women within capitalism. Our aim has been to demystify economics' role by showing that economists, their theories and their policies are often gender-blind, but not gender-neutral.

One of our main goals has been to try to extend feminist economic analysis beyond the issues that have traditionally been defined as 'women's concerns'. For this reason we have chosen case studies that are not usually associated specifically with women. The government's overall economic strategy is rarely seen as being of particular concern to women. However, in Chapter 3 we have tried to show that the macroeconomic strategy pursued by the Hawke Labor government has profoundly affected women. The government's conservative economic strategy has sometimes resulted in policies that have been against the economic interests of most women. An additional effect of this strategy is that Labor has been less able to introduce reforms in other areas of potential benefit to women. We argue that, in their own interests, women should not only oppose the Labor government's conservative strategy, but also support and be involved in the development of an alternative economic strategy based on more progressive state interventionist policies.

The two remaining case studies in Chapters 4 and 5 are also of issues that have not traditionally been seen as of particular concern for women. Under the Hawke government, however, taxation has become one of the few areas of broad economic policy debate in Australia in which women have been active participants. Superannuation, on the other hand, remains a policy area to which very few women give priority. In both these areas, the state's policies have not improved women's economic position. However, as part of a feminist strategy, there is scope for the state's policies to result in better economic outcomes for women.

Underpinning the entire book, of course, are assumptions about the existence and extent of sexual inequalities in Australia. We expect that, for most of our readers, the extent of the problem is well known. What they will be looking for are explanations of the situation and strategies to change it. However, some brief summary of what is known about the degree of sexual inequality in Australia seems appropriate here.

INCOME AND WEALTH DISTRIBUTION

The overall distribution of income between Australian men and women is extremely unequal. The 1986 Census revealed that 68 percent of adult men earned annual incomes of more than $9000, compared to only 36 percent of women. While 24 percent of men earned more than $22 000, only 6 percent of women did so. At the top end of the scale, 4 percent of men earned more than $40 000 compared to 0.4 percent of women. At the bottom end, however, 8 percent of men earned less than $2000, compared to 25 percent of women (Australian Bureau of Statistics Census Australia, 1986).

While overall economic inequalities are usually measured largely in terms of income distribution, the ownership of wealth is a more important indicator of inequality. The ownership of property and assets within a capitalist economic framework confers many economic advantages that are of greater importance than income. Wealth provides increased access to credit and the ability to generate greater income and wealth. Wealth also provides security, status and power.

Wealth in Australia is distributed even more unequally than income. While a major study of wealth distribution is yet to be carried out, the available research evidence overwhelmingly reveals a high level of inequality (Raskall, 1978, 1986 and 1987; Williams, 1983; Piggott, 1984; *Business Review Weekly* 14 August 1987). Overall, wealth is highly concentrated amongst a very small group. The top 5 percent of wealth holders own more assets than the bottom 90 percent of the population, (Raskall, 1978). In 1987, it was estimated that there were 32 000 millionaires in Australia. At the same time, two million Australians were living below the poverty line (Raskall, 1987:24). Very few women are represented in the lists of millionaires. For example, only two women appear as wealth owners in their own right in the *Business Review Weekly's* most recent annual list of the wealthiest 200 Australians (*Business Review Weekly* 14 August 1987). One of the few available studies of the comparative wealth ownership of men and women found that at no stage of their lives were women as a group likely to possess as much wealth as men (Raskall, 1978:9). Using estate-duty records for the year 1970, Phil Raskall concluded that, overall, twice as many men as women owned assets in excess of $15 000 (in 1970 money terms).

The extent of women's economic inequality is also reflected in their over-representation among the poor. Women and their dependent children comprise the majority of the two million Australians who live below the official (Henderson) poverty line. Between 1972–73 and 1981–82 the proportion of Australians living in poverty increased from 8 to 13 percent. At the same time, the proportion of children in poverty increased from 8 to 19 percent (Cass, 1986a:6). The household units most likely to be found in poverty are female-headed one-parent families and single (especially aged) women (Cass, 1985:80–2). Furthermore, women comprised almost 60 percent of social security pensioners and beneficiaries in June 1987 (Department of Social Security, 1987). The numbers of women in poverty have dramatically increased in recent decades, as separation and divorce have risen simultaneously with unemployment. Between 1972–73 and 1981–82, for example, the poverty rates for female-headed, single parent households increased from 38 to 50 percent (Cass, 1986a:7).

WOMEN'S POSITION IN THE LABOUR MARKET

Another major area of women's inequality in Australia is the paid labour market. Women now constitute 40 percent of the paid labour force. Almost 50 percent of all adult women are now in the workforce at any one time. The biggest increase has been among married women workers, whose workforce participation rate has risen progressively from 6.5 percent in 1947 to 48.6 percent in August 1987 (Eccles, 1984:81; Women's Bureau, 1987). Women are, therefore, by no means marginal to the labour market. They are a central and essential component.

However, within the paid labour force women continue to face severe inequalities and exploitation. In particular, they occupy jobs that tend to be highly concentrated in a narrow range of industries and occupations. In May 1986, 82.3 percent of all women workers in Australia were concentrated in just a few occupational groups—clerical, sales, service and professional (primarily nursing and teaching). Over 50 percent of all women workers were located in just two industry categories— wholesale/retail and community services (Women's Bureau, 1987). Within these areas they are systematically subjected to pay, status and working conditions that are inferior to those of men.

In spite of the formal introduction of equal pay for male and female workers, real wages remain considerably lower for women. In the November quarter of 1986, women workers' total full-time earnings amounted to only 78 percent of full-time male earnings. The total earnings for all women workers (including part-time employees) was 64 percent of all male workers (Women's Bureau, 1987). Furthermore, 20 percent of women employees did not receive any form of non-wage employment benefits. Only 7 percent of men employees failed to receive such benefits (Australian Bureau of Statistics, Employment Benefits Australia, August 1987). Superannuation is the third most widely received male employment benefit (after annual leave and sick leave). Only a quarter of women workers in August 1986 had occupation superannuation coverage, compared to half of men workers (see Chapter 5).

In February 1987, women comprised 80 percent of all part-time employees, and 40 percent of all women who worked were employed only part-time (Women's Bureau, 1987). While part-time and casual employment may be attractive to women with domestic and childcaring responsibilities, it almost invariably is accompanied by wages and working conditions that are substantially lower than those of full-time workers. An Australian Bureau of Statistics (ABS) survey of the conditions of part-time work in South Australia, taken in May 1985, reported that some 77 percent of part-time workers were 'casual' without the benefits of permanent employment (Sharp, 1987:37–8). Women also comprise the majority of home-based workers, or outworkers, who have particularly poor pay and working conditions. In 1985, it was estimated that there were up to 60 000 women outworkers in the textile, clothing and footwear industries in Australia (*Women at Work* March–May 1985).

In spite of quite dramatic increases in the numbers of women participating in the labour market, women also have higher rates of unemployment than men. Official figures for February 1987 reveal that 304 000 women were unemployed in Australia—an unemployment rate of 9.9 percent compared to 8.5 percent for men. According to the ABS, however, there were another 653 600 women who could be described as the 'hidden unemployed'. If these were included in the labour force statistics, the real unemployment rate for women would have been 26 percent compared to a real male unemployment rate (including hidden unemployment) of 12 percent (Women's Bureau, 1987).

WOMEN'S ECONOMIC POSITION IN THE HOME

In the household, women in Australia do not always have equal access to the family's economic resources. While wives play a more prominent role in the management of family finances, those finances are more often controlled by husbands than by wives. Women with low incomes or without their own earnings are in the most unequal position in the family because of their near total dependence on their husbands' incomes (Edwards, 1983:133). Furthermore, wives are less likely to have personal spending money other than housekeeping money. They are also less likely to know their partners' earnings and the value of items, other than family allowances, that increase family disposable income (Edwards, 1983; Brotherhood of St Laurence, 1985; Office of Status of Women, 1985).

Women's position in the family is also characterised by a division of labour and power that disadvantages them economically. Women's economic inequality in society, therefore, begins with unequal responsibilities for unpaid domestic work. Research on the relative contribution of husbands and wives to childcare and housework in Australia indicates that, despite minor changes since the 1940s and 1950s, women remain overwhelmingly responsible for these activities (Bryson, 1984:135). Moreover, while the nature of domestic work has changed, the amount of it undertaken by women has not declined (Game and Pringle, 1984:66–73). Clearly, the relatively high proportion of domestic work undertaken by women is a major barrier to their equal participation with men in the paid workforce.

WOMEN AND CLASS

Of course, gender inequalities are not the only determinants of women's economic position. Women's economic welfare is also profoundly influenced by their inferior economic position in the class structure in relation to men as a group. This is not to say that *all* individual women are economically inferior to *all* individual men.

Class also divides women. For example, 12 261 women in Australia were recorded as earning incomes in excess of $50 000 in the 1986 Census (ABS, Census Australia, 1986). Although these represent only 0.2 percent of all women, it must be recognised that their economic interests are clearly different from the 50 percent of women whose incomes were below $6000. Similarly, a recent survey of Australian company shareholders discovered that four in every ten individual shareholders are women (*Times On Sunday* 1 November 1987:17). As the survey pointed out, women are often only the nominal shareholders (since a husband often places stock in his wife's name to minimise income and capital gains taxes). However, these women are likely to perceive their economic interests in different class terms from other women. While the majority of women workers have low-paid, low-status jobs, there is a significant minority who hold professional, semi-professional and managerial positions. These women clearly occupy a different place in the class structure from other women and in many instances will be quite differently affected by government policies. A feminist analysis of economic inequalities must recognise these differences in women's economic positions.

In addition, it is important that a woman's class position is not assumed to be determined simply by her husband's position. One of the problems with traditional sociological analyses of class is that they invariably take the family as the basic unit of analysis. Consequently, a woman's class is to be determined by the male with whom she lives. As Hilda Scott has commented, 'The slippery downward slope that awaits the nominally middle-class woman when she loses her husband through separation or divorce is another side of the picture' (Scott, 1984:18). The 'middle-class' position of many women is, in fact, secured only by a toe-hold and is maintained only as long as their marriages remain intact.

CONCLUSION

Apart from this brief outline of the dimensions of women's economic inequality in Australia, this book does not seek to demonstrate further the existence of such inequalities. The argument we develop mostly assumes an acceptance by the reader of the existence of such inequality. In fact, it tends also to assume the reader's commitment to the desirability and need for radical changes to the existing distribution of power and economic resources between men and women. For this, of course, we make no apology. However, we have written the book in the hope that it will be read by both women and men and influence their thinking. We would like to think that the book might help to convince all politically progressive men and women that the struggle for socialism and the struggle for women's economic equality can and should be integral parts of a progressive strategy for change in Australia.

I

THEORETICAL PERSPECTIVES

1 Women and the capitalist state

From its beginnings the women's movement has been engaged in a relationship with the state. In a wide range of struggles, campaigns and engagements, feminists have attempted to use the various institutions that make up the state system in a capitalist society to achieve social changes and economic reforms to benefit women:

- First wave feminists struggled for the right of women to vote and participate equally in the political processes of the state.
- Modern feminists struggle for influence in political parties that aspire to govern the whole state apparatus in liberal democracies.
- Feminist reformers struggle within the state's bureaucracies for the introduction of progressive policies for women.
- Women trade unionists campaign for equal pay through the state's industrial and arbitration system.
- The women's movement generally has struggled for an enormous range of state-provided reforms—childcare, women's shelters, equal opportunities in employment and education, and many others.

There are, however, feminists who have consciously shunned the state as a potential agent of progressive change for women. Many of the most active radical feminist projects have sought to minimise their connections with the state and remain independent and self-sufficient. Rape crisis centres, women's shelters, health centres, bookshops and so on, have all been constructed by radical feminists utilising a strong anti-bureaucratic, anti-patriarchal state strategy.

In either case, theories about the state are implicit in the strategies being employed, but are rarely articulated. Consequently, the implications of using a particular theory of the state may not consciously be recognised by those involved in the political struggle for feminist goals. Certainly, recent feminist literature contains numerous comments on the lack of a formal theory about the relationship between the state's activities and the subordination of women (Randall, 1982:126; Franzway, 1986:46; Barrett, 1980:242; MacKinnon, 1983:644). Some feminist activists and writers may dismiss theoretical analysis as of only academic interest (Baldock and Cass, 1983:xi), but the development of a clear theoretical understanding of the role of the capitalist state in relation to women is of critical importance in developing political strategy. The central questions that a feminist theory of the state needs to address are these:

- What role does the state play in either causing, or at least maintaining, the subordinate position of women?
- To the extent that the state *does* participate in the subordination of women, for what reason and in whose interests does it act? In particular, does it act primarily as the agent of capitalism or patriarchy?
- Are there aspects of the state's policies and actions that have benefited women and reduced sexual inequalities? In what circumstances, and in what ways, can the state be utilised by feminists to improve the position of women?

By clarifying these questions it is possible to better understand how far progressive changes are possible through the agencies of the state. Political activity in the state arena can then be concentrated on those areas where changes are achievable. Changes that cannot be achieved or are unlikely to be achieved through state intervention need to be pursued using other strategies and means.

This chapter aims to analyse and extend existing feminist theories of the state—particularly in relation to the economic position of women. In any attempt to theorise about the role of the state there are certain problems. One of the major dangers is the tendency towards functionalism—whereby the theory becomes an all-embracing explanation for everything the state does. All general theories of the state, ranging from pluralist to Marxist, tend towards an analysis of the role of the state in terms of its functions for the wider society. Feminist theory is likely to explain the state purely in terms of its pursuit of goals that support patriarchy and/or capitalism. Such an approach may leave little room for the existence of contradictions and ambiguities in the state's behaviour, or for the role of political struggle to influence the end result. Therefore, a feminist theory of the state must consciously identify the complexities in the state's role. It also needs to be historical, and sensitive to changing circumstances rather than static. Above all, it needs to be informative and useful in guiding the day-to-day struggles of feminists and progressive organisations with the various agencies of the state.

FEMINIST VIEWS OF THE STATE

Although feminist political struggles have been underpinned by implicit assumptions about the role of the state, there has been very little formal discussion of these. Nevertheless, a fairly coherent picture can be drawn about the very different assumptions concerning the state that influence the political activities of various broad feminist groupings.[1]

LIBERAL FEMINISM

In their political strategy, liberal feminists have firmly embraced the state as potential agent for change. In choosing a reformist strategy based on an incrementalist approach to pursuing the rights of women, liberal feminists have assumed that the state is an arena within which interest groups can compete and succeed in having their demands met. While they acknowledge that in the past women have done very badly from the state, this failure is attributed to discrimination against women and women's failure, or inability, in a sexist society to achieve protection of their interests. Liberal feminists have assumed that the state is capable of, and likely to respond to, pressure to allocate resources to women. Application of pressure is likely to come both from organised women's groups and internal infiltration of the previously male-dominated state by individual women. So, although the state is seen as patriarchal up to the present, there is no structural, economic or biological obstacle to changing the role of the state once its present domination by men and male interests has been overcome.

Liberal feminists have in practice focused their strategy for change on achieving equal rights and opportunities for women. They have attempted to utilise the state to achieve this through a number of specific policy initiatives. These include:

- legislation to remove discrimination against women in society and particularly in the workplace
- attempts to place more individual women in positions of influence—in employment, politics and the state itself

- attempts to promote more individual women to higher paid, prestigious jobs
- attempts to change sexual stereotyping—especially in schools and in advertising

The term liberal feminist can be applied to a range of individuals and groups in Australia. One of the distinctive characteristics of feminism in Australia has been the degree to which feminists have occupied positions within the state itself, in areas nominally established to improve the position of women (Franzway, 1986). Many, but by no means all, of these 'femocrats' have held, or have adopted, a liberal feminist perspective on the role of the state. Some femocrats who held more radical views when they took up their positions have appeared to adopt a liberal feminist framework over time. Others who began with liberal assumptions appear to have moved closer to a socialist feminist view as a result of the experience (Dowse, 1984:159). Nevertheless, liberal feminism has certainly been the dominant ideological perspective to be found amongst women working in 'women's areas' in the bureaucracies of the Australian state.

The term liberal feminist can also be used to describe many of the women who belong to the mainstream political parties in Australia. Although the Australian Labor Party (ALP) is nominally a social democratic party committed in principle to socialist goals, in practice many of its policies and strategies are liberal ones aimed at achieving relatively minor reforms to the existing distribution of economic resources. Many women active in the dominant right-wing and centre-left factions of the ALP hold liberal feminist views of the role of the state. There are other liberal feminists in the centrist Democrat Party and to a lesser extent in the liberal-conservative Liberal Party. A number of the women's pressure groups in Australia in the past decades have adhered to a liberal feminist perspective. There have been only a handful of women academic economists in Australia—but a number of these have advocated policies for reform based on liberal feminist principles.

While liberal feminists have undoubtedly achieved gains for women, the theory of the role of the state behind their political approach is ultimately limited in its potential for achieving significant change. In the first place, the view of the state adopted by liberal feminists is essentially pluralist, presupposing a relatively open policy-making process. The pluralist view of power assumes that power is distributed fairly evenly over a wide range of groups in society and that no individual group or class dominates. Similarly, the state is seen as a relatively neutral organisation that arbitrates between the conflicting pressures from the various interest groups in society. However, a wide range of socialist and feminist analyses have clearly demonstrated that the state is not a neutral actor in this process (Wilson, 1977; Ferguson, 1984; Miliband, 1969). Historically, through its policies and activities, the state has played an important role in maintaining and reinforcing the inequality of women in the economy and in society generally. Above all, the pluralist assumptions of liberal feminists can result in a failure to recognise the influence of both capitalism and patriarchy on the state's behaviour towards women, or at least to underestimate that influence.

Secondly, as a result of their liberal assumptions, these feminists tend to rely on an individualistic approach to solving what are actually deeply-rooted structural inequalities. Such an approach is often perceived as elitist by other feminist activists who, for example, are inclined to be sceptical about policy decisions made on behalf of working-class women by middle-class femocrats. Radical feminists, in particular, have been scathing in their scepticism of the ability of individual feminist policy-makers to overcome existing sexist structures and processes (Ferguson, 1984:192). One of the major problems with the liberal feminist approach is that it seriously underestimates the forces that are opposed to equality for women. In particular, it fails to recognise the enormous hostility of some powerful men and the deep-rooted, though subtle, structural sexual bias in social institutions. It also fails to recognise and understand the constraints imposed by capitalism on the state's ability to achieve social and economic equality (Dale and Foster, 1986:174). Furthermore, liberal feminists tend to overestimate the power of the state to achieve changes in society. As a result, liberal feminists have focused almost exclusively on working for changes within the state arena itself. They have not directly challenged the powerful economic and patriarchal structures in society, which cannot be transformed simply by changes in government policies.

These criticisms do not necessarily lead to the conclusion that the liberal feminist approach is totally wrong or useless as a strategy. However, this approach is certainly seriously inadequate as a theory to explain the state's role in determining women's economic position, and its reformist policy goals are far too narrow to effect the changes required to alter significantly that position.

RADICAL FEMINISM

Radical feminists have on the whole firmly rejected the state as a potential agent for change. Radical feminism insists that sex is the fundamental division in society to which all other differences, such as social class or race, are merely secondary (Randall, 1982:5). In this view, virtually all societies are marked by an unequal division of labour in which male dominance is systematically institutionalised as a result of men's ability to exploit biological differences between the sexes. Key radical feminist theorists such as Shulamith Firestone and Kate Millett have, therefore, tended to link politics and the state fundamentally with patriarchy. The state is seen simply as one of the means by which men subordinate the interests of women to their own (Randall, 1982:127). Radical feminists tend to argue, therefore, that women should not look to the state in its present form to play any role in ending the subordination of women to male power (Leonard Barker, 1978; MacKinnon, 1983).

Within radical feminism there is a range of views about how separate the strategy of the women's movement should be from the state's institutions of male power. Some radical feminists have been prepared to work within the state's institutions for strategic reasons, but still maintain a profoundly critical attitude to its patriarchal nature. Some have been drawn reluctantly into a relationship with the state when their originally autonomous projects have floundered and become dependent upon state support for their survival (Dowse, 1984; Curthoys 1984:167–9). Many radical feminists have focused on the family as the primary source of oppression in society and have rejected that the state can have any role in a strategy for change, since it is another bastion of male domination. Others, however, view the state as a major source of male oppression and therefore a primary target for feminist struggle. For example, Kathy Ferguson argues that the domination of male-constructed bureaucracies in society is a primary source of the oppression of women (Ferguson, 1984:ix). Although writing as a radical feminist she describes her critique of the state as 'anarchist feminism' and advocates the destruction of the state apparatus itself (Ferguson, 1984:214). Similarly, Christine Delphy advocates that a prime feminist strategy should be directed towards overthrowing the patriarchal system by the 'seizure of political power over ourselves presently held by others' (Delphy, 1984:75).

Radical feminists have correctly argued that state policies

towards women overwhelmingly tend to reflect male interests. In other ways, however, this argument has not made a significant or systematic contribution to understanding the role of the state and public policy in a capitalist society. Radical feminism tends to see patriarchy as completely independent from the capitalist economic system within which it exists (Kronemann, 1981:220). As a result, radical feminist theory of the state is somewhat static and ahistorical, and makes little attempt to understand the relationship between patriarchy, capitalism and the state in a particular historical and social context (Barrett, 1980:38). Furthermore, by artificially separating sexual and economic issues, radical feminist theories avoid confronting the difficult issue of how the state is forced to attempt to reconcile the often contradictory pressures placed upon it by capitalism and patriarchy.

For radical feminism, the state is simply an agent of patriarchal oppression, with little or no room for any concept of conflict within the state apparatus. It is not seen as an arena in which some degree of struggle occurs between competing interest groups or between dominant and subordinant sexes and classes. Consequently, the radical feminist view of the state is somewhat functionalist and determinist, providing little insight into the complex and dialectical nature of the state's role.

Radical feminism can also be criticised for its lack (or rejection) of an adequate class analysis (Simms, 1981:237). The patriarchal oppression experienced by all women is seen to override all other forms of power relationships in society. There is no room, therefore, in the radical feminist view, to examine how the state relates to women of different classes and races (Phillips, 1987:Chapter 1).

Finally, radical feminist approaches to the state have tended to ignore the mechanics of the state's role in the oppression of women. The contribution of radical feminist theory to feminist theories of the state remains primarily its focus on the state's usual, but not totally consistent, role in maintaining policies that tend to support male domination and female subordination. It has not, however, provided a suitable framework for examining how and why the state plays this role. Neither does it indicate how this role relates to the state's other roles and how the interaction of these roles affects women.

SOCIALIST FEMINISM

Socialist feminists have shared some of the suspicion of the radical feminists towards the state, without embracing the separatist approach of that group. While at times being prepared to utilise the state as part of a women's strategy, socialist feminists have strongly emphasised the limitations of this approach (Simms, 1981:227–39). They have been careful, therefore, to distinguish between the short-term reforms for women that are possible within the framework of the state and the long-term strategies required to end the exploitation and subordination of women in society. Since the fundamental causes of women's oppression are located in the structures of patriarchy and capitalism, it is in these arenas that the key struggles must be fought. However, because the state is seen to play a role in maintaining the existing oppression of women it must inevitably be the target for feminist struggle.[2]

Socialist feminists have in practice struggled for a range of state policies and reforms that have not been the primary concerns of liberal feminists. These have included attempts to place on the political agenda issues such as childcare, equal pay, the breakdown of sexual labour-market segmentation and the incorporation of women into industry policy. Socialist feminists have attempted to develop a strategy that will benefit women collectively, rather than only a few individuals, and to focus on policies that will primarily benefit working class women instead of those who are already relatively well-off.

There is by no means universal agreement, however, among socialist feminists either on the nature of the state's role in women's oppression or on its corollary, the state's possible role in a progressive feminist strategy. A subtle but important distinction can be drawn between different strands of socialist feminist thought on the interaction between capitalism, patriarchy and the state in relation to women's position. Some socialist feminists, though critical of traditional Marxism's inadequate analysis of women's position, adopt its basic concept of the capitalist nature of the state (Wilson, 1977; McIntosh, 1978). In this view, the state has historically maintained the subordination of women because women's unequal position in the family and in the workforce has been in capital's interests (Power, 1983). It is assumed, however, that women's subordination will not always inevitably be in capital's interests. As capital's needs change, the state's policies towards women can also change. The state, therefore, can be vulnerable to pressure from feminists to introduce policies to benefit women, particularly when the interests of capital do not coincide with those of patriarchy.

Some socialist feminists tend to see women's subordination as the result of a partnership between capitalism and patriarchy—a dual system of oppression (Hartmann, 1981). In this view, the state acts consistently to reinforce women's inferior position as a result of the demands of both capitalism and patriarchy. While the two systems are perceived as relatively independent, historically they have evolved a form of working partnership that overwhelmingly influences the state's behaviour towards women. Although those supporting this view usually still argue in favour of feminist struggle in the state arena, they are inclined to be more pessimistic of the state's role in improving women's position. Attempts to change the role of the state can be expected to meet enormous resistance from capital and patriarchy.

In a third strand of socialist feminist thinking, the state is seen less as an agent of either capital or patriarchy and more as an arena where different forces struggle for influence (Barrett, 1980; Burton, 1985; Randall, 1982). Capital and patriarchy may still be the dominant influences, but the demands of each may not always easily be reconciled. In addition, the state is seen as having to accommodate demands upon it from other sources, including other classes and women themselves. In this view, therefore, while the state can still be expected basically to reflect the influence of the dominant class and sex, it is certainly an arena in which feminists can and should act.

In terms of political activism, the name socialist feminist may be applied to a wide range of individuals and groups in the Australian political scene. It includes, for example, some feminists whose formal political affiliation may be with the social democratic ALP but whose analysis of class and gender inequalities has led them to reject the narrow liberal reformism of the mainstream of that party. The long-term aim of this group is the transition to a socialist society. Their short-term goals, however, are based on the reconstruction of capitalism along more equal class and gender lines. Many femocrats are committed to similar goals, even though in practice they usually find that the structures within which they work frustrate the achievement of these goals. Other socialist feminists, while striving for the reform of class and gender inequalities within capitalism, have as their goal the more rapid achievement of a socialist society. Many feminists with these views have focused their political activism on the more progressive wing of the trade union movement.[3] A significant number of feminist academics also adopt a socialist feminist analysis in their work.

One of the strengths of socialist feminist thought about the state's role is that it has drawn upon a relatively sophisticated and coherent existing body of theory by non-feminist neo-Marxist writers. The weakness of Marxist theory from a feminist viewpoint has always been that it has not focused specifically on the crucial questions of how and why the state plays a role in the oppression of women. However, the reason neo-Marxism has been basically accepted as a starting point by many feminist writers (including some who are not Marxists) is that, unlike pluralist theory, it can be extended to accommodate a feminist analysis that is historical, dialectical and can link women's subordination to the economic system.

Unfortunately, there as yet exists no comprehensive feminist theory of the state based on the neo-Marxist framework. Very few socialist feminists have consciously sought to develop a theory of the state and women. Our own aim here, therefore, is to attempt to identify the main elements of a fairly embryonic feminist theory of the state developed intermittently by socialist feminist writers. As well as identifying the strengths and weaknesses of these diverse views of the role of the state, we attempt also to draw out the implications of incomplete analyses and to extend their framework of analysis where gaps exist.

NEO-MARXIST THEORIES OF THE STATE

First, it is important to identify the key elements of Marxist and neo-Marxist theories that have influenced socialist feminist attempts to construct a theory of the state.

The starting point of these theories is the historical perspective on the origins of the state developed in the writings of Marx. In Marx's works, the origins of the capitalist state are located in the struggle between the newly-emergent bourgeois class and the previously dominant feudal aristocracy. As the modern bourgeoisie gained economic ascendency over the former ruling class they also struggled for, and gained, political power. Hence the former autocratic feudal political structures, based on the hereditary and absolute rights of monarchy and nobility, were replaced by a political structure that reflected the new dominant power of the capitalist classes. Consequently, the establishment of the liberal-democratic state in Western capitalist countries was the product of the victory of the capitalist classes. While the new state structure usually took a democratic form that was structurally independent of the bourgeoisie, it was certainly not neutral or above class interests. In broad terms, Marx argued that it is through the state primarily that the capitalist class establishes and maintains its political dominance over the rest of society. In addition, the state ensures the level of political stability and economic development required for the efficient running of the capitalist economy.

Modern Marxist or socialist writers have said a great deal about the economic role of the capitalist state. Beginning from Marx's basic standpoint, they have refined and developed this theory in a number of directions. Above all, they have tried to identify the functions of the state in the wider society. For example, one the of the main protagonists of the debates about the capitalist state, Ralph Miliband, has portrayed the state as having four types of function—economic, repressive, ideological and international (Miliband, 1969). However, the main focus of Marxists, particularly those writing within a more functionalist framework, has been the state's critical and continuous role in assisting the process by which capital, or business, is able to operate and successfully make profits ('capital accumulation'). The activities by which the state does this are extensive. They include, at the broadest level, the state's general involvement in trying to stimulate or restrain the economy. More specifically, the state promotes an economic and social environment that minimises the costs of production for capital. This includes not only the provision of benefits and assistance to business through a range of measures such as subsidies, tariffs and social infrastructure, but also the implementation of policies to reduce the cost of labour power and maximise its availability.[4]

In the early 1970s a number of socialist feminist writers began to criticise the Marxist analysis of capitalism strongly for focusing on the production/accumulation process and ignoring the preconditions that made it possible. This critique was most explicitly outlined in a series of socialist feminist articles that comprise what is known as the domestic labour debate. Here it was argued in particular that women's domestic labour is a vitally important 'behind the scenes' precondition of capitalist production. It is integral both to the reproduction of the labour force and also to the reproduction of the class system and the ideological structures that sustain it.

While socialist feminists were seeking to expand the Marxist analysis of capitalism to include an understanding of the role of the family and domestic labour, at the same time a number of male neo-Marxist writers were producing radical reformulations of the theory of the state that opened the way for Marxism to accommodate the feminist critique. Although each used slightly different terminology—Louis Althusser ('social reproduction'), James O'Connor ('legitimation') and Ian Gough ('social consumption')—all argued that the capitalist state has developed a crucial role, not only in the process of capital accumulation but also in assisting the legitimation and reproduction of capitalism as a social system. A great number of the state's activities were identified as related to this role. For example, the state has taken upon itself the major responsibility for education. This was to produce workers not only with skills to suit the labour market but also with values that accepted the legitimacy of the existing form of property relations. The state has also intervened heavily in industrial relations, specifically in Australia through the development of a complex arbitration system. The state's goal here is to sort out conflicts between the classes in an orderly and manageable way—in a way that does not threaten the class system itself. Similarly, the state has developed an enormous welfare system that protects and nurtures those who are alienated from, or brutalised by, the economic system itself. The welfare state, in particular, was portrayed by these writers as a crucial weapon in the ideological struggle to gain legitimacy for capitalism as a moderately fair, equitable and humane system.

The strength of these neo-Marxist writings on the state from a feminist perspective is that, while they themselves have not done so explicitly, they do have the potential to include an analysis of the state's role in influencing women's unequal economic position. Neo-Marxism attempts to understand how the capitalist state assists both in capital accumulation and in the social reproduction of capitalism as a system. This provides a framework within which the relationship between women's economic subordination in the home and in the paid workforce can be understood. Socialist feminism has consistently drawn upon this framework, added to it and, to some extent, transformed it. Consequently, socialist feminists have potentially been in a much stronger position than either liberal or radical feminists to develop an adequate theory of the capitalist state's role in women's economic subordination and liberation.

Socialist feminist writers have tended to approach the role of the state indirectly rather than directly. For example, rather than analysing how the state oppresses or benefits women, Mary McIntosh poses the crucial question: What part does the state play in establishing and sustaining systems in which women are oppressed? (McIntosh, 1978:259) The two systems she identifies as crucial are the patriarchal family structure and the paid labour market. These two systems have, in fact, been the foci for the vast majority of all feminist analyses of women's economic inequality.

THEORIES OF THE FAMILY AND THE WELFARE STATE

Clearly, in modern capitalist society the state has developed a highly interventionist role in its relationship with the family. While the dominant conservative view might hold that the family is part of the private sector of people's lives and any role played by the government in this area is interference, the reality is that in a multitude of ways and for a variety of reasons the state's policies and actions affect the family—and women's role in particular.

The role played by the state, however, is a controversial and complex one. The New Right lays the blame for the decline of the family on state intervention. For example, state policies that provide assistance to single parents are seen to encourage the breakup of families. At the other extreme, radical feminists have argued that the central goal of the state's policies towards the family has always been the subordination of women for the benefit of men. Radical feminists, therefore, have stressed the role of the state in supporting and maintaining the patriarchal family structure. The reasons for the state's role have not been explored in detail but have been generally attributed to the patriarchal nature of the state and the domination of patriarchal ideology.

Similarly, socialist feminists have generally attempted to demonstrate that the consistent principle behind state intervention in the family has been the maintenance of the patriarchal family structure. However, whereas radical feminists have identified the state's motives as being the subordination of women for the benefit of men, socialist feminists have tended to interpret the state's goal as being primarily to maintain the family as a unit that serves the needs of capitalism. Within this general approach, of course, socialist feminist analyses have differed in the degree to which they have seen capital alone or a combination of the demands of capital and patriarchy as the dominant influence over the state's behaviour. Theorists have also disagreed as to how far the state's role simply maintains and reinforces women's subordinate position within the family. Some have seen the state's policies in relation to women and the family as somewhat ambivalent or even contradictory—aimed both at benefiting women and oppressing them, as a result of conflicting pressures on the state. These debates have been conducted in two main areas of feminist writing—those concerning domestic labour and the welfare state under capitalism.

Socialist feminists have written prolifically on the relationship between women's domestic role and the capitalist economy. Over 50 articles appeared on the topic between 1969 and 1979. However, few of those who participated in what came to be known as the domestic labour debate explicitly addressed the question of the role of the state (Buechler, 1984:23–4; Barrett, 1980:172–83). Nevertheless, the questions addressed influenced later attempts to develop a feminist theory of the state and therefore are worth canvassing briefly.

The domestic labour debate developed from feminists' critiques of Marxism's failure to acknowledge or analyse the important role played by women and domestic labour within capitalism. Participants were agreed that women's subordinate position in the family benefits capitalism. Furthermore, most agreed with the general proposition, later outlined by Elizabeth Wilson and Mary McIntosh, that in fulfilling the needs of capitalism the state generally has sought to maintain the patriarchal structure of the family (Wilson, 1977; McIntosh, 1978). However, there was serious disagreement concerning the associated question of whether the existing domestic role of women was constructed by capitalism itself or by patriarchy. Controversy also continued over whether the exploitation of women in the family is essential for capitalist production and reproduction or merely convenient. These questions have important implications for the role of the state. For example, if women's domestic subordination is essential to capitalism's economic functioning then presumably there is little chance that the capitalist state can ever play a positive role in breaking down inequality in the family. Unfortunately, questions about the nature of the state's role were not seriously addressed by these socialist feminist writers.

The domestic labour debate contributed a great deal to developing a more detailed analysis of the relationship between capitalism and the family. In particular, the debate focused attention on the importance of the relationship between women's domestic role and their subordinate position in the economy and in society. In the end though it became clear that the debate was too narrowly focused and inclined to a somewhat crude and functionalist approach. It provided little insight into the complexity of the issues. By and large, the interest in the role of the state shown by participants in the domestic labour debate was limited to the question of what functions does it perform for capital or patriarchy.

On the other hand, one of the areas of state activity in relation to women most explicitly analysed by feminists has been the welfare state. The obvious importance of the welfare state to women's position has focused feminist theorists' attention much more clearly on the question of the role of the state as a whole.

While liberal feminists have tended to perceive the welfare state as a purely progressive development for women, socialist feminists have stressed its important role in the production and reproduction of capitalist society. As the Australian feminist Lois Bryson stresses, the term welfare state is itself an ideological one and disguises the fact that any of the state's welfare activities can be seen as contributing both to capital accumulation and to reproduction of the system (Bryson, 1984:122–3). Elizabeth Wilson has argued that the development of the welfare state has represented nothing less than a comprehensive attempt by the state to organise domestic life in a way that maintains the family structure and women's dependency for the benefit of capitalism (Wilson, 1977:9).

One of the most developed theoretical socialist feminist analyses of the role of the welfare state has been provided by Mary McIntosh (McIntosh, 1978:254–89). She argues that the most fundamental way in which the state has intervened in the family sphere has been by seeking to maintain the dependent status of women. To the extent that the family has successfully fulfilled the needs of capitalism, the dependent role of women within the family structure has been seen by the state as desirable and has been actively supported by state policies. However, in many ways the family has proved to be both ill-suited and seriously inadequate to meet these needs. The welfare state emerged as a result of the failure of the patriarchal family to meet the severe demands placed upon it by advanced capitalism.

The breakdown of the family and its inadequacy to meet the economic tasks demanded of it have, therefore, required actions by the state that have sometimes cut across the goal of the preservation of the family structure and women's dependency upon men. In cases where the family structure has obviously proven inadequate, the state has attempted to help these families to behave more like normal ones. For example, the state assists single parents in the process of childrearing, which normally requires two parents. In other areas, however, the state has come to intervene far more directly and systematically in the process of social reproduction, in effect taking over these functions. For example, the state has taken almost total responsibility for the education of the young as well as financial support for those who are out of work. In other words, the state assumes that neither the economy nor the family is able to perform tasks adequately.

Mary McIntosh emphasises that while the role of the state is a complex one, its fundamental nature is capitalistic rather than patriarchal (McIntosh, 1978:260). Although the state operates in accord with prevailing assumptions about gender roles, it does not usually act with the sole purpose of subordinating women to men. Furthermore, since the state has had to take over the family's traditional roles in some areas, it has itself partially undermined the bases of the patriarchal system and helped improve the position of women.

Adherents to the dual systems school of socialist feminism, such as Heidi Hartmann and Zillah Eisenstein, suggest that the welfare state is constructed not just by the needs of capitalism, but under the influence of patriarchy and male needs as well (Hartmann, 1981; Eisenstein, 1979). Heidi Hartmann, for example, argued that men have a direct interest in maintaining the existing family structure regardless of its benefits to capitalism. Consequently, she portrays capitalism and patriarchy as powerful independent systems that are joined in a partnership—mutually benefiting from women's oppression. Heidi Hartmann's analysis is pessimistic about the potential role of the state. Clearly, the state's role is unlikely to be other than oppressive for women because of the dual pressures on the state from capitalism and patriarchy.

Other socialist feminists of the dual systems school have argued that the welfare system has served to lock women into a new form of dependency that continues to serve the interests of both capital and men. Carol Brown refers to this process as the substitution of public patriarchy for private patriarchy. The implications of this analysis are even more negative. A woman who succeeds in leaving an oppressive husband only to become dependent on state welfare is not freed of patriarchy—she has simply become 'less subject to private patriarchy and more subject to public patriarchy' (Brown, 1981:259). Her conclusion not surprisingly is that women should not expect liberation and equality to be pursued by the state. In fact, by struggling at all for an extension of the welfare role of the state women are helping to increase the scope of public patriarchy. Unlike some radical feminist analyses, however, socialist feminists who adopt this analysis do not completely reject the state as an arena for feminist political activity. Carol Brown concludes that in spite of the patriarchal nature of the welfare state 'there is no question that women must make demands on the public patriarchy' (Brown, 1981:262). To do otherwise would be to allow capitalism and patriarchy to force women into greater dependency on individual men.

Most theories that have stressed the domination of the state by capital or a partnership between capital and patriarchy tend towards functionalism. In contrast, a few socialist feminist writers have regarded the state's role as far more complex and ambiguous. In particular, Lois Bryson has argued that the overall effect of the state's policies and actions is clearly not entirely oppressive to women. In fact the state, through its family and welfare policies, both benefits women and reinforces their oppression. On the one hand, state welfare measures have afforded women opportunities to survive financially without having to be dependent upon a male breadwinner (Bryson, 1984:129). Sheila Shaver has argued that even though the social security system is constructed by a 'patriarchal logic', the net effect is a substantial transfer of spending power from men to women (Shaver, 1983:151). On the other hand, while offering a subsistence survival, welfare simultaneously locks women into a powerless and subordinate position.

This strand of socialist feminist thinking about the welfare state tends to understand the state not in terms of its functional role in meeting the needs of either capitalism or patriarchy but rather as an arena where various groups, including women themselves, strive for influence. A number of socialist feminist writers have recognised the importance of class and feminist struggles in the development of the welfare state (Beechey, 1977:60; Roe, 1976; Hicks et al., 1978; Land, 1975; Rose, 1978). Few, however, have pursued a detailed analysis of their impact.

These analyses imply the state's confused attitude towards women in relation to the family is due to its attempts to reconcile many different pressures. These pressures derive from the capitalist economy in general as well as from individual capitalists, from the patriarchal ideological and social systems, and from the organised demands of a range of other groups—including women themselves and the working class. Consequently, the subordination of women is not necessarily the primary aim of the state in the construction of its welfare policies, but rather the outcome of political processes. This view of the state as the mediator of many pressures is not to be confused with the pluralist view adopted by liberal feminists, which sees various interest groups competing more or less equally for the support of a class neutral state. What distinguishes this version of socialist feminism from liberal feminism is its insistence that the state is not neutral and the competing groups do not possess equal amounts of power. In particular, the fact that women wield so little power in the economy means that women's issues have only a toehold on the political agenda. Political and state structures are naturally dominated by the concerns of the powerful.

THEORIES OF THE STATE AND WOMEN'S PAID WORK

The paid labour market is the other major arena of women's inequality to be analysed by socialist feminist writers. On the one hand, women's lack of access to the labour market is commonly seen as one of the major contributors to their inferior economic position. On the other hand, even when women participate in the paid labour force, they experience inequalities and exploitation. In particular, women's jobs fall within a narrow range of industries and occupations where the pay, status and working conditions are inferior to men's occupations.

Feminist theory has grappled at length with complicated historical questions of why women have been marginalised from the mainstream of the paid workforce and why the labour market has been so segmented along sexual lines. The socialist feminist analysis has concentrated on identifying the activities of the state that have tended to reinforce women's inferior position. A number of analyses have also addressed the more complex question of why the state has pursued the role that it has. Overall, theoretical analyses in this area have again been predominantly functionalist. However, a few writers have sought to explore the role of the state within a more complex framework.

The state is perceived as contributing to women's disadvantaged position in three ways. Firstly, the state has pursued policies that have either reinforced women's dependent position in the home or locked them into dependency on state welfare (Barrett, 1980:231). From this position women have been restricted to an inferior and temporary role in the labour market—serving in effect as a 'reserve army' of labour for capital, to be called upon when required but expelled when not (Beechey, 1977:56; Barrett, 1980:158–60). For example, state welfare and taxation policies have discouraged women from becoming permanent members of the workforce (McIntosh, 1978:277).

Secondly, socialist feminists portrayed the state as pursuing policies that reinforce the existing sexual division of labour. For example, historically the state has determined and regulated terms and conditions of work in a way that has excluded women from areas of male employment. One key example is the development of protective legislation, ostensibly to protect women from dangerous work, but in reality to protect male jobs from cheaper female competition (Barrett, 1980:231; McIntosh, 1978:277). Similarly, the state's industrial arbitration system endorses male workers' definitions of skilled jobs—a system that has effectively excluded women from the better paid and more secure areas of employment (Barrett, 1980:158; McIntosh, 1978:233).

Thirdly, socialist feminists view the state as playing an important role historically in maintaining a discriminatory wage structure. The concept of the family wage for male workers, which emerged in the nineteenth century and dominated the wage structure until recently, was adopted and enforced by the state arbitration system. The family wage concept not only reinforced the assumption that every male worker had a dependent wife engaged in domestic labour but it also provided ideological justification for unequal pay for women workers (Hartmann, 1981:16; Power, 1983:71).

In explaining why the state has acted thus, many socialist feminist writers have emphasised the benefits that accrue to capital from women's subordination. Socialist feminist writers have stressed the strong link between the state's support for women's domestic position and their role in the workforce. The role of the state, Mary McIntosh argues, is intended at least in part to maintain women in a 'semi-proletarianized' position in the economy (McIntosh, 1978:276–7). The state's policies are geared towards maintaining married women in a position of economic dependence on their husbands and unmarried women in a position of dependence on the state itself. Because women are not fully dependent on their own wages, they can be persuaded to accept casual and low-paid employment and they can be drawn in and out of the workforce as the changing employment needs of capital dictate. The state, therefore, effectively acts on behalf of capital in assisting to establish and maintain women as a reserve army of labour.[5]

Others have argued that, contrary to the reserve army of labour theory, capital and the state have not consistently sought to maintain women in a marginalised labour market position. Lynda Yanz and David Smith have suggested that capital's natural tendency has been to seek to bring women into the labour force both because of their cheaper wages and also in order to deskill male areas of employment (Yanz and Smith, 1983). They argue that the outstanding feature of women's work in the past 40 years has been the dramatic increase in their workforce participation rates. The increasing integration of women into wage labour has fundamentally changed all aspects of women's labour force position, including their competitiveness, availability and cheapness as a reserve army of labour. Marilyn Power has similarly argued that capitalism has gradually incorporated women into an active labour force and the state has supported this transition, assuming more of women's traditional functions of social reproduction—education, childcare, care of the aged, and so on (Power, 1983).

Another interpretation of the role of the state is provided by socialist feminists who emphasise the dual labour role of women. Nancy Holmstrom has suggested that capital stands to profit most when women are able to participate fully in the labour market while still maintaining their domestic role (Holmstrom, 1981). While some socialist feminists have seen this as a contradiction between capitalism's different demands from women, Nancy Holmstrom argues that capitalism has a strong economic interest in finding ways of maintaining both roles for women.

Unfortunately, socialist feminists who have embraced the dual labour theory have not speculated on its implications for the role of the state (Buechler, 1984:25). Nevertheless, the dual labour theory clearly implies that the state's role has been to pursue policies that assist women in both areas—a somewhat complicated role to say the least. In practice, of course, many writers have observed that the state has rarely acted consistently in this area. State policies tend to be a confused mixture aimed on the one hand at maintaining women in the home (such as the dependent spouse taxation rebate), and on the other at facilitating women's participation in the workforce (such as the increasing provision of state childcare services).

The socialist feminist theories of the state's role in relation to women in the workforce that have been discussed so far have all concluded that both women's position and the state's role are fundamentally determined by the needs of capital. Other socialist feminists, however, although agreeing that the state has been an important agent in women's oppression, have stressed the profound influence of patriarchy. These writers have portrayed capitalism and patriarchy as engaged in an 'unhappy marriage', of which the offspring has been women's subordinate labour market position. They have focused on two major pressures deriving from patriarchy that have reinforced the similar pressures from capital for the state to maintain women's subordinate workforce role. These are, firstly, the restricting influence of women's domestic responsibilities within the patriarchal family structure and, secondly, the key role of sexism and patriarchial ideology within male-dominated trade unions (Barrett, 1980:152).

In the most influential statement of the theory of the partnership between capitalism and patriarchy, Heidi Hartmann argued that male demands for services in the home ensure that women's freedom to seek paid labour will be limited (Hartmann, 1981). Thus, even though women's restriction to both the home and the secondary labour market can be perceived as benefiting capital, a key determinant is still patriarchal relations in the home. The inferior position of women in the paid workforce should therefore be seen partly as a manifestation of patriarchy.

A number of socialist feminists have also argued that male-dominated trade unions have been a key factor in influencing the behaviour of the state. However, while most agree that historically trade unions were engaged in constructing a definition of skill that excluded women from certain areas of the workforce, there is disagreement about whether this was conducted by the working class as a whole or simply by male workers. Jane Humphries has argued that it was the working class as a whole that struggled to prevent employers using cheap female labour to deskill work and undermine the wages of skilled workers. In her view, the family was defended by all the working class, including women, on the grounds that it provided a degree of self-sufficiency and a refuge from capitalist exploitation (Humphries, 1977).

Heidi Hartmann, however, contended that in resisting capital's attempts at deskilling and undercutting male wages with female labour, male workers had the choice of including (through unionisation) or excluding women workers. Instead of fighting for equal wages for men and women, unions generally chose to exclude women from skilled work and seek a family wage for male workers. The concept of a family wage for men implied at least an acceptance of lower wages for women. The family wage was supported by male workers, unions, management and the state. Hartmann argued that the motivating force behind the struggle by male workers and unions for the sexual division of labour was not simply to defend their skills, but, even more important, to maintain male domination in the working class family. The sexual division of labour and the family wage were accepted by capital because they also benefited its needs—particularly by reinforcing the family's role in social reproduction and maintaining women's role as a reserve army of labour. Hartmann argued, therefore, that the adoption of the family wage by the state effectively cemented the partnership between capitalism and patriarchy in the late nineteenth century. She also argued that the sexual division of labour and wage differentials were further cemented by the state's involvement both in enacting so-called protective legislation, which actually excluded women from certain key areas of work, and in establishing separate wage structures for males and females.

Heidi Hartmann's argument about the key role of male worker sexism in the development and maintenance of the sexual division of labour and the role of the state has greatly influenced socialist feminist writers (Barrett, 1980:152). However, a number of other recent socialist feminist writers have extended the somewhat functionalist analysis of the partnership of capitalism and patriarchy thesis (Burton, 1985:104–11; Dale and Foster, 1986; Franzway, 1986; Dowse, 1984). Michele Barrett has argued that although the sexual division of labour is both disastrous for women and beneficial to capital and men, it is false to conclude that it is created by capitalism and patriarchy and reinforced by the state in a simple functionalist way. She believes that the situation is more complex than this. The existing sexual division of labour has been constructed historically in a long and uneven process that involved struggles between capital and workers on the one hand and between male and female workers on the other. The state's involvement has been an important aspect of this process, but it cannot be characterised as simply serving the interests of either capital or patriarchy (Barrett, 1980:165).

EXTENDING FEMINIST THEORY

An attempt has been made in this chapter to draw together the different strands of socialist feminist theoretical writings and to show that they constitute a much more comprehensive analysis of the role of the state and women than many commentators have recognised.[6] Nevertheless, it is clear that a complete theory is still required. Our aim here is to pinpoint the main areas of weakness and to suggest a few directions in which the theory needs to be developed. The main inadequacies of the existing theory are in two areas:

- Socialist feminist analyses of the role of the state in relation to women have dealt with only a very limited range of the state's economic activities that actually affect women. Similarly, they focus on the state's activities that have served to maintain women's subordination with little attention to those state interventions that have benefited women.
- Most socialist feminist analyses have sought to understand the causes of the state's behaviour towards women in a fairly narrow functionalist framework. They have consequently been strong on analysing the pressures on the state from capital and patriarchy to reinforce women's subordination but weak on analysing other pressures that affect the state's behaviour and how the state responds to these pressures in reality.

EXTENDING THE ANALYSIS OF THE STATE'S ROLE

In the first place, socialist feminist analyses of the role of the state have been primarily limited to state activities that have directly related to women's role in the home and in the workplace. These areas of state intervention are obviously of crucial concern to women, but the actions of the state in a wide range of other areas also profoundly affect the economic position of women. The limited focus of theoretical analyses has most likely been partially responsible for the rather restricted framework within which the organised feminist movement has sought to influence the behaviour of the state. Overwhelmingly, feminist struggles over state policies have been directed to the welfare area and to state labour market policies.

In advanced capitalist societies the state plays a very significant role in the distribution of incomes and resources. The state welfare system and the state's role in regulating the labour market are of course, two key ways in which the state's intervention affects women. However, the state's interventions in many other areas are also profoundly important. Firstly, income available to individuals and families is determined not only through the wage and welfare systems but increasingly through the government's fiscal (or budgetary) and monetary policies as well. Taxation policies obviously are of importance in determining final take-home wages and affect women either through their own wages, their partners', or both. Just as importantly, the taxation system plays a key role in the redistribution of incomes in society through the extensive system of allowances and benefits that are transferred through the process referred to as fiscal welfare (Titmuss, 1958; Keens and Cass, 1982:1).

A further and increasingly important area of state intervention is the system of transfers and benefits associated with, but additional to, remuneration from paid employment. Such nonmonetary fringe benefits, referred to by Richard Titmuss as 'occupational welfare', constitutes a major form of state welfare available by and large only to privileged male workers and members of the capitalist elite. Because of their overall inferior position within the labour market, few women have benefited equally from these workforce fringe benefits. The state has actively supported and subsidised a range of occupational welfare measures. The most significant example of such a policy has been the state's provision of, support for, and subsidisation through the taxation system of occupational superannuation.

In a major study of gender and class biases in Australian tax policy, Carol Keens and Bettina Cass concluded that fiscal welfare and occupational welfare provided by the state reinforced and augmented the position of the privileged. They also argued that these activities of the state effectively negated and even reversed the direction of the redistribution provided by social welfare towards women (Keens and Cass, 1982:1).

Similarly, budgetary expenditures affect women not only because they are the primary recipients of social welfare services but also because of what has been termed the social wage components of government expenditure programmes. These include privately provided goods and services that are subsidised by the state, such as housing and health, as well as services provided directly by the state, such as education, communications and public transportation. In addition, the state has a significant effect on the economic position of women by regulating key areas of the capitalist economy that have a significant impact on consumption. For example, state policies on bank interest rates can dramatically affect a family's or individual woman's housing situation by determining their ability to get credit.

Even more broadly, however, government macroeconomic strategies affect the economic position of women by influencing general patterns of economic development and distribution of incomes. For example, a non-interventionist approach to the operation of the free market is more likely to produce a pattern of development and distribution that leaves women worse off than would a more interventionist approach. A critical point to recognise here, however, is the class-based nature of the state's fiscal and general economic policies. The government's policies certainly do not impact equally on all women. The implementation of different economic policies will affect women in different class positions in very unequal ways.

The relationship between class and gender inequalities
It is interesting to note that while government economic policies affect women in different class positions in very unequal ways this is an area rarely analysed by feminist writers. We suggest that this is because it raises the complex issue of the relationship between sexual inequality and class inequality. While most socialist feminist writers at least acknowledge the importance of combining a class analysis with a feminist analysis, in practice there has been a tendency to develop analyses only of those economic issues that either affect women as women in a fairly uniform way (for example, the dependent spouse rebate), or that affect only a specific group of women (for example, welfare policies). However, analysis of general economic policies by the state, such as the pattern of government budget expenditures and taxes, raises the question of the very different impact of such policies on women in different classes and class positions. Of course there is an element of truth in the argument that women actually form a separate class in the sense that, for many, their class position in society is held only by a toehold, maintained only so long as their marriage exists. Nevertheless, so long as women do maintain different class positions, whether indirectly through their dependency on a male, or directly through their own economic activities, they will be affected differently by state economic policies. Any feminist analysis of the economic role of the state in relation to women must acknowledge and incorporate this reality.

The complexity of the state's role
Socialist feminist theoretical analyses of the state have focused almost exclusively on the state's role in maintaining women's subordinate position. As Ann Curthoys has commented, the fundamental question of most socialist feminist analyses has been how is women's oppression functional to capitalism? (Curthoys, 1984:170). Analyses of the role of patriarchy in influencing the role of the state have focused almost totally on those activities of the state that are intended to maintain women's oppression.

An adequate theory of the state's role simply cannot be constructed on the basis of an incomplete caricature of the empirical reality. Many socialist feminist writers have in fact acknowledged that the state can play, and has played, an important role in improving women's economic position in society (Barrett, 1980; Dowse, 1984:142-4). Certainly, socialist feminist political struggles are clearly based on the assumption that the state can play a progressive role in relation to women. In Australia socialist feminist and other feminists have been at the forefront of campaigns to defend and extend the public sector on the grounds that they believe that the public sector can benefit women. However, the positive side of the state's role in relation to women has not been adequately theorised by socialist feminists. The consequences of this failure are to be found not only in an inadequate theory but in a less coherent political strategy.

THE STATE AS AN ARENA OF CONFLICT

As we have seen, socialist feminist theories of the state have followed three distinct strands of thinking concerning the causes of the state's policies towards women. These have contended respectively that the state's role is:

- determined fundamentally by the needs of capital;
- determined by the common needs of capitalism and patriarchy;
- relatively autonomous—in the sense that the state's policies are determined by a political process in which a range of groups and classes (including capital, men, the working class and women) compete to have their needs fulfilled by the state.

Clearly these three strands overlap and elements of more than one strand can sometimes be detected in the writing of individual theorists.[7] Nevertheless, most socialist feminists theories are inclined to one or other of these three strands and most analyses of the role of the state are firmly located within the first two.

The first two are clearly based on a functionalist approach to understanding the causes of the state's behaviour. The strength of these theories is their analysis of the ways in which capital as a class and patriarchy as an ideology and a social system place demands on the state. Their weakness is their failure to identify and analyse other pressures that affect the state and the degree to which the state's behaviour reflects those other pressures. In particular, neither strand of functionalist theory is able to explain why the state at times pursues policies that are progressive for women.

Rather than seeing state economic policies towards women as deliberately constructed to serve the economic needs of capital or men, the state is best seen as an arena of struggle producing outcomes that represent an accommodation to the existing balance of power between different interest groups. Of course, given that the balance of power in capitalism has historically been overwhelmingly in favour of capital over other classes and of men over women, it is hardly surprising that the interests of capital and patriarchy have generally dominated the policies of the state. However, although state policies are naturally dominated by the powerful, they must also be seen as the products of a process that includes a number of modifying elements. These elements include:

- the contradictions in the demands of capital and patriarchy themselves;
- the conflicts and political struggles that occur over competing demands from other classes and from women;
- the effects of the policy process itself, by which competing needs and demands are refracted, mediated and translated into actual policies.

In the first place, contradictions exist both within and between the demands made by capitalism and patriarchy on the state in relation to women. These contradictions in themselves make it impossible for the state to respond to these demands in a simple, functionalist way. The relationship between capital and patriarchy is one of conflict and accommodation rather than simple functional compatibility. The state cannot always neatly reconcile the conflicting demands of the two. As Sheila Rowbotham has observed, capitalism has historically tended to whittle away at the economic and ideological basis of patriarchy (Rowbotham, 1973:119). Similarly, as Mary McIntosh has argued, the structures of patriarchy, particularly the patriarchal family inherited by capitalism from feudalism, have not always been the most efficient ones to meet the dynamic and changing economic needs of capital (McIntosh, 1978:284). The state has often found itself caught in the middle of this conflict. While feminist theorists have understandably tied themselves up in knots trying to identify which of these forces has predominated in determining state policies, perhaps it is simply not possible to resolve this question absolutely at a theoretical level.

Secondly, the fundamental tendency of the capitalist state to act in the interests of both the dominant class and patriarchy is further modified by the degree to which the state itself becomes an arena of class conflict and feminist struggle. Socialist feminists have frequently acknowledged the importance of taking account of the role of class conflict in influencing both the position of women and the role of the state. However, there have been few attempts to incorporate an analysis of the role of women's own political activities on the state's policies—either through the feminist movement or through other organisations such as trade unions. The state, which traditionally has acted to maintain women's inferior position, has also at times acted in a way that has improved women's economic position. It is responsive not only to the demands of capital and patriarchy but also to struggles by women workers, feminists and those trade unions that have attempted to represent the interests of women workers.

Thirdly, a further major qualification to the functionalist theory of the role of the state is the extent to which the system's needs are mediated while being converted into policies. In the first place, as Suzanne Franzway has pointed out, knowing that the state defines its role in terms of meeting certain economic functions does not tell us whether it actually succeeds in fulfilling this role (Franzway, 1986:46). Its success may depend on a range of variable political factors, which may include the strength and cohesion of the dominant classes in a particular society; the degree of government centralisation; and the accepted boundaries within which the state is able to operate legitimately (Randall, 1982:128–36).

The needs of capital are also mediated by the extent to which the state itself participates in the political struggles that occur over policy. Joni Lovenduski, for example, in a major comparative study of women and public policies in Europe, portrays the state as an important actor in the arena of conflict, with its own clearly identifiable interests (Lovenduski, 1986:245–96). Vicki Randall takes the view that every state has certain interests of its own separable from, or at least not reducible to, the interests of any dominant social category. Those who achieve positions of influence in the hierarchy of the state will find themselves inevitably constrained by the need to reconcile the interests of the state with the demands of external powerful groups (Randall, 1982:129).

In the process by which the state translates external demands into policies, one of the key factors influencing the final outcome is the structure of the state institutions themselves. The state is a highly complex set of institutions, often seen to be pursuing different goals. For example, the government of the day can sometimes find that its policy goals are not necessarily those of its public service hierarchy. A crucial aspect of the state's internal structures that must invariably influence the state's policies towards women is the extent of male domination of the policymaking process. Since men dominate in not only the hierarchy of the state apparatus but also the class organisations and interest groups that seek to influence the state, policymaking becomes, in effect, a process of accommodation between dominant and subordinate men. This is a process from which historically women have been largely excluded. This exclusion is not an inevitable aspect of the state's nature. The experiences of femocrats who have recently penetrated the internal structures of the bureaucracy have illustrated both the possibility that the state's policies can be influenced in a more progressive direction for women as well as the enormous difficulties involved in doing so (Dowse, 1984; Franzway, 1986; Summers, 1986).

Another factor influencing the final determination of the state's policies and actions is the role of ideology. Feminists have consistently recognised and developed an analysis of patriarchal ideology's powerful influence over the state. For example, Michele Barrett has argued that the state has unquestioningly accepted the ideology of women's subordinate role and dependency in society. In particular, she points to the assumptions of female dependency deeply imbedded in the state's regulations regarding welfare payments (the cohabitation rule), the taxation system (the dependent spouse rebate) and the concept of the family wage, which assumed that every working male has a dependent wife to support (Barrett, 1980:229-30). Even when bureaucrats and politicians apply policies that they assume to be gender neutral, upon close analysis these can often be shown to be based upon patriarchal assumptions.

However, feminist analyses have been less inclined to recognise the ways in which the ideology underlying orthodox economic theories have profoundly affected the state's policies towards women. Feminists have begun to confront this important conservative force as a result of their recognition of the need to counter the repressive effects of New Right economic policies. However, New Right policies are only the most extreme expression of a set of ideas and assumptions about the role of the state that they share with mainstream orthodox economic theory. The ideological influence of mainstream economic theory upon the economic policies of the state plays an important but little recognised role in reinforcing women's subordination. This influence is analysed in greater detail in the following chapter. Equally, alternative economic theories can play a critical role in the struggle by feminists to use the state in a strategy for achieving economic equality for women.

In summary, none of the existing feminist theories of the state appears entirely satisfactory. In particular, they are limited in their ability to provide an adequate basis for developing strategies for change that incorporate the state. The liberal feminist view tends to be somewhat naive concerning the power structure within which the state operates. As a result, the strategy adopted by liberal feminists is inclined to be individualistic and hence inadequate to effect the major structural changes required. The radical feminist view, on the other hand, tends to focus on the patriarchal nature of the state. Radical feminists, therefore, are inclined to unduly neglect the state as an important arena of struggle for change. The socialist feminist view of the state has likewise focused on its oppressive role. Their analysis, however, has often presented the role of the state in a more complex way. This has encouraged socialist feminists, at the very least, to struggle to prevent the state actively pursuing the conservative interests of capital and men. To some extent also this view has resulted in some socialist feminists viewing the state as an arena in which progressive changes can be achieved by means of organised pressure and struggle.

Nevertheless, while socialist feminist theories have undoubtedly contributed much to our understanding of the role of the state in relation to women's economic position, they certainly need further development. Our aim in the remainder of this study is to attempt to understand in more detail the complexities of the state's role and to draw conclusions about the ways that the state can be incorporated in a feminist strategy for change.

2 Women and economics

Mainstream economic theories have had very little to say explicitly about women. In this sense, the discipline of economics has been gender blind. However, economic theory has not been gender neutral. The theories of economics have been used by the state to develop and to justify policies that serve to reinforce and exacerbate women's economic inequality within capitalist society. At the same time, the gender and class bias of economic theory itself has often limited the state's own ability to pursue policies likely to improve the economic position of women. Consequently, mainstream economic theory, and the policies derived from it, have historically been active agents in women's economic subordination.

A substantial body of feminist research in Australia and overseas has identified the ways in which economic theory and policy has contributed to reinforcing women's oppression (for example, see Amsden, 1980; Edwards, 1983; Phillips, 1983; Power et al., 1984; Savage, 1984). However, a feminist analysis of mainstream economic theory and policy needs also to understand and clarify why this has been the case and to ask to what extent feminists and progressive economists can work within the existing frameworks to develop policies more likely to promote women's equality. Furthermore, to what extent do feminists need to seek alternative frameworks of economic analysis to challenge existing sexual inequalities?

MAINSTREAM ECONOMIC THEORY AND POLICY

Mainstream economic policies have their basis in neo–classical economic theory. Neo–classical economics is a generalised term for several strands of theory which are distinguished by a common methodology and shared assumptions. The model emerged in the latter part of the nineteenth century as a reconstructed version of Adam Smith's original economic theory.[1] Post-war thinking has been based upon the two main strands of modern neo–classical economic theory—Keynesianism and neo–liberalism (including monetarism, supply-side economics and rational expectations theory).[2]

Following World War II, most capitalist countries were strongly influenced by the theories of John Maynard Keynes.[3] The adoption of Keynes' economic ideas partly reflected the crisis in economic theory produced by the Great Depression and the inability of neo–classical theory to either explain the collapse or to provide governments with effective policy responses. In reality, Keynes' theory shared most of the traditional neo–classical model's assumptions and methodology. Where it differed fundamentally was over its perception of the inherent instability of the unregulated capitalist economy. Neo–classical theory has traditionally argued that capitalism tends towards a full employment equilibrium and is inherently stable. Keynesianism argued that, on the contrary, capitalism was an inherently unstable system prone to cyclical fluctuations and underemployment. It also provided a radically different approach toward the 'nature, scale and need' for state intervention. Neo–classical theory advocated a strictly limited economic role for the state and emphasised the key role of the free market in maximising economic growth and individual welfare. Keynesianism, however, stressed the positive and necessary role of the state in regulating the economic system and promoting full employment whilst minimising inflation. Keynes believed that the public sector would provide a stabilising factor and curb the volatility of private investment using an active fiscal policy (government spending and taxation policies) and monetary management policy.

To post-war governments Keynesianism appeared to offer the means to avoid major depressions and ultimately the collapse of capitalism. However, Keynesianism did not mark a radical departure from neo–classical theory. In the first place, it basically adopted most of the neo–classical model's central assumptions. Markets were assumed to be competitive; consumers pursued their own self-interest and maximised their economic choices; and firms made decisions on the basis of profit maximisation. While Keynesians emphasised the importance of state intervention to overcome market failure, they fundamentally accepted the dominant role of the market in allocating resources. The market would best respond to the free interaction of the welfare maximising consumer and the profit maximising producer—each making their own economic choices. Secondly, the link between Keynesianism and neo–classical theory was further consolidated in the 1950s and 1960s by the submerging of Keynesianism into the neo–

classical model. This hybrid model is variously described as 'neo–classical synthesis', 'bastard Keynesianism' or 'classical Keynesianism'.

One of the effects of the re-emergence of economic crisis in capitalism in the 1970s was the collapse of conventional Keynesian economic theory. Keynesianism's strength had been its recognition of the inadequacy of the 'free market' if left to itself to solve the contradictions of capitalism. However, as a theory, it did not itself have the resources to solve these deep-rooted problems. The emergence of stagflation (the simultaneous occurrence of unemployment and inflation) in the early 1970s destroyed the credibility of the Keynesian policy approach. This left the way open for a resurgence of the more conservative tradition of neo–classical theory. This strand of neo–classical theory had not disappeared during the period in which (bastard) Keynesianism was dominant. It was kept alive by a group of conservative neo–classical economists who emphasised the role of the market and opposed the role of the state in the economy. Two key figures in both the survival and the revival of conservative neo–classical economics were the Austrian Friedrich von Hayek and the American Milton Friedman. The economic theories of both were based on the principles of individualism; the virtue and stability of the free market; and opposition to almost any form of government intervention. Because of its total commitment to individual 'freedom' and the market, this economic theory is best described as neo–liberalism. Although in many ways neo–liberalism is a theoretical regression to the classical liberal theories of Adam Smith, it nevertheless shares most of the economic assumptions and the methodology of neo–classical economics.

Both Keynesianism and neo-liberalism have promoted the introduction of economic policies by the state that have discriminated against women. Nevertheless, the impact of the two policy frameworks on women have been very different. In particular, Keynesian economists have tended to be more inclined to pursue a degree of income redistribution and increased economic equality as part of their strategies. Policies based on state intervention to alleviate the inequalities created by the market have historically been more beneficial to women than neo-liberal laissez-faire policies, which have tended to reinforce the inequalities.

Leaving these important differences aside for the moment, all mainstream economic policies, whether Keynesian or neo-liberal, have much in common with neo–classical economic analysis. A feminist critique of the assumptions, methodology and policies of neo–classical economics is an important step in the process of developing economic strategies to change women's unequal economic position.

FEMINISTS AND ECONOMICS

One of the first statements on the importance of economics for women was made by the American activist Charlotte Perkins Gilman. At the time her book *Women and Economics* was published in 1898, winning the right to vote was seen as the means of securing true equality. Charlotte Gilman, however, argued that women's equality with men could only be achieved by women acquiring economic independence from men. She identified two factors that remain central to modern day feminist critiques. Firstly, she argued that women's unpaid work makes an economic contribution to society. Secondly, she pointed out that there exists a distinction between making an economic contribution and being economically independent:

> The labour of women in the house certainly enables men to produce more wealth than they otherwise could; in this way women are economic factors in society. But so are horses. The labour of horses enables men to produce more wealth than they otherwise could. The horse is an economic factor in society. But the horse is not economically independent, nor is the woman. (Gilman, 1966:13)

Although modern feminists would disagree with much of Gilman's analysis, her perception of the importance of women's unpaid work to the economy, the right of women to paid work and the economic and social gains to society from organised childcare were far-sighted. Nearly a century later these issues still remain outside the mainstream of economic theory and policy.

More recently, while women still comprise only a minority of the economics profession, there is a growing body of critical feminist economic analysis.[4] Feminist analyses of mainstream theory and policy cover a range of specific areas—labour market economics, development economics, the new home economics and public sector economics.

In Australia, the most developed feminist critique has been in the area of taxation theory and policy. Contributors such as Elizabeth Savage and Meredith Edwards have shown ways in which taxation analyses have been blatantly biased towards serving patriarchal interests. Others have pointed to the systematic ways in which taxation policies are class biased. These taxation analyses have shown, for example, that:

- Taxation policies that discriminate against women are also economically inefficient (Apps, 1987; Jones & Savage, 1986).
- Empirically false assumptions underlay discriminatory taxation policies in relation to women (Edwards, 1980, 1983).
- The taxation system involves a system of fiscal welfare that favours higher income groups and men (Keens & Cass, 1982).
- The development of taxation theory and policy in isolation from social welfare theory and policy perpetuates gender inequities and class biases (Harding, 1984; Harding & Whiteford, 1985).

More generally, however, it is in the area of women's paid work that the most detailed theoretical and empirical feminist critiques have arisen. In Australia, feminists have inevitably been led to question how women's labour market position is perceived by economists. An important early contribution was made by Margaret Power in her 1974 article 'The Wages of Sex', which challenged the assumption of economics that institutional discrimination against women in the labour market does not exist (Power, 1974). Feminist critiques have also highlighted that:

- The labour market is characterised by sex segmentation (Power, 1975; Eccles, 1984; Rubery, 1980; Kramer, 1983).
- The sexual division of labour in the home is an important determinant of women's labour market position (O'Donnell, 1984a; Bryson, 1984; Brennan, 1977).
- Skill and its rewards are defined by male-centred institutions in a way that disadvantages women (Cockburn, 1983; Rubery, 1980; Phillips & Taylor, 1986; Short, 1986; Pocock, 1988).
- The determinants and patterns of unemployment for women are different to that of men's and are not adequately understood using conventional economic concepts (Dex, 1985; Women's Bureau, 1984).

One particularly important area in which feminist analyses have gained some recognition is in the literature on development economics and Third World women. Western economic theories and policies have had a poor track record in promoting growth and development in the Third World. Two key reasons for this have been their failure to take into account the distributional impact of economic growth and the human element (as opposed to the technical inputs) in the growth and development process. Feminist critiques such as the pioneering work of Ester Boserup in her book *Women's Role in Economic Development*, published in 1970, have not ignored the distribution question nor the significance of social factors. In particular Boserup focused on the fact that the sexual division of labour affects the pattern of growth and development. Feminist analyses of growth and development have also drawn attention to the following:

- Women are invisible in the economist's theories, data and policies. Consequently, economic theories and policies have rarely been a mechanism for positive change for women (Boserup, 1970; Pala, 1977; Rogers, 1980).
- Economic growth is not a sufficient condition for reducing women's poverty and raising their economic and social position. That is, the trickle-down assumption is invalid for women (Anard, 1983; Karl, 1983; Palmer 1979; Boserup 1970).
- Growth and development is impeded if women's specific role is ignored (Taylor, 1985; Rogers, 1980).

Feminist contributions in the area of Third World growth and development have had little impact on mainstream economics in industrialised countries such as Australia. Their broad conclusions would, however, appear to be equally valid if applied to mainstream economic analyses of the developed economies. As the conclusion of one feminist critique of mainstream economics in Australia has recognised:

> ...the approach taken by economists and policy makers has not only prevented them from providing anything but a superficial explanation of women's true place in the economy, it has also caused them to reach misleading and erroneous conclusions about the true nature of the economy itself. (Power, Outhwaite, Rosewarne, Templeman & Wallace, 1984:30)

TOWARDS A FEMINIST CRITIQUE

To date, however, the impact of feminist critiques on mainstream economics has been relatively minor. This is reflected in the frequency with which many feminists say that they remain intimidated by the language and methodology of economics. Undoubtedly, economics intimidates many people, men and women, because of its unnecessarily technical and jargonistic language. However, this failure to break down the mystique of economics is also due to the fact that feminism has not yet developed an overall critique of neo–classical economics. Existing feminist critiques have tended to be specific, and somewhat technical and jargonistic themselves. As a result, a coherent framework to apply a feminist analysis to current economic debates does not exist.

There are two main facets of neo–classical economics that an overall feminist critique needs to analyse. Firstly, neo–classical economics has a profound effect on women's economic position because of its ideological link with the capitalist system. Secondly, neo–classical economics' methodology has consistently produced policies that disadvantage women.

NEO–CLASSICAL ECONOMICS AS AN IDEOLOGY

Neo–classical economics developed largely as an attempt to provide an answer to Marx's devastating critique of capitalism and classical economic theory (Fusfeld, 1986:83–95). From the beginning, therefore, neo–classical economists saw the task of economic theory, at least in part, as justifying the economic system. A further indication of this ideological dimension is the emergence of major revisions within the model whenever capitalism has experienced crises that have called the legitimacy of the system into question. In explaining the historical development of neo–classical thinking Daniel Fusfeld suggests 'that ideas are not accepted because they are "right" and rejected because they are "wrong", but they are accepted when they are useful and rejected when their usefulness ends' (Fusfeld, 1986:95).[5] Consequently, neo–classical economics has not only sought to explain the operation of the capitalist economic system, but it also serves to legitimate and justify the economic order which capitalism creates. Because women occupy an unequal position in the capitalist economy, economics effectively acts to justify this inequality.

The neo–classical theoretical model is imbued with the values and assumptions of nineteenth century liberalism and capitalism. It presents an idealised version of the economic system of capitalism as a universal 'given'. Its analysis is based on the assumed existence of a world of rational self-interested individuals exercising free economic choices in an economic framework dominated by self-adjusting markets. While individuals act separately and selfishly, the operation of the private enterprise market ensures the best and most efficient outcome for all. The free market ensures that the economy produces what consumers want, allocates resources efficiently, and normally operates at full employment levels. It is not, however, assumed that all individuals benefit equally from the economic system. On the contrary, individuals are seen to be rewarded according to their own efforts and initiatives.[6] Therefore, although it is recognised that capitalism creates inequalities these are justified as the fair result of individuals' own actions. It is also perceived as the most efficient way to organise the economy. Moreover, all individuals will benefit in the long run from a 'trickle-down' effect as economic growth raises the living standards of even the poorest members of society.

The validity of this theory depends on the existence of perfect competition. However, the real world of modern capitalism is not this 'theoretical Nirvana'. Consequently, neo–classical economic theory lends itself to being used to justify a political preference rather than present an economic reality. Joan Robinson, the late Cambridge University Economics professor, succinctly identifies the existence of such laissez-faire ideology in her book *Economic Philosophy*:

> It is possible to defend our economic system on the ground that, patched up with Keynesian correctives, it is, as he put it, the 'best in sight'. Or at any rate that it is not too bad, and change is painful. In short, that our system is the best system that we have got. Or it is possible to take the tough-minded line that Schumpter derived from Marx. The system is cruel, unjust, turbulent, but it does deliver the goods, and damn it all, it's the goods that you want. Or conceding its defects, to defend it on political grounds—that democracy as we know it could not have grown up under any other system and cannot survive without it. What is not possible, at this time of day, is to defend it, in the neoclassical style, as a delicate self-regulating mechanism, that only has to be left to itself to produce the greatest satisfaction for all. (Robinson, 1962:130)

The application of neo–classical economic theory to policy-making by the state has very significant implications for women. Firstly, the theory inclines economic policymakers to a view of the world that does not identify women's economic inequalities as a 'problem'. Since resources are assumed to be allocated efficiently by the market, women are assumed to be rewarded according to their contribution to the economy. If women do not occupy highly rewarded positions within the economy it is because they have chosen not to invest their own resources in obtaining such positions. Economic policymakers, therefore, tend to hold a set of ideological or moral values that predisposes them to a view of the existing economic distribution of resources as a just one. Secondly, the theory's ideological assumptions predispose policymakers against any attempt to utilise the state to improve women's economic position. While Keynesian economists recognised the need for state intervention to alleviate poverty and stabilise the capitalist economic and social order, they still perceived the market as the most efficient way to allocate resources. Any attempt by the state to interfere in the overall distribution of incomes and resources to promote increased equality usually had to be traded off against a reduction in the efficient operation of the market.

NEO–CLASSICAL ECONOMICS AS A METHODOLOGY

Neo–classical economics further contributes to policies that discriminate against women because of the methodology it has developed for analysing the economic process within capitalism. Understanding this methodology and the assumptions upon which it is based is crucial to understanding the ways in which economic theory and policy affects the position of women. Above all, economics is a method or a technique of analysis, or as Keynes put it, economics is an 'apparatus of the mind'. By understanding how economics 'explains' it soon becomes apparent to feminists why economic policies consistently discriminate against women.

In the first place, neo–classical economics aspires to be universal in its application. For example, it seeks to be valid for capitalism as it exists in industrialised and Third World countries and at any point in the history of the development of capitalism. Its methodology transcends the very things feminist analyses have emphasised—history, culture, power, class, race and gender. The notion is that economic behaviour has a universal form and, as such, it can be understood outside these contexts. Alice Amsden sums this up as well as indicating its patriarchial bias when she notes that 'the human subject of neo–classical investigation is a timeless, classless, raceless, cultureless creature; although male, unless otherwise specified' (Amsden, 1980:13).

Secondly, neo–classical economic theory has sought universality by a highly reductionist methodology. That is, it uses models with a limited number of general or 'universal' economic variables. This gives economics a level of mathematical sophistication and abstraction not seen in the other social sciences. However, as one feminist economist has noted, the 'power' of such a framework has been 'purchased at the price of obliterating most of the trees from the forest' (Sawhill, 1980:133). For example, income and prices are taken as the major determinants of an individual's economic behaviour. Other influences on economic behaviour such as beliefs, caring and prejudice are lumped together as 'tastes'. Occasionally some of these tastes may be given prominence in an economic theory. Employers' discrimination against women is acknowledged to exist by some neo–classical economists as a taste and its impact on women's earnings has been analysed (Becker, 1971; Phelps, 1972; Arrow 1973). However, the framework does not allow the neo–classical economist to see discrimination as being structurally imbedded in capitalism. In most cases, as two of neo–classical economics' most influential proponents have put it, 'the economist continues to search for differences in prices or incomes to explain any differences or changes in behaviour' (Stigler and Becker, 1977:76). Tastes therefore remain as 'constants', and for the purposes of explanation and prediction are disregarded. However, it is in this way the structural features of economic society are eliminated from neo–classical economic analysis (Lawrence, 1987:307). The fundamental question for feminists is how useful is such reductionism in providing an adequate understanding of the economy and women's place in it.

Thirdly, the 'universal' behavioural assumptions the theory proceeds from are imbued with the philosophy of individualism. They include:

- individuals are driven by self interest
- individuals behave rationally in that they maximise their economic and social returns
- individuals have freedom of choice

The underlying premise is also that an individualistic society will provide the basis for a stable social order. Inherently selfish people left to pursue their own interests in a competitive market environment will not only maximise their own returns but will maximise the welfare of the community as a whole. The philosophy of individualism, of course, is the basis of capitalism's political ideology. The behavioural assumptions of individual selfishness, rationality and freedom of choice give the neo–classical paradigm an internal logic that simply defines women's problems out of existence. For example, the sexual division of labour in the home can be shown to be the rational outcome of women and men 'choosing' to specialise in a way to maximise family welfare. Not only is there no 'problem' but neo–classical economic theory also effectively legitimates women's disadvantage. The philosophy of individualism is given further support by the theory's inclination towards the principle that economic, social and political phenomena can only be understood if they are constructed in terms of the beliefs, attitudes and decisions of individuals (Blaug, 1980:49). Such a methodology is opposed to analysing social structures and processes that are not reducible to individual actions or attitudes, for example, class, structural discrimination and the state itself.[7]

Fourthly, the methodology of neo–classical economics is designed fundamentally to explain market behaviour. The market is the device for translating the actions of self-interested individuals into affluence for all. The competitive market acts as the 'invisible hand' which can most efficiently promote the public interest. The methodology used to achieve this is described by Geoffrey Lawrence:

> Economic theory takes what seems at the level of appearances to be 'real' (free buyers, free sellers in the market, price movements resulting from supply and demand etc.) and constructs an account of the world on this basis. In taking such a partial view of the economic and social order it not only provides a distorted picture of real economic relations under capitalism but elevates the market to a position of absolute importance in the process of theoretical formulation and policy recommendations. (Lawrence, 1987:309)

There are three main implications of this for women. Firstly, many of their activities are ignored by neo–classical economics because they have no market value. As a result, women's economic contribution and role are not reflected in economic policies. Secondly, neo–classical theory's presentation of markets as self-regulating devices predisposes it against the state having an active role. Alice Amsden has noted that 'one almost never associates orthodox neo–classical economics with the advocacy of government policies to change the position of women in the economy' (Amsden, 1980:34). Thirdly, choices are posed in a way that implies an inherent conflict between equity and efficiency (McClellend, 1987:107). Consequently, women's demands for greater equity are perceived to involve reduced efficiency. Neo–classical analysis ignores the positive role government plays in shaping society's choices in the first place.[8]

Finally, neo–classical economics has adopted an adapted version of the methodology and philosophy of 'logical positivism' called 'positive' economics.[9] This approach has been the means by which the discipline has sought to be scientific in its method. One result has been to promote economic theory as being 'value free'. Many economists believe that they only enter the realm of value judgements when they deal with policy. Even proponents of neo–classical economics, such as Mark Blaug, have pointed out that on issues of value judgements economists are prone to 'self-deception'. While arguing for economics to be scientific in its method, he argues that modern economics is imbued with more value judgements than is commonly admitted:

> [Economists'] skills, such as they are, are largely underdeveloped because of a long-standing tradition in modern economics to deny both the value aspects of economic beliefs and the realities of policymaking. The scope of positive economics is smaller and that of normative economics larger than is frequently made out by economists. (Blaug, 1980:152)

Since grave doubt has been cast on the 'scientific' validity of neo–classical economic theories (Robinson, 1962; Blaug, 1980; Katouzian, 1980), economics doesn't always fulfil its own stated tests. Joan Robinson has argued that this failure resulted in economics limping along 'with one foot in untested hypotheses and the other in untestable slogans' (Robinson, 1962:25). Nevertheless, neo–classical economics has achieved a dominant status within the social sciences as a result of its 'scientific' method. Even more importantly for women, however, is that the positivist framework adopted by economics has served to disguise the conservative values contained in both economic theory and policymaking.

These five aspects of the methodology of neo–classical economic analysis serve as a powerful restriction on the state to develop policies likely to benefit women. Conversely, it is only by challenging its restrictive methodology and assumptions that feminists might pressure the state to introduce more progressive policies.

The methodological approach of neo–classical economics results in a number of important consequences in terms of the way it treats women within its analysis and policies:

- Neo–classical economic analysis and policy systematically ignores the specific position of women in the economy.
- Economic analysis and policy divides economic activity into a public/private dichotomy. Women's economic activity thereby tends to be marginalised into a 'non–economic' private category and the important relationship between women's unpaid and paid work is ignored.
- Economists make a series of unrecognised assumptions about the role and position of women that produce policies that tend to disadvantage women.

An awareness of these consequences is crucial for any feminist critique of economic policy and the development of feminist economic strategies. The ideology and methodology of economics are ultimately the constraining factors on the ability of neo–classical economics to produce genuine equality for women. However, some of its consequences could be, and have been, modified by feminist analyses and political action.

Economics ignores the specific position of women
A common textbook definition of economics is that it is the study of the choices arising from our unlimited wants in the context of a scarcity of available resources. These choices can be categorised as: what to produce; how to produce; and for whom? As the authors of the major Australian first-year university and college economics textbook put it:

> Man, unfortunate creature, is plagued with wants. He wants, among other things, love, social recognition and the material necessities and comforts of life. Man's striving to improve his material well-being, to 'make a living', is the concern of economics. More specifically, economics is the study of man's behaviour in producing, exchanging and consuming the material goods and services he wants. (Jackson and McConnell, 1980:3)

If we give the authors the benefit of the doubt about their sexist language, we can assume that they intended to suggest that economics in its broadest sense should be about the everyday decisions made by all men and women.[10] All aspects of our lives involve economic choices—the work we do; what we buy; our leisure activities; whether we study at university; whether we have children. All such choices affect not only our own economic welfare but also the economy as a whole.

However, there is a major contradiction within this approach. Economics is fundamentally concerned with every-day decisions concerning production and consumption with which women are intimately involved, yet, in practice, economics makes little specific reference to women. As Anne Phillips has commented, 'economics has never had much to say about women'. Issues of economic policy are rarely thought of as being related to women in any specific or different way. In fact, issues related to women are usually dealt with under the label of 'social policy' (Phillips, 1983:1). The usual explanation provided by economists for this omission is that economic policy changes and changes in the economy affect women and men similarly. That is, economic policy is seen as gender neutral.

This assumption of gender neutrality in the impact of economic policies is derived from a methodological approach which systematically ignores the specific economic position of women. Women, however, do not occupy an equal position in society. They are placed in a different and often disadvantaged social and economic position from that of men. Their experiences and location within both the family and the labour market place them in a subordinate position in most industrialised capitalist countries. Compared to men, women:

- comprise a lower proportion of the workforce
- form a high proportion of part-time and casual workers
- earn substantially lower wages
- experience a higher level of unemployment
- typically experience a more broken workforce pattern
- work in highly segmented, and lower status, occupational and industry groupings
- form a higher proportion of social security recipients and poverty groups
- undertake a far greater share of the unpaid economic activities carried out in the home

Of course, not all women are economically disadvantaged compared to men, but significant differences do exist in the economic experiences of most women compared to most men—even where they occupy similar class positions. This has crucial implications for economic policy. Only where women and men have identical social and economic circumstances could one logically presume a gender neutral impact. However, if women's different economic position is ignored by policy-makers, even policies which are intended to be gender neutral will affect men and women in general quite differently. In many cases such policies will further exacerbate existing inequalities.

There are numerous examples of major economic policies in Australia which do not take into account women's specific position. Labour market training programmes are illustrative. Since the late 1970s Federal and State Australian governments have played an increasingly interventionist role in the labour market. In particular, governments have provided training and retraining opportunities and job creation as a means of reducing unemployment. Despite women's lower level of qualifications and skills in the workforce and their higher unemployment rates, they have not had equal access to such programmes. Although these programmes have not set out to discriminate against women, the effect has nevertheless been discriminatory. Programmes that centred on apprenticeship training, construction projects and full-time jobs simply missed women. On the other hand, the Hawke Labor government's Community Employment Program (CEP) might be regarded as an exception. In this, an atypical case, gender equality in placement numbers was achieved directly as a result of the government's recognition that women would be treated unequally unless their specific labour market position was recognised (Women's Budget Program, 1986–7:99).

Economics ignores or undervalues women's economic activity in the home

Feminist writers have argued that capitalism has split the process of economic production into two separate spheres—the public world of paid work and the private world of unpaid domestic work. The consequence of this split for women is that their economic activities become concentrated in the unpaid and lower status area of the domestic economy. Since capitalism allocates resources and incomes virtually solely through market mechanisms, those who are excluded from, or marginalised within, the market inevitably receive poor rewards for their economic activities. Neo–classical economic theory has unquestioningly incorporated the existence of this public/private dichotomy into its framework of analysis, and by so doing it has played an active role in reinforcing women's economic inequality.

Since the methodology of neo–classical economics is based on an analysis of market behaviour, economists have not widely studied activities that do not directly involve a financial transaction. Women's economic activities that do not occur within a market framework have been perceived as belonging to the 'private' sphere and not the appropriate subject of economic analysis. Traditionally, economics has viewed the household as the place where the consumption of goods and services produced in the market takes place. The process of consumption in this view is equated with 'leisure'. As one traditional economics text states, leisure is valued for 'relaxation, recreation and the accomplishment of assorted household tasks' (Dolan and Vogt, 1981:516).

The failure to analyse the unpaid domestic labour of women has led to its undervaluing within the overall economy. Feminist analyses, dating as far back as Charlotte Perkins Gilman's *Women and Economics*, published in 1898, have pointed out that domestic labour plays a crucial role in the process of capital accumulation. In the first place, since women's domestic and caring work in the home is economically and socially necessary, without it capital would be required to pay much higher wages. A recent study in the United States concluded that to replace women's unpaid domestic labour with paid labour in 1976 would have cost the economy US$566 billion. This represented about one-third of the total United States gross national product (Peattie and Rein, 1983:38). Secondly, other writers have argued that one area in which women's unpaid labour is economically most beneficial for capital is that of consumption (Galbraith, 1973:29–37). Consequently, while capitalism appears to split the activities of individuals into the public productive sphere and the private non-productive sphere, both spheres are actually integral parts of the overall system of production.

The failure to acknowledge the importance of women's domestic labour is not accidental. Rather it plays an important ideological role in giving moral sanction to what otherwise might be perceived as unjust. As John Kenneth Galbraith observed:

> The notion that economic society requires something approaching half of its adult members to accept subordinate status is not easily defended. And it is not easily reconciled with a system of social thought which not only esteems the individual but acclaims his or her power. So neo–classical economics resolves the problem by burying the subordination of the individual within the household, the inner relationship of which it ignores... The economist does not invade the privacy of the household. (Galbraith, 1973:35)

If women's unpaid economic contribution were more explicitly analysed and valued by mainstream economics, 'it might invite inconvenient rejection' (Galbraith, 1973:33).

Although neo–classical economics has traditionally ignored non–market activities, one particular branch of analysis emerged in the 1960s and 1970s in the United States, known as the 'new home economics'. Utilising human capital theory, Gary Becker and others attempted to analyse aspects of the 'private' sphere such as marriage, divorce, sex-roles, fertility and childrearing within the framework of neo–classical economics (Becker, 1973; Schultz, 1974; Mincer & Polacheck, 1974). The 'new home economics' sought to formulate the economics of the family in terms of costs, benefits, resources, scarcity and choice. It used the same tools of analysis and applied the same assumptions about market behaviour to behaviour in the household (Cohen, 1985:290).

Nevertheless, an important innovation was that it included an analysis of production (i.e., unpaid work) as well as leisure/consumption in its range of home activities (Cohen, 1985:291). However, even these attempts maintain the public/private dichotomy. This is illustrated by the fact that individuals in the family are treated as one unit. The neo–classical economists' concept of the household includes several individuals (wife, husband, children), but in practice individual and household choices are treated as interchangeable or identical (Galbraith, 1973:31). As Isabel Sawhill puts it:

> ...everyone's preferences are swept into one household utility function because different family members are assumed to care enough about one another to weigh up each others preferences in arriving at family decisions... Why is it then that marriage sometimes leads to positive and sometimes negative caring among family members? The economist has no answers. (Sawhill, 1980:134)

It should be noted that this heroic assumption about the family has troubled some economists. For example, Richard Lipsey in his widely-circulated economics text *Introduction to Positive Economics* makes the point that it is a simplification to equate the household with the individual (Lipsey, 1963). However, having mentioned it (and Lipsey is an exception for doing so), neo–classical economic theory and policy rarely returns to the question of what goes on inside the household. Consequently, the public private dichotomy is effectively maintained through a methodological sleight of hand.

The failure of mainstream economics to analyse adequately women's unpaid economic activities also reduces its ability to explain women's paid work. In particular, economic analysis is unable to explain the sexual division of labour in the workforce. It argues that the division of labour within the family is determined by the relative ability of family members to earn an income. Thus women tend to be responsible for the home and men for earning an income since it seems rational to have the lower-income earner raise the children. The key question here is why do women earn less than men? Economic analysis resorts to human capital theory for the answer. According to this theory women invest less in education and training (i.e., human capital) than men. Women acting rationally allocate their time to training and education in the light of:

> ...human and financial capacities in the family but also to the prospective utilisation of the capital which is being accumulated. Expectation of future family and market activities of individuals are therefore important determinants of the levels and forms of investment in human capital. (Mincer and Polachek, 1974:577)

In other words, women earn less because of their special role in the family, but their special role is related in turn to their investments in their own education and training. In explaining the sexual division of labour in the workplace, the sexual division of labour in the family is simply treated as a given, and vice versa. Consequently, 'we have come full circle' (Sawhill, 1980:133). Mainstream economics, with so many important 'givens', cannot make the necessary connections between unpaid activities and paid activities. In other words, its analysis is severely impaired by its adoption of a public/private dichotomy.

This in turn means the importance of the sexual division of labour in determining women's economic position is neither recognised nor challenged. One example of this is government economic policies which seek to increase the number of women in paid work without taking into account the quality of the jobs. The likelihood of this is reinforced by the 'trickle down' assumption of mainstream policymakers. As Margaret Power and her co-authors have put it:

> ...an economic analysis which takes the sexual division of labour fully into account does not mistake the expansion of lower paid, low status jobs for a more equitable distribution of employment opportunities between women and men. (Power, Outhwaite, Rosewarne, Templeman, Wallace, 1984:36)

Similarly, during recessions the implementation of economic policies that ignore women's hidden unemployment and underemployment, and produce cuts in public expenditures on the assumption that a family welfare system exists, take the sexual division of labour in the family as 'natural' or a 'given'. For this reason women are likely to bear a disproportionate share of the burden of economic downturns and the 'belt-tightening' economic policies that usually accompany them.

The public/private dichotomy is also reflected in economic policies that treat childcare as a purely private concern. For example, the state's employment policies do not make childcare for working women a priority. Maternity and parenting leave is not treated as legitimate for the purposes of superannuation. Taxation policies provide a greater level of subsidy to gold miners than to families with children.

Economics adopts assumptions about women that reinforce inequalities
Economic theory and policies contain a number of unstated assumptions that reflect widely-held societal views regarding women's role and behaviour. Two such important assumptions are that women are the dependents of men and that families pool their income and wealth.[11]

The notion that households comprise a breadwinning male and a female spouse dependent upon, and benefiting from, the man's earnings and assets pervades public policies. The dependent spouse rebate is the most explicit manifestation of this assumption in current Australian economic policy. With few exceptions it is paid to male taxpayers with spouses with little or no earnings of their own. This assumption also underlies many income-support policies whereby married women are ineligible for unemployment benefits and income support for education, training and retraining if their spouses are earning. Although married men with an income-earning spouse would also be excluded from these benefits, the point is that far more women than men are excluded on the assumption that their spouse (married or de facto) will support them.

The assumption that women are the dependents of men has two corollary assumptions that make for tidyness. One is the value judgement that women's primary role is in the home. This was widely upheld in forums such as the *Australian Financial Review* during economic policy debates about unemployment remedies. The other is that family resources are pooled, or that women as dependents have access to husbands' incomes and assets. This perpetuates the view that the household is a benign place where the preferences of individual family members can be treated as one. In any case, one of the central tenets of neo–classical theory is that individuals exercise freedom of choice. Therefore, if women are economically dependent it is presumably out of choice.

The assumption that women are the dependents of men reinforces and exacerbates sexual inequalities in a number of ways.

Firstly, this assumption perpetuates the view that women's unpaid work makes no economic contribution. As a result the importance of women's economic role is never reflected in policies. Accordingly, women are assumed, like children, to make no economic contribution as a result of their dependent position. Secondly, the assumption of dependency undervalues the importance of women's paid work. This is despite the fact that the Henderson Poverty Commission Report points out the number of two-parent families in poverty would have doubled if mothers had not been employed (Henderson, 1975:204). Nevertheless, the assumption of dependency continues to undervalue women's paid work in arguments such as married women are the cause of high youth unemployment rates. Thirdly, policies built upon the assumption of women's dependency often reinforce that dependency. For example, in practice the dependent spouse taxation rebate acts as a disincentive for women to work. Fourthly, policies that assume women's economic dependency usually do not protect them economically. For example, occupational superannuation schemes that exclude married women (because of their presumed dependency on a spouse), do not in any way guarantee their right to their spouse's superannuation benefit in the event of his death or marital breakdown.

Similarly, the assumption that the income (and assets) of a household is pooled amongst family members underlies many economic (and social) policies. A corollary assumption is that the economic and social position of one spouse can be ascertained by reference to the income (and assets) of the household. This is regardless of who has legal title to that income. In many ways this is a curious assumption because in the event of divorce, separation or death, legal title is paramount in policies concerning the division of income and assets, which women generally receive on an unequal basis.

Economic policies reflecting the assumption of pooled income include proposals for joint or married unit taxation with income splitting and home ownership schemes. In addition, the vast majority of state-provided social security benefits and pensions are based on this assumption.

It is not an assumption based on empirical investigations. The empirical research does not support the view (Edwards, 1983, 1985). Instead the assumption is derived from neoclassical economic theory and societal views about marriage. Economic theory treats the economic behaviour of individual family members as a unit. Society views marriage as a partnership of equals, a value judgement that is the least troublesome for policymakers. In any case, the public private dichotomy in economics provides a rationale for not being seriously concerned with what goes on the family. Economic policies are not neutral with respect to economic relationships between family members. For example, the payment of family allowances to the mother rather than the father, directly increases the access and control women have over income. Policies of the state such as these can be more significant than commonly recognised. A survey by ANOP Market Research commissioned by the Office of the Status of Women (OSW) in 1985 found that of the 2000 women with children surveyed, the family allowance was the only source of outside income for 40 percent of mothers (Office of the Status of Women, 1985b:3). Furthermore, when the Hawke Labor government income tested the family allowance in 1987 on joint husband and wife earnings, it was reported by the Department of Social Security that many women could not reapply because they simply did not have the necessary information about their husbands' incomes (*The Australian* 26 September 1987). Such tax-transfer policies serve to reinforce and increase women's economic inequality. If family resources are not pooled, policies that reduce women's, or increase men's, disposable income will redistribute income from women to men. Moreover, the empirical evidence on financial arrangements within Australian families indicates that different income classes have different arrangements. Meredith Edward's study showed that in higher-income families husbands were more likely to give wives a set housekeeping allowance than lower-income groups. In the latter the wife was more likely to 'manage' (not control) the family finances with husbands receiving personal spending money (Edwards, 1983:134). Therefore, the same tax-transfer policy can have differing effects for women of different classes. An important policy implication of this is that the impact of economic policies on intra-family income and asset distribution should be an essential element of a poverty alleviation strategy. Poverty in the community can be seriously understated if the distribution of income within the family is not taken into account.

THE ECONOMICS OF THE NEW RIGHT

The recent revival of conservative neo–classical theory was in large part due to the election of right wing governments in the United Kingdom and the United States in 1979 and 1980. With the coming to power of Margaret Thatcher and Ronald Reagan the political ground in Western capitalism shifted towards the conservative forces of the New Right. Similarly, neo-liberalism, the economic theory of the New Right, became the orthodoxy of the economics profession. As one commentator put it, 'economic doctrines move with the tides of politics and provide the intellectual letters of credit that justify specific political strategies' (Fusfeld, 1986:186).

In Australia, these adjustments can be observed clearly in the economic philosophy and policies of the Federal Treasury. Following World War II, Treasury, influenced in part by the existence of a Labor government, adopted a predominantly Keynesian economic model. The maintenance of full employment was given top priority. However, over the next twenty years, under a conservative Liberal/Country Party government, there occurred a gradual shift in Treasury's outlook 'from a predominantly Keynesian model to a predominantly neo–classical model' (Whitwell, 1986:262). This shift meant that Treasury's view of the role of government changed dramatically over time from favouring active state intervention in the economy to a strong belief in restricting the role of the state. By the mid-1970s Treasury, under the control of the New Right economist John Stone, actually perceived the actions of government as a major source of unemployment and inflation (Whitwell, 1986:262–3).

The onset of the 'Stone Age' in Treasury resulted in greatly increased influence for neo-liberal economic theory over Australian policymaking (Hughes, 1980). This was reflected in the Fraser government's application of elements of monetarist, supply-side and rational expectations policies. Above all, it was reflected in the strategy developed by the Fraser government from 1975–1983 around the neo-liberal theme of 'fighting inflation first'. This was supposedly aimed at reducing the size of government and the scope of state intervention in pursuit of economic expansion and full employment. Its principal policy thrusts, however, were to attempt to force a reduction in real wages while simultaneously transferring state expenditures away from the 'social wage' areas of the budget (education, health, social security, housing and regional development, culture and recreation) towards increased resources for capital (Broomhill, 1978).

Therefore, while these policies were justified by the invocation of neo–liberal economic rhetoric, the underlying political motivation was the development of a class-based strategy to generate an economic recovery that minimised the costs to capital at the expense of wage and salary earners and the unemployed. Wage restraint was seen as crucial to recovery and became a key element in the Fraser government's economic strategy. The lowest paid and least organised workers were, of course, least able to defend themselves against the erosion of real wages. Not only were women workers' living standards eroded by falling real wages but so too were their working conditions as the state accepted and even encouraged an expansion in part-time, casual and volunteer work. Women also bore the brunt of the government's increasingly harsh cutbacks in spending in social wage areas. Young, Aboriginal and migrant women took the brunt of unemployment, while married women's right to work came under ideological attack (Power, 1980:42)

Under the increasing influence of New Right political and social ideology, the Fraser government moved further away from social and economic policies likely to improve the position of women. Not only were policies to promote income redistribution shelved, but pressures developed for the reversal of previous reforms which benefited women.

Ultimately, the economic strategies pursued throughout the late 1970s and early 1980s failed to deliver economic recovery. In Australia inflation remained at around 11 percent in 1982 while unemployment averaged 9.3 percent for the year 1982–83. Of course this is hardly surprising, since the causes of the recession were global and largely beyond the scope of national governments to overcome. However, the strategy pursued by the government between 1975 and 1983 not only failed to produce economic recovery but worsened the impact of the recession on both women in the paid workforce and those dependent on the state.

In spite of the failure of the somewhat inconsistent attempt by the Fraser government to implement New Right economic policies, a new wave of these ideas arrived in the mid-1980s and gained considerable influence on the Australian political agenda. Although promoted by a relatively small group of academics, business people, employer organisations and newspapers, the ideas of the New Right have penetrated the three major political parties.

Neo-liberal economic theory continued to dominate policy-making in Australia under the Hawke Labor government. While Labor came to office supporting a mildly expansionist Keynesian approach, economic policymaking since 1985 has effectively been dominated by the 'rationalist' approach of neo-liberalism. In fact, early in 1987, the director of one of a number of New Right think-tanks stated:

> The Labor government is an irrelevancy. It is our policies that are being put in place. We have made the running on financial deregulation, privatisation, big government, taxation and cutting back the welfare state. We have influenced the media. We have initiated the debates. We have influenced the politicians. It is our political agenda being followed in Canberra. (Botsman, 1987:18)

While this claim is undoubtedly highly exaggerated, it is true that the New Right have profoundly influenced the issues addressed by the Labor government.

The primary target of New Right activity has been the push for deregulation of the labour market. A strong ideological attack on the established industrial relations system, combined with a coordinated industrial campaign aimed at using common law provisions against trade unions, have been the bases for asserting 'employer prerogatives'. While claiming to want to base the employment relationship on an individual contract between employer and worker, the New Right's campaign is actually aimed at breaking the power of trade unions, reducing wages and working conditions and increasing employers' power over the work process. The implications of these policies for women workers are enormous. Being among the most vulnerable and powerless group in the labour market, women workers would undoubtedly experience a dramatic drop in working and living standards as a result of such policies while a small elite group of highly skilled (usually male) workers could benefit. The huge increase in sweated labour (or outwork) in the female-dominated clothing industry is a vivid example of what labour market 'flexibility' can look like in practice.

The New Right has also directed a sustained attack on the role of government in Australia. In particular, it has focused on demands for the privatisation of key state utilities and public enterprises. It has mounted a campaign for reduced government expenditures, particularly in welfare and other areas of benefit to women and disadvantaged groups. It has also campaigned strongly for significant reductions in taxation, which in turn would further reduce government expenditures in the 'social wage' area. These ideological attacks on the role of the government, combined with pressures generated by the fiscal crisis of the state, pose a serious threat to the economic status of women in Australian society.

The economic libertarianism of the New Right has been allied (particularly in the United States and the United Kingdom) with extreme conservatism on moral issues. Ultimately there is a deep contradiction in the alliance of free-market libertarianism with the Moral Right, since many of the moral 'problems' that horrify the conservatives are actually products of the free enterprise system itself. However, both groups are acutely aware of the need to broaden their appeal and consequently an increasing alliance between the two is quite likely to develop in Australia. Although some women who have been individually successful have been attracted by the New Right's emphasis on individualism, the alliance of this economic theory with a moral world-view that places women in a rigidly traditional social role is a further guarantee that women's economic position cannot be improved by such policies.

As extreme as the New Right's economic policies may appear to women, it is important to recognise they are merely extensions of mainstream economics. Neo–classical economic theory and policy are incapable of delivering genuine equality. Feminists might, therefore, ask if there is much to be gained by bothering with neo–classical economics. However, it is important that women participate in the mainstream economic debate to stop the very worst scenarios from occuring and to achieve the best outcomes possible within this framework. As Joan Robinson has argued, 'the purpose of studying economics is not to acquire a set of ready-made answers to economic questions, but to learn to avoid being deceived by economists' (Galbraith, 1973:11). Given the ability of neo–classical economics to shape both the overall public policy framework as well as particular economic policies, a feminist strategy cannot afford to ignore economics.

II

CASE STUDIES

3 Women and the Hawke Labor government

The Hawke Labor government was elected in March 1983 after seven years of conservative administration in Australia. It was by no means a radically reformist party that took up the reins of government. In this sense, the Hawke government contrasted starkly with the previous Whitlam Labor administration, which was elected in 1972. Labor under Whitlam had promised to change radically the status of women in Australian society. The Hawke government, although supporting the goals of sexual equality, made few specific promises. A great deal had changed between December 1972 and March 1983.

The Hawke government came to office at a time when global recession and structural changes had created a major fiscal crisis in virtually all capitalist countries. This has had profound implications for women. In the first place, it produced an economic climate hostile to achieving progressive changes for women through the use of state intervention. Even more seriously, however, the policies introduced by the state as a result of these forces have in some cases caused considerable hardship to women and have actually reduced their economic status.

Over the past decade we have seen severe expenditure cuts in areas important to women, reductions in the growth of public sector employment, a squeeze on wage and salary-earning taxpayers and families, and real wage cuts for low-income earners. Above all, a more general effect of the economic recession and the fiscal crisis of the state has been the increasing dominance of ideological conservatism within the state policy making process. In both the United Kingdom and the United States conservative governments were introducing neo-liberal, or New Right, economic policies. Under the Fraser government (1975–83) Australian economic policymaking had also moved away from the Keynesian approach. The economics profession as a whole adopted a more market-oriented approach and the Federal Treasury, the state's most important policymaking body, had shifted firmly towards the neo–liberal camp.

In this economic, ideological and political context, there was clearly little hope that the Hawke government would adopt a radical programme of reform for women. In terms of specific economic policies to benefit women, the Labor government has taken few initiatives. It has been accused by feminists of failing to implement policies to significantly improve the position of women. These have included, for example, childcare, family allowances, taxation and labour market policies to overcome women's disadvantaged position in the workforce (Brennan, 1986; Lamaro, 1985; Savage, 1987; Power, et al., 1984).

Progress has been more discernible in legislative and social policy areas such as affirmative action and sex discrimination legislation, small increases in a number of welfare areas and a major reform of assistance for low-income families in the 1987/88 budget. Overall, however, it is clear from the following examination of government policy that Labor's record on more general economic reform measures for women is not good. Not surprisingly, therefore, the Hawke government has come under sustained criticism from women's groups (Hall, 1983; Blackman, 1984; Council of Action for Equal Pay, 1984; Jackson 1986).

LABOR'S MACROECONOMIC STRATEGY

In response, the Labor government argued that its first priority in such a severely constrained economic environment has been to develop a set of macroeconomic policies that will restore economic growth and create an environment in which a long-term recovery can occur. In the current circumstances, therefore, the best chance for improving women's economic situation is for the government to concentrate on overcoming Australia's broader economic problems. This was clearly articulated in Labor's 1987/88 Women's Budget Statement:

> Ultimately, it is sustainable economic growth and the associated opportunities for productive employment that afford the greatest protection against poverty and provide government with the financial capability to assist the disadvantaged. Economic policies which enhance the prospects of the Australian economy for sustainable growth are the means by which the government can best ensure a bright and secure future for present and future Australians.
> (Women's Budget Statement, 1987/88:3)

> **Macroeconomic policy:**
>
> Policy which deals with the functioning of the whole economy rather than with the individual units—such as the consumer or the corporation (which is microeconomic policy)

Women should not, and have not, been convinced by this argument. Even if Labor's overall strategies prove successful in establishing economic recovery, the benefits to women are, at best, likely to be indirect. Labor has based its strategy on setting the economic fundamentals in position to allow the market to produce its long-awaited recovery. The unspoken assumption here is that benefits will eventually 'trickle-down' to all groups, including women. This argument deserves to be treated with some scepticism and scarcely begins to respond to the long list of claims that women have struggled to place on the political agenda in Australia.

This is not to imply that a government's macroeconomic strategy is unimportant to women. The allocation of resources in a capitalist society is carried out primarily by the market, or rather, by the small number of giant corporations that dominate the market. Nevertheless, governments can have an important influence on the overall creation and distribution of economic resources, in particular by intervention through budgetary policy in general (the pattern of government revenue-raising and expenditures), combined with specific policies on wages, housing, welfare, the labour market and trade and industry.

THE 'TRICKLE-DOWN' STRATEGY

The macroeconomic strategy that Labor sought to apply in its first two years in office involved an expansionary budgetary policy to generate growth and employment while restraining inflation by controlling wage growth in particular. While the previous conservative government had pursued a consistently restrictionist policy aimed at fighting inflation first, Labor aimed to reduce both inflation and unemployment simultaneously. In contrast to the restrictionist school of economists, which had dominated the thinking of the Fraser/Howard government, the neo-Keynesian expansionist school of thought initially adopted by Labor argued that it was possible for the economy to be gently reflated and full employment restored without fuelling inflation (Indecs Economics, 1986:18-24). In

> **Expansionists:**
>
> Those economists who argue that government economic policy should consciously permit and, where necessary, assist economic growth.
>
> **Restrictionists:**
>
> Those economists who argue that government assisted growth can only produce an inflationary or balance of payments crisis.

order to control inflationary pressures, however, it was argued that some device was needed to provide a temporary truce in the ongoing struggle between employers and workers over wages and prices.

In office, Labor set about attempting to generate increasing demand in the economy through a combination of mildly expansionary public-sector spending together with expansionary tax cuts. Simultaneously, inflationary pressures were to be kept under control by maintaining a tight monetary policy and negotiating wage restraint through the Prices and Incomes Accord. The Accord was an agreement made between the Australian Labor Party and the Australian Council of Trade Unions whereby unions agreed to limit wage demands in return for a range of non-wage benefits for workers. While these policies involved a high degree of Keynesian-style state intervention within the economy, in other areas the Labor government introduced policies more in tune with free-market neo-liberal thinking. In particular the government introduced a high degree of deregulation in the financial sector. It adopted the neo-liberal view that deregulation would stimulate the private sector and make the economy as a whole more competitive and dynamic.

Underlying this strategy was at least one significant similarity to the policies of the Fraser government. Both relied heavily on the 'trickle-down' process. While the Fraser government had preferred to rely on a market-led recovery, Labor aimed initially to stimulate growth in the economy through public-sector led expansion. It was assumed, however, that this public expansion would in turn lead to private-sector expansion as a result of restoring profitability. With rising profits, regulated labour costs and increasing demand in the economy, private business would increase investment, which in turn would lead to expanded growth and employment in industry.

LABOR'S RETREAT

In spite of outstanding but temporary growth in the economy in 1983/84, the government did not succeed in sustaining the recovery that it claimed would provide the basis for improving women's position. Even the potential benefits for women that may have derived from the re-introduction of an expansionary economic policy were not realised. From the beginning of 1985 the Labor government was faced with a continually worsening decline in Australia's terms of trade, increasing balance of payments problems, rapidly increasing national debt and a falling dollar. In addition to these external problems was the internal problem of the failure of business to increase productive investment within Australia.

This produced a quite dramatic upheaval in Labor' macroeconomic strategy. Focusing on the growth of the trade deficit as the key problem facing the economy, Labor targeted its entire strategy to the goal of restoring Australia's international competitiveness. In turn, Australia's terms of trade were to improve and the national debt was to be reduced. Labor emphasised three key factors as crucial to improved competitiveness. Firstly, it welcomed the dramatic devaluation of the Australian dollar, which reduced the effective price of our exports and made them more attractive to overseas buyers. Secondly, it argued that further reductions in real wages were required to decrease production costs for local producers over and above the benefits brought by devaluation. Thirdly, in order for devaluation to be successful it needed to be accompanied by a more restrictive budgetary policy. The government abandoned its previous full-employment goal and placed priority on reducing the budget deficit in order to restrict the growing demand in the economy that was drawing in imports. Increasingly restrictionist policies moved the government further away from any reform strategy likely to attack women's inequality.

A WRONG STRATEGY FOR WOMEN

The government has argued that the international environment has been a major constraint on its economic policy options. However, the reasons for the Labor government's problems and its inability to achieve progressive goals for women were related in large part to serious weaknesses in its own macroeconomic strategy. In particular, Labor has pursued an almost obsessive attack on the budget deficit at the expense of economic and social equity goals. Similarly, in addressing the severe structural problems within the economy it has focused almost exclusively on the trade deficit and ignored other equally serious structural problems.

Above all, the government's strategy has relied ultimately on a naive belief in the free-market's ability to restore productive investment to the economy with a subsequent flow-on of benefits to the community. This simply has not happened. In spite of an improved environment for profitability, business had not engaged in substantial new investment, particularly in industry. Clearly, an economic policy based merely on getting the economic environment right while relying upon market and business entrepreneurial endeavour is not enough to ensure increased productive investment in the economy.

Furthermore, financial deregulation has locked the Australian economy firmly into a greatly increased dependence on the international economy. Progressive government policies are now likely to trigger a major loss of confidence within the international money markets. Economic policies to significantly benefit women are not likely to emerge without more, rather than less, public control over the economy and without a far more interventionist government macroeconomic strategy and trade and industry policy.

The government has argued that economic recovery is the first step towards being able to introduce equity policies. Certainly a macroeconomic strategy that will genuinely produce economic recovery and industry restructuring is an essential accompaniment to policies to improve women's economic position. However, economic recovery and restructuring are only the first steps. Women's inequality is so deeply entrenched in our economy that a fundamental and radical programme of redistribution is required. Labor's chosen macroeconomic strategy has been disastrous for women in particular, because not only has it not produced economic recovery but it has also made progressive policies in the specific areas considered below extremely difficult.

BUDGETARY POLICY

Through the period 1983/84, the government's expansionist budget strategy appeared to be highly successful, producing significant public-sector led growth in the economy. During 1983, through the mini-budget in May and the August budget,

> **Budget deficit:**
>
> The difference between the government's domestic budget expenditures and its incoming revenue (when expenditures are greater than its revenue). Governments can finance budget deficits by three methods:
>
> - producing more money
> - borrowing from the private sector (local or overseas)
> - increasing taxes

the government managed to pull back the deficit while still increasing government expenditure outlays by 7.7 percent in real terms. It further stimulated the economy by introducing small tax cuts, by ending the conservative government's wage freeze and restoring wage indexation, and by increasing the public capital works budget by 22 percent.

The year 1984 was extremely successful for the Labor government. Expansionist policies, combined with temporary external factors, produced a remarkable restoration of growth in the Australian economy. The recovery in turn produced substantial increases in tax revenues. The government was therefore able to introduce further measures to stimulate demand. It introduced further tax cuts totalling $1.3 billion, slight increases in welfare payments, a 44 percent increase in job creation schemes and, finally, a 6.1 percent real increase in total budget outlays. Public-sector spending reached the near record level of 30.8 percent of Gross Domestic Product (GDP) in 1984/85.

For women on low incomes the overall trends within the economy during 1983/84 were hopeful. In the lead-up to the December 1984 election, the Labor government seemed to be in an unassailable position and well placed to go into a second term with a record majority. In this environment it would have been reasonable to expect the government to implement an even more expansionary economic strategy, from which most women would have benefited, and to adopt a programme of reforms to benefit women on low incomes or dependent on the state.

FROM EXPANSION TO RESTRICTION

However, the period following the 1984 election produced a very different policy framework. This was partly the result of the dramatically changed global economic outlook. But it was also due to weaknesses in the government's macroeconomic strategy. The result was enormous pressure for the abandonment of an expansionist budgetary policy.

No doubt increasing awareness of the emerging problems in the economy was a key factor in Prime Minister Hawke's decision to call an early election in December 1984. During the lengthy election campaign the Prime Minister suddenly announced a major change of direction in budgetary policy. The government publicly committed itself to a set of fiscal policy constraints, which came to be known as the Trilogy. The Trilogy commitments put an extraordinary restriction on the range of budgetary policy options available to the government. Firstly, there would be no overall increase in taxes during the next parliamentary term. Secondly, there would be no increase in the budget deficit as a percentage of GDP. Thirdly, government expenditure increases would be held below the rate of growth in the economy as a whole. The principles adopted by the government in the Trilogy represented a total capitulation by Labor to neo-liberal economic thinking. They also represent an abandonment of any possibility of a progressive and equitable solution to the government's budgetary crisis. Cuts in government spending areas of benefit to women were made inevitable.

In order to meet the goals set out in the Trilogy, not only was the government forced to abandon its earlier strategy of using public sector expansion to stimulate the economy but it was forced to cut back dramatically on expenditures such as welfare, health and childcare. In practice, the cut backs actually exceeded the guidelines presented in the Trilogy. In May 1985 the government announced overall expenditure cuts of $1.25 billion from the forward estimates of the 1985/86 Budget. In the August Budget itself the projected budget deficit was further reduced to $4.9 billion. This was about $2.3 billion lower than the ceiling implied by the Government's Trilogy commitment (Stilwell, 1986:65). The 1986/87 Budget posed a major problem for the Treasurer. A considerable amount of revenue was lost to the government as a result of promised tax cuts and a significant fall in the price of crude oil on the world markets. In addition, the government had been obliged to hand out substantial subsidies to both banks and farmers during the previous year (Stilwell, 1986:66). By substantially restricting loans and grants to the states, freezing public service staff levels and applying a further $900 million cuts in expenditure programmes, the government was able to bring in a planned deficit figure of only $3.5 billion.

The biggest cuts, however, were introduced in a May 1987 mini-budget. At that time, Treasurer Keating announced projected cuts to the 1987/88 Budget amounting to $4 billion. Savings were to come from a reduction of $1 billion in grants to the states and $1.6 billion worth of cuts to Federal expenditures. Government income was boosted through the sale of $1 billion of government assets and $400 million in extra revenue from sales tax. The *Australian Financial Review* (14 May 1987) commented that the cuts were cleverly concentrated on sectors where the backlash would be minimal. These included cutting the dole for sixteen and seventeen-year-olds, scrapping the Community Employment Program, which had provided jobs for a large number of women, and cutting family allowances for women living in families earning more than $50 000. Further minor cuts combined with increases in revenue in September produced a projected budget deficit for 1987/88 of only $27 million—virtually a balanced budget (*Australian Financial Review* 16 September 1987).

THE IDEOLOGY OF THE MARKET

While these budgetary cutbacks at first sight seem in total contradiction to the expansionary policies pursued in 1983/84, in retrospect it can be seen that, although marking a change of direction, they were not incompatible with the underlying assumptions of Labor's previous strategy. In particular the Treasurer, Paul Keating, had always argued that the government's role in stimulating the economy was a strictly limited one. He argued that while the recovery of the first two years of Labor's administration was public-sector led, the recovery should thereafter be fuelled by the private sector. Thus, while the impetus for the change of direction to a less expansionist policy was the need to cut off inflationary pressures that were drawing in imports, the change was actually very compatible with Keating's and the Labor right wing's own policy preferences.

In opposition, the Labor Party had adopted a broad expansionist approach to economic policy under the then leadership of Bill Hayden and the centre left faction of the ALP. In office, and under the right wing leadership of Bob Hawke and Paul Keating, the party felt less comfortable with this strategy. In fact, the emergence of a more adverse economic climate was to some extent seized upon by the dominant right wing faction of the Labor government as an opportunity to shift to their preferred policy approach. Paul Keating in particular was concerned that following the 1984 election there would be strong pressures building within the government and ALP for a more rapid expansionary policy through major increases in spending. This was a policy the right wing strongly opposed, due to their closer attachment to mainstream economic assumptions (Indecs Economics, 1986).

RESTRICTIONISM AND WOMEN

Labor's emphasis on the need to get the macroeconomic environment right first resulted in little progress being made in improving women's economic position. Furthermore, this policy resulted in the introduction of severe budgetary cutbacks that led to the worsening of women's position. Given the commitment of Labor to reducing the budget deficit without increasing taxation, it was inevitable that cuts had to come in areas of importance to women—including welfare, housing, education and employment.

The switch to a restrictionist budgetary policy not only had negative effects on all lower-income groups, including women in particular, it also failed to achieve the goals intended. Its major theoretical justification was the conservative 'crowding out' thesis adhered to by Treasury. In this view government spending should be restricted to make room for private-sector expansion. The role of the state is assumed to be limited to providing the environment for successful private capital accumulation. This theory is based upon a very conservative neoclassical view of the role of government. It also denies the need for any form of economic redistribution. Furthermore, the theory is unsound in its disregard of the role state expenditures play in stimulating the private sector by generating multiplier effects that boost the level of economic activity (Stilwell, 1986:67-8).

The development of what Frank Stilwell has termed Labor's 'deficit fetishism' was also related to its increasing political vulnerability to capital's demands on policy issues. Labor perceived the success of its policies to be dependent upon the willingness of local business to invest and that of the international money market to support the Australian dollar. Both groups were demanding a lower budget deficit. Hence Labor was obsessed with producing an ever-decreasing deficit, budget after budget. The problem for the government was that in spite of ever increasing cuts business never seemed satisfied. In reality, the size of the budget deficit, through its impact on interest rates, is only one of many factors that affect business decisions. In fact, restrictionist policies are more likely to prolong the recession. The failure of the increasing cutbacks to produce the expected response from business led to a great deal of frustration, not only within the government, but echoed in the conservative financial press as well. The *Australian Financial Review* castigated Australian and foreign business alike for its lack of entrepreneurial flair:

> Business is happy to have a favourably disposed government bending over backwards to avoid upsetting the delicate sensibilities of overseas lenders and local investors but it is either not prepared to accept that the private sector has a major role to play in any sustained national recovery or it simply will not believe that a genuine recovery is possible. (*Australian Financial Review* 22 August 1985)

An expansionist budgetary policy is clearly in the interests of most women, provided the expansion is in areas of state expenditure that produce growth, employment and economic redistribution. However, the experience of the Hawke Labor government makes it clear that the adoption of an expansionist budgetary policy is in itself not adequate to produce economic results likely to benefit women in the long term. While certainly producing a degree of growth and redistribution of economic resources in the shorter term, an expansionary budgetary policy that is not backed up by an interventionist trade and industry policy will, for example, run the risk of creating serious balance of payments problems. On the other hand, the Labor government's experience also clearly demonstrates that a restrictionist budgetary policy is unlikely to be in the interests of the majority of women. It did not produce the macroeconomic results that the government had hoped for and claimed. It certainly did not economically benefit women as a group and the cutbacks in key areas important to women were unjustified, unnecessary and disadvantageous.

THE PRICES AND INCOMES ACCORD

In the face of a restrained budgetary policy, the government held up the Prices and Incomes Accord as the means by which workers and their families would be protected and economic equity promoted. The Accord certainly contained aspects that offered benefits to women. In return for wage restraint by stronger sections of the workforce, unions were offered a return to a centralised wage fixation system. The aim was to guarantee the maintenance of real wages in the context of economic recession and over time provide for an increase in living standards in line with increases in national productivity. Women with low incomes, who generally have a low level of trade union participation and little industrial bargaining power, stood to benefit from a return to a centralised system of wage indexation. Simultaneously, the government promised to take measures to restrain prices and non-wage incomes. Such a move would certainly benefit women as managers of household budgets. The Accord also identified as one of its key objectives the achievement of 'an equitable and clearly discernable redistribution of income' (Stilwell, 1986:163). This was to be done through restructuring and reform of the taxation system and a gradual increase in the 'social wage'. The latter was to occur particularly through expanded government expenditure on social security, essential services and social infrastructure—health, education and the public service (Stilwell, 1986:166). These policies too, if implemented, would clearly have been beneficial to the majority of women as well as to all disadvantaged groups. Finally, the Accord provided for the development of a strong industry policy with the objective of full employment through government interventionist policies and incorporating significant trade union involvement in economic planning. A highly interventionist industry policy aimed at restructuring Australian industry and the labour market was potentially of great benefit to women. It opened up the possibility of major reform of many of the structural inequalities facing women.

FEMINIST RESPONSES

In retrospect, the Accord has produced at best only limited benefits for women. Many feminists have perceived the Accord as totally negative for women (Hall, 1983; Blackman, 1984; Power et al., 1984). Their criticisms of the Accord have focused on two aspects. Firstly, the process by which the deals were done have been seen as effectively excluding women. While the Accord advocated the increased participation of unions and workers in economic decision making, this participation involved only a handful of key union leaders. Women, either individually or as a group, had little input in its formulation. Secondly, partly as a result of women's absence from the decision making process, the policies implemented under the Accord have themselves been severely criticised as ignoring the special needs of women or, even worse, as actually worsening the position of women.

In a strong feminist critique of the Accord, Danny Blackman characterised the arrangement as 'a compact with the patriarchy' (Blackman, 1984:17). She argued that the working class with which the Accord is concerned is seen as being predominantly male. The Accord document's single reference to women is in the specific area of equal opportunity in education and training. The economic strategy of the Accord is directed primarily at producing recovery in the manufacturing sector at the expense of areas where women are primarily employed. Furthermore, in spite of the rhetoric of the Accord, in reality the government and unions themselves placed a low priority on redistribution through expansion of the social wage, effective price control and tax reform. Finally, Danny Blackman voiced a criticism commonly heard from women in the union movement when she argued that the commitment to real wage maintenance contained in the Accord failed to raise the vital question of equal pay for women. In addressing the issue of what women would have argued for if they had been able to participate in negotiations over the Accord, she identified the following claims: equal pay/comparable worth; adequate childcare; a higher priority for increases in the social wage; genuine taxation reform; effective price control; and a commitment to public sector development (Blackman, 1984).

WOMEN'S WAGES

The major plus for women workers from the Accord has actually been the re-introduction of a centralised wage fixation system. This has helped lower paid and poorly organised women to achieve at least some wage progress at a time when none may have otherwise been possible. There is some evidence that under the Accord women's wages were higher than they would have been without the centralised wage fixing system it provided. Certainly, in the preceding period of Liberal/National government, 1975–83, the gap between male and female earnings had begun to widen as pay claims were resolved increasingly outside the wage indexation system (Prendergast, 1986).

From March 1983 to February 1987, adult women's full-time earnings increased by 35.9 percent while inflation as measured by the Consumer Price Index (CPI) changes increased by 32.1 percent. Women's full-time earnings also continued to improve slightly in relation to men's, rising from 77.3 percent of the male average to 78.6 percent over the same period (Women's Bureau, 1987). However, when the increasing number of part-time workers is also included in the comparison, women's total weekly earnings declined slightly in relation to men's, from 66.1 to 65.3 percent. These figures, of course, need to be further adjusted to take account of the rapidly growing number of women who have been forced outside the normal wage fixing system through the growth of home based work.

The introduction at the end of 1986 of a two-tiered wage system initially appeared to have benefits for women workers. Under the first tier, all workers received a flat increase. Within the second tier, however, they had to bargain with employers over a possible additional 4 percent. The fixed first tier increase improved women's relativities, but the crucial test for women was the extent to which they were able to obtain increases under the second tier. The Australian Council of Trade Unions (ACTU) argued that women would gain access to second tier rises through the inclusion of claims for supplementary payments and increases based on industry restructuring and changed work practices. In practice, however, it appears that second-tier increases proved much harder to obtain than unions expected. Few women workers appear to have gained agreements, and progress on negotiations over supplementary payments stalled. Of course, women workers have rarely been able to make progress in the industrial relations marketplace, where their bargaining power is at a minimum.

While women's full-time wage relativities improved under the Accord, the framework within which the Accord operated effectively inhibited progress on equal pay claims. While some gains were made, as through the nurses' comparable worth case in 1986, the overall effect of the Accord has been to slow down progress on achieving equal pay through the formal processes of the arbitration system (Short, 1986).

THE ACCORD AND THE STATE

In retrospect, the Accord illustrates two key points about the state's role in relation to women's economic interests. In the first place, it is a manifestation of the state's need to reconcile a number of conflicting pressures from different classes and economic interest groups. It clearly represents an attempt by the Labor government to respond to pressures on it from both capital and unions. While extreme differences exist in views about the particular economic advantages accruing to capital and labour as a result of the Accord, it does at least show that the state can be forced to respond in a formal way to the demands of economic interests other than capital. This is especially so when a Labor government comes to office. Secondly, however, the Accord's failure to address even the most fundamental specific economic issues of concern to women illustrates how crucially important it is for women to gain effective representation in trade unions and peak union organisations. Historically, the state has responded to union pressures to adopt policies that result in protection for male workers at the expense of female workers. As long as the ACTU and trade unions generally continue to see themselves primarily as the representatives of male workers, the influence they exert over the state will naturally continue to represent the interests of men.

THE SOCIAL WAGE

One area within which the Accord appeared to promise most for women was through its commitment to increasing the social wage. Certainly, in the first two years of government under Labor the level of spending in this area increased significantly. Thereafter, however, the social wage was subjected to quite severe cutbacks as the government's overall fiscal policy changed from a mildly expansionist approach to a restrictionist one.

The concept of a social wage is somewhat vague. In the Accord it is defined as 'expenditure by governments that affect the living standards of the people by direct income transfers or provisions of services'. This definition leaves room for debate about which government expenditures most directly affect the living standards of women. Most analyses of the social wage have included all Federal government expenditures on education, health, social security and welfare, housing and regional development, culture and recreation. From the point of view of women, it is debatable whether expenditures in all of these areas are equally beneficial to their own living standards. For example, attempts made in the Federal Women's Budget Program to disaggregate departmental expenditures in areas such as Sport and Recreation have shown that men are the major beneficiaries of these government outlays (Women's Budget Statement, 1987/88). Nevertheless, there is no doubt that women are major beneficiaries of government outlays in the important areas of health, social security and welfare to the extent that they are the main users of these services. Women also benefit from increased social wage spending to the extent that these areas of government are major employers of women.

In a recessionary environment, government expansion of the social wage area is attractive to women as a method of stimulating the economy, both because of its almost immediate impact on the level of aggregate demand for goods and services and because of its redistributive potential.

In the first two years of Labor government the overall level of expenditure in the areas of education, health, housing and social security/welfare increased significantly. Using outlays for 1975/76 as a base, social wage expenditures in 1983/84 were 115.6 percent of the 1975/76 figure (see table 3.1). The following year outlays increased to 124.8 percent of those in the last Whitlam government budget. Of course, as can be seen from Table 3.1, these aggregate figures disguise the fact that the bulk of the increased expenditure occured in the area of social security and welfare. This increase was partly the result of steadily increasing numbers of recipients of unemployment benefits and partly the result of administrative changes to unemployment and supportive parent benefits, which increased the value and availability of these benefits. Nevertheless, small increases did occur in government expenditures in education and housing and community amenities. Quite substantial increases occured in health expenditures as a result of the introduction of Medicare. Undoubtedly the restoration of a public health benefits system was a progressive step for women in Australia, since they receive over 60 percent of medicare benefits payments (Women's Budget Statement, 1987/88:69).

As the government increasingly resorted to a restrictionist budgetary policy from early 1985 onwards, the commitment in the Accord to significant increases in the social wage has fallen by the wayside. Overall spending on the areas of education, health, housing, social security and welfare barely grew in real terms at all, increasing by 1.8 percent in 1985/86 and by only 0.7 percent in the 1986/87 budget. Further substantial cuts in the May 1987 mini-budget actually produced a real cut in the social wage areas over 1986/87. The 1987/88 budget restored social wage spending to a level 1.9 percent above the situation following the May 1987 cuts.

Looked at as a percentage of total Federal government outlays, (Table 3.2), the overall social wage under the Hawke government has actually remained well below the levels achieved in the mid 1970s, including during the early years of the Fraser government. This is in spite of continual growth in the numbers requiring government support as a result of rising poverty and unemployment. Spending on education and housing in 1983/84-87/88 still fell well below expenditures in those areas

Table 3.1 Social wage outlays 1972/73–1987/88 as a proportion of 1975/76 outlays (expressed in constant prices)

	education %	health %	social security & welfare %	housing & community amenities %	total 'social wage' %
1972/73	38.4	43.0	67.3	15.3	51.2
1973/74	65.5	45.5	70.1	71.3	62.6
1974/75	104.1	50.6	85.9	133.8	83.5
1975/76	100.0	100.0	100.0	100.0	100.0
1976/77	104.8	77.2	113.7	74.7	98.8
1977/78	105.3	75.8	122.4	60.2	101.3
1978/79	103.8	76.3	125.0	41.7	100.7
1979/80	97.3	75.7	123.4	26.0	97.4
1980/81	98.7	78.7	126.0	28.4	99.9
1981/82	100.7	56.3	130.6	30.6	96.4
1982/83	103.1	59.6	144.4	44.4	105.4
1983/84	105.3	71.4	156.2	56.8	115.6
1984/85	109.5	93.4	159.6	66.7	124.8
1985/86	111.2	97.7	160.3	66.9	126.6
1986/87	109.2	98.8	159.2	70.3	126.3
1987/88	111.4	101.2	163.9	54.1	128.2

Source: Australian Government, *1987/88 Budget* Statement 6, Table 3, p. 389

as a percentage of total government outlays during the latter part of the Whitlam period and the early years of the Fraser government.

Although comprising a major element of the Accord agreement, the Hawke government has set a low priority on increasing the social wage to provide a degree of redistribution towards wage and salary earners and the poor. The budgetary policy adopted by Labor has made any further expansion of the social wage since 1984 virtually impossible. In fact, as the government has committed itself to a lowering of the budget deficit, it has been forced to look increasingly into the social wage for programmes and benefits that might be cut. Labor's 'Razor Gang' has actually proven far more effective than the previous conservative government's. Labor has claimed that it has cut spending in welfare areas only as a result of the overwhelming pressures for budgetary restraint. However, from a feminist perspective the government appears to have chosen the restrictionist strategy as the politically easiest solution. Cutting the social wage was perceived as a politically less painful way of reducing the deficit than, for example, increasing taxation for high and middle–income groups and corpora-

Table 3.2 Social wage outlays as a percentage of total outlays 1972/73–1987/88

	education %	health %	social security & welfare %	housing & community amenities %	total 'social wage' %
1972/73	4.4	7.8	20.7	0.9	33.8
1973/74	7.0	7.8	20.4	3.8	39.0
1974/75	9.3	7.2	20.8	6.0	43.3
1975/76	8.5	13.6	23.1	4.3	49.5
1976/77	9.0	10.6	26.5	3.2	49.3
1977/78	8.8	10.1	27.8	2.5	49.2
1978/79	8.6	10.0	27.9	1.7	48.2
1979/80	8.1	10.1	27.9	1.1	47.2
1980/81	8.0	10.1	27.5	1.1	46.7
1981/82	7.9	7.1	27.8	1.2	44.0
1982/83	7.6	7.0	28.8	1.6	45.0
1983/84	7.2	7.8	29.0	1.9	45.9
1984/85	7.1	9.6	27.9	2.2	46.8
1985/86	7.0	9.8	27.4	2.1	46.3
1986/87	7.0	10.0	27.4	2.2	46.6
1987/88[a]	7.3	10.5	28.9	1.8	48.5

Note: [a] forward estimates
Source: Australian Government, *1987/88 Budget* Statement 6, Table 1, p. 387

tions (see Chapter 4). While the government claimed its actions were motivated by economic pragmatism and 'rationalism', it was also a class and political decision to implement a strategy that would place the burdens on the politically weaker groups. It is in the two areas of housing and welfare where the effect on women has been most severe.

HOUSING

The cost and availability of housing is of crucial economic importance to women. At the time of the election of the Hawke government a major housing crisis existed in Australian cities for people on low incomes (Rossiter et al., 1985:21-2).[1] Women predominate in those types of households most likely to experience housing problems—single-adult households and one-parent families.[2] Housing costs are a major contributor to the economic stress faced by the estimated 700 000 Australian families who have incomes below the poverty line after they have paid for their housing (Vipond, 1986:19-21).

In order to stimulate the housing construction industry, the Hawke administration during 1983/84 introduced a new First

Home Owners Scheme (FHOS) and dramatically boosted housing funds for state governments under the Commonwealth-State Housing Agreement (CSHA). Under the FHOS, over 90 000 were given assistance to buy homes during its first year of operation (Paris, 1987:9). Commonwealth government outlays peaked at $306 million for FHOS in 1984/85 and declined to $222 million in 1987/88. The Labor goverment also injected substantial funds into housing by increasing direct grants to the states for public housing by 230 percent over the three years to 1985/86. Over the same period, allocations under CSHA for repayable loans to the states increased by 61 percent in real terms (Peetz, 1985:53). Overall, Commonwealth housing assistance to state and local governments increased from $444 million in 1982/83 to $ 1191 million in 1986/87.

Critics of the government argued that the achievement of Labor's policy was less than it claimed. Chris Paris described the FHOS as having been 'little more than middle-class welfare'. He also pointed out that the rapid growth in housing commencements during 1983–85 was not sustained and there have been few significant Commonwealth housing initiatives since the December 1984 election. Overall outlays for housing were actually cut quite drastically in 1987/88 budget allocations.

To some extent also, the benefits to home buyers provided by the FHOS were undermined by aspects of the government's broader macroeconomic policy. In particular, the government's policy of maintaining a tight monetary policy, which contributed to sustaining very high levels of interest, had a severe effect on the housing sector. This problem was worsened by the government's decision to deregulate the financial system. In April 1986 the government agreed to remove controls on interest rates for all new mortgages while protecting the loans of existing borrowers. The decision to make new homebuyers bear the burden of the increased rates was not only inequitable but also directly contradicted the government's own policy of attempting to stimulate the housing industry.[3]

In terms of its benefits for women, an even more important criticism of Labor's policy approach was that it failed to tackle the issues of poverty and gross inequalities in access to housing. Labor gave priority to the use of housing as part of its macroeconomic policy. Far less priority was given to housing inequalities. Instead, the government preferred to rely on the market to 'trickle-down' the benefits to those with fewest resources. For women in housing difficulties, the government's increased spending on housing provided little concrete assistance.[4]

WELFARE

Of all the budgetary expenditures of the state, social security and welfare outlays are the most directly redistributive towards women. Sixty percent of all recipients of government pensions in Australia are women. At the end of June 1987, 1.6 million adult women in Australia were dependent upon a government pension or benefit for their livelihood (Department of Social Security, 1987). In other words, over 25 percent of all women basically relied upon state welfare for their economic existence.[5]

Under the Accord, the ALP and the ACTU agreed that in government Labor would give priority to welfare policies (Stilwell, 1986:171). From its first budget in 1983 the Hawke government's welfare policies have come under strong criticism from both women's organisations and welfare groups. The most common criticism has been based on Labor's failure to implement reforms regarded as long overdue. These groups have been extremely critical of the government's failure to index welfare benefits to cost of living increases or even to increase payments of some benefits at all. For example, family allowances decreased in real value by 34 percent between 1976 and 1987.

In practice, Labor's rhetorical commitment to the goal of greater equity translated into a more limited policy of targeting resources to people in greatest need, especially 'the dependent, the disabled and the disadvantaged' (Elliot, 1986:135). The Labor government's welfare goals became the efficient management of limited resources rather than an expansion of welfare expenditures.

However, as the government moved to a more restrictionist budgetary policy after 1985 it began to apply actual cuts to the welfare area. Publicly, the Hawke government has taken great care to stress that in applying a restrictionist policy it has sought to protect the position of the least advantaged in the economy—'restraint with equity'. But in order to achieve the sort of reductions in the size of the budget deficit applied in 1986/87 and 1987/88, the government has been forced to cut into the welfare areas.

Many of the changes to the welfare system introduced under Labor have clearly disadvantaged women. The most outstanding example of such a decision is the introduction of means testing for family allowances in the 1987 May mini-budget. The impact of means testing is to reduce or eliminate family allowances for 200 000 women with 370 000 children (Women's Budget Statement, 1987/88:254). In addition, changes to windows' and supporting parents' pensions and benefits mean that when their children are over sixteen they must apply for unemployment benefits. The harsher income test and loss of children's allowance and pension concessions left many women worse off.

During the 1987 election campaign the Labor government announced the introduction of what it claimed was a major reform initiative that would eradicate poverty among children by 1990. The policy involved the introduction of a new family allowance supplement to be paid on top of existing family allowances and to be available to all welfare recipients and low-income families. The reform was estimated to cost an additional $600 million per year. Undoubtedly, this increase in resources for the alleviation of poverty will benefit large numbers of welfare-dependent and low-income earning women. On the estimation of researchers from the Social Welfare Research Centre the package will reduce the number of children in welfare-dependent families living in poverty by between 135 000 and 180 000. However, even with these welfare increases there would remain between 450 000 and 500 000 children in poverty in Australia (Saunders and Whiteford, 1987:22–4).

The eradication of poverty is a crucial economic goal for women, since they form the vast majority of those adults affected by it. However, poverty is the result of very deeply-rooted structural problems and inequalities. It is not likely to be eradicated merely by increasing welfare payments. In itself the provision of welfare by the state poses a dilemma for feminists. On the one hand, the development of the welfare system has increasingly locked women into a dependent relationship with the state. On the other hand, state welfare is the only support available to many women. In practice the women's movement in the 1980s has found itself spending an increasing part of its energies fighting battles to prevent welfare cuts. Inevitably, this is a limited strategy. The focus of any proposed economic strategy by progressive forces must be directed towards achieving increased equality in society rather than merely extending the welfare system.

For this reason the most important progressive step taken by the government in the welfare area has been the introduction of a major Social Security Review. In February 1986 the Minister for Social Security, Brian Howe, announced the review, which was to be based on the objectives of achieving vertical and horizontal equity, and facilitating the entry of welfare recipients into the workforce. This radical shift in social welfare policy indicates a recognition of the importance of assisting people in poverty away from welfare dependence and into paid work. The idea of developing such a strategy has been applauded within the welfare sector. However, encouraging welfare recipients to obtain jobs depends for its success on employment being available. It also depends upon state assistance to overcome the barriers that have partly prevented them from previously obtaining employment, such as childcare. Since the Labor government has not shown any signs of changing its policies to work towards full employment or adequate childcare, the new welfare strategy is unlikely to succeed. Reforms in one policy area are usually dependent for success upon an overall progressive economic strategy. Even worse, Labor's reforms may end up leaving many of the poor without access to either employment or welfare.

LABOUR MARKET POLICY

While the Labor government has effectively abandoned the Keynesian economic goal of full employment, one of the real successes since it came to office has been the substantial growth in employment. Between August 1982 and August 1987 over 830 000 new jobs have been created and 60 percent of these have been occupied by women and girls (Wajcman and Rosewarne, 1986:15). The total number of women in employment rose by almost half a million over this period, an increase of over 20 percent. Women's overall labour market participation rate increased from 44 to 48 percent while men's continued to decline from 77 to 75 percent. Similarly, women's measured unemployment declined between August 1983 and August 1987 from 9.9 to 8.3 percent (ABS, *Labor Force Australia*). Furthermore, there was a substantial reduction in the huge numbers of women classified as hidden unemployed and discouraged jobs seekers. By adding these women to the official unemployment figures, we find that 28.9 percent of women in the labour force were actually unemployed in September 1983. Three years later, however, this had been reduced to 23.4 percent (Women's Bureau, 1987).

Of course, it is impossible to identify with certainty the degree to which the government itself was responsible for this.

The government has naturally claimed that it has been the result of its macroeconomic policies. Some of it can certainly be related to expansion of jobs in the public sector. Of the 431 300 female jobs created between August 1983 and May 1987, 22 700, or 5.3 percent, were in the Commonwealth public sector. Over that period, women's employment in the Commonwealth public service expanded by 17.1 percent compared with only 3.1 percent for men. A further 84 000 new women's jobs were generated by state and local governments (ABS, *Employed Wage and Salary Earners Australia*).

However, by far the largest increase was in the private sector, where over 300 000 new jobs for women were created in this period (ABS, *Employed Wage and Salary Earners* 1987). This result is in line with the government's strategy of seeking to generate economic recovery from within the private sector. The nature of these jobs, however, raises some critical questions. In the first place, a high percentage of private sector jobs, in contrast to those in the public sector, were part time. Between 1983 and 1986 almost one half of these new jobs were part time, a trend that appears to be accelerating. Over the year 1986/87 almost three out of four new jobs for women were part time. The increasing trend to part time employment represents a deterioration in the working conditions of women's work. A study of part time work by the Australian Bureau of Statistics in 1986 suggests that more than three-quarters of these jobs are casual, without the benefits of holiday pay, sick leave and other fringe benefits. They offer little or no job security and rates of pay well below full-time employees (Sharp, 1987).

Of concern also is the fact that labour market sex segmentation has actually continued to worsen under Labor.[6] The overall concentration of women workers in the four main female industry groups increased from 72.6 to 73.6 percent between 1982 and 1987 (ABS, *Labour Force Australia*).

Clearly the Labor government cannot be blamed for these trends. Rather they are a direct result of restructuring and recession within the Australian economy. However, the government's basic commitment to a non-interventionist, 'trickle-down' economic strategy has left women workers largely at the mercy of an extremely harsh labour market. In spite of a number of worthwhile, but minor, labour market programmes introduced by the government, there have developed no real labour market policies capable of protecting women from these negative changes. Neither has there been any sign of a commitment to a wider strategy on the scale required to attack the historical inequalities. The labour market policies applied by the government that have attempted to address women's workforce problems are of four main types—legislative reforms; job creation schemes; training programmes; and childcare provisions.

LEGISLATIVE REFORMS

Labor has introduced a number of legislative reforms in the areas of affirmative action, equal opportunity and anti-sex discrimination. The Affirmative Action (AA) Act (1986) covers all women employed in private sector organisations with 100 or more employees and in tertiary educational institutions. The AA Act is essentially an educational strategy to raise employers' awareness of discriminatory employment practices and encourage organisations to improve women's career opportunities by removing discriminatory obstacles. In the public sector, Labor introduced an Equal Employment Opportunity (EEO) programme to ensure that departments adopted personnel practices enabling women to compete equally for promotion as well as eliminating all forms of discrimination. On a broader scale the Sex Discrimination Act (1984) provides a conciliation based mechanism for resolving complaints of discrimination within a wide range of areas, including the workplace. Where conciliation by the Human Rights and Equal Opportunities Commissioner is unsuccessful the complainant has ultimate access to a court.

Labor's equal opportunity legislative reforms have been strongly supported by women's groups and endorsed by the ACTU and many individual unions. However, even though equal opportunity legislation had previously operated for a number of years in some states, opposition from conservative parties forced the weakening of the legislation. In the final format it contained few punitive provisions and avoided establishing any quotas or targets for its goals.

The establishment of the legislation itself demonstrates that the state can successfully adopt equal rights policies in relation to the workplace. The form in which it was adopted, however, also illustrates how reforming policy initiatives by governments often fail to go to the root of the problems facing women. AA and EEO programmes are only of benefit to a strictly limited number of women working in already relatively well paid and high status jobs. The vast majority of women workers have little or no access to the benefits of these programmes. Such legislation cannot in itself provide equality to women. Other structural obstacles exist that prevent women from competing equally in a male-oriented working environment. While token legislation may be an important symbolic first step, in itself it has only limited potential to combat the 'totality of women's inequality' (Lovenduski, 1986:251).

JOB CREATION SCHEMES

Labor introduced two job creation schemes in an attempt to boost employment while maintaining the workforce experience of unemployed people. The Community Employment Program (CEP) was introduced in 1983 to create employment in projects sponsored by community groups and local government. A special attempt was made within the CEP project to provide equal opportunities for unemployed women and also to employ women in non-traditionally female work areas. In 1986/87, 9584 women occupied CEP jobs, which was 46 percent of total placements. Although the numbers were small, the CEP helped some women gain experience in the workforce. In September 1987, however, the scheme was abolished. Another scheme—JOBSTART—provided subsidies to employers for six months as an incentive to employ disadvantaged workers. In 1986–87 JOBSTART provided places for 68 000 workers, with just over one-third going to women. Unlike the CEP, however, there is no guarantee that JOBSTART creates new jobs. Rather it bears more resemblance to the schemes introduced under the Fraser government, which were criticised for merely subsidising existing jobs. In terms of JOBSTART's goal of opening up employment opportunities for women, the results have been extremely limited. Industry take-up of the programme has been heavily concentrated in male-dominated industries. Only 8 percent of places occured in the female dominated industries of finance, property, business and community services (Women's Budget Statement, 1987–88).

TRAINING PROGRAMMES

The Labor government has focused a lot of attention on labour market training for young women to combat sexual segmentation and increase women's workforce participation. In 1985 the Australian Traineeship system introduced a twelve-month training programme to improve both the long-term employment prospects of young people and the skill base of the workforce. A special attempt was made to place young women in industries and occupational areas in which they are underrepresented. The government's other labour market programmes also aim to improve the representation of women. These have included training allowances available to long-term unemployed persons and adult and youth training programmes to encourage the unemployed to use existing training programmes. In addition, a Working Group on Women in Apprenticeships was established in 1986 to encourage employers to broaden employment opportunities for women through formal apprenticeships. Apprenticeships provide about one-third of all full-time employment opportunities for school leavers but females have traditionally obtained only a small fraction of these (Women's Budget Statement, 1987–88).

In practice, the training programmes implemented by the government have had little success in breaking down labour market sex segmentation. Although women were well represented in the traineeship system—holding 68 percent of the positions in 1986/87—they did not succeed in breaking into traditionally male occupations. Similarly, in spite of the small initiatives in apprentice training, women still accounted for only 12 percent of all apprenticeships in 1986–87. While individual women certainly benefited, the schemes were clearly inadequate to tackle a problem the size of the existing labour market segmentation in Australia. The Labor government made a genuine effort to reform existing labour market programmes, but as Margaret Power has pointed out, such inadequacies cannot be overcome simply by including equity guidelines. Labour market programmes themselves are usually based on the assumptions of human capital theory (Power et al., 1984). That is, the strategy assumes that the sexual segmentation of the labour market is caused primarily by women's failure to invest in their own 'human capital'. Merely attempting to push young women into training programmes for the often hostile environment of male-dominated skilled work cannot in itself overcome the numerous structural barriers that determine the segmentation of the labour market.

CHILDCARE PROVISIONS

In the area of childcare the Labor government at first made a number of impressive advances. In the 1984/85 Budget, for example, the Treasurer announced a $30 million increase in new initiatives in children's services. Following the huge cutbacks implemented under the previous Liberal/National government, this increase restored the level of expenditure to that of the mid-1970s. Over the first two years of Labor government the proportion of children under the age of five with access to childcare rose from 3.6 to 5.8 percent. While pointing out that Australia still had a long way to go before a comprehensive, free, high-quality childcare system was available to all women with children, women's groups welcomed the direction of the Hawke government's policies. However, in the May 1985 minibudget, Treasurer Keating produced quite dramatic cuts in childcare. Later in the same year a new formula for childcare funding was introduced. This linked government subsidies solely to numbers of children catered for—ignoring the quality of care provided. It thereby placed enormous pressure on management in childcare centres to reduce the number of trained staff. The second major consequence of the new funding system was significantly higher fees. Deborah Brennan has pointed out that fees in Commonwealth funded childcare centres are now higher than the fees charged by elite private schools (Brennan, 1986).

While the Labor government has acknowledged the importance of childcare by substantially raising the level of spending in this area, it has failed to accept the overall significance of childcare in improving the labour market position of women. It has backed away from the idea of a universally available childcare system for women workers. The Finance Minister, Senator Peter Walsh, has estimated the cost of providing subsidised childcare for every child under five with one parent working at $1.3 billion a year. An initial capital injection of $2 billion would also be required. Eva Cox has challenged Peter Walsh's figures on the grounds that they are based on overestimated calculations (*Times On Sunday* 4 October 1987). For example, he assumed that 100 percent of all under fives would utilise childcare if it was available. But even accepting Peter Walsh's figures, the cost is certainly well within the government's reach. Commitment is what is required.

TRADE AND INDUSTRY POLICY

Government policies on trade and industry can have a profound influence on women's workforce situation. At the broadest level these policies strongly influence the macroeconomic scenario within which women live and work. Even where governments' choose to pursue basically non-interventionist policies on trade and industry, such policies have the result that women are more likely to be subject to the full, rather than the modified, impact of market forces. Secondly, when industries are changing and restructuring, government policies can significantly affect the availability of jobs for women. Finally, trade and industry policy debates are currently raising fundamental questions about the nature of employment, skill divisions, work organisation, retraining and many other crucial questions for workers. These debates could be used to put women's employment concerns on the political agenda as a legitimate part of the claims of all workers.

THE ROLE OF THE ACCORD

As we have seen, the version of trade and industry policy laid out in the Accord contains no mention of the specific position and needs of women in industry. The proposals outlined in the Accord's industry strategy have been perceived by women's groups as primarily concerned with preserving male jobs in manufacturing industry (Hall, 1983; Power et al., 1984) Recovery in the manufacturing sector has been emphasised at the expense of the public and service sectors where employment is more crucial for women. Similarly, the strategy outlined by the ACTU in its important publication *Australia Reconstructed* in 1987 focuses almost exclusively on manufacturing industry. While sexual segmentation of the labour market is identified as a problem, no significant specific strategies are recommended for combating it. Again women are totally invisible in trade and industry proposals (ACTU/TDC, 1987). From women's perspective a central component of any industry restructuring has to be a strategy for ending gender inequality in the labour market. Without such a strategy even a successful programme of industry restructuring may simply leave women workers further behind in the labour market.

DEVALUATION AND THE BALANCE OF PAYMENTS CRISIS

The Labor government has consistently asserted that its strategy for industrial development was based on establishing the correct macroeconomic environment for industry. The emergence of the balance of payments crisis, however, caused the government to allow interest rates to rise to try to shore up the exchange rate by encouraging capital inflow (Brain and Gray, 1986:24–6). However, in the longer term the government's policy has been to rely primarily on the market to solve the balance of payments problems.

Basically, the government believed that by encouraging the devaluation of the dollar the problems of the adverse balance of payments would be reversed. Australian exports would be cheapened in overseas markets and Australian export-oriented

> **Balance of payments:**
>
> A series of financial statements summarising Australia's external trading position. It tabulates the credit and debit transactions of Australia with foreign countries, international institutions, individuals and corporations. The balance of payments is in deficit if Australia's outgoing debits are greater than its incoming credits.
>
> Overseas transactions are divided into two broad groups:
>
> - The *current account* is made up of 'visible' trade (imported and exported goods) and 'invisible' trade (services such as banking, insurance, tourism, shipping, company profits and interest payments).
> - The *capital account* is made up of money flows from borrowing, lending and the sale and purchase of capital assets between Australian overseas companies, individuals and governments.

manufacturers would be provided with an effective reduction in labour costs. Similarly, the price of imports would be increased, thereby depressing demand for imported goods and boosting local import-replacing production. Although there would be a delay in the response to the devaluation, in the longer run the benefits to Australian industry would be substantial. Hence the concept of a J-curve to describe the delayed, but ultimately beneficial, effect of the devaluation on trade and Australian manufacturing industry. The Treasurer in particular has made it quite clear that having placed the economic 'fundamentals' in order, the government perceived no further need to develop an interventionist industry policy (Stilwell, 1986:93).

In a general sense, Labor's approach to trade and industry policy has been weak and inadequate. By relying on devaluation to overcome Australia's trade problems the government has placed a rather naive faith in the market to make the necessary changes to Australian industry. This approach ignores the severe structural problems in the Australian economy, which make it highly unlikely industry will suddenly change direction and move to export-oriented and import-replacing production. Only through a highly developed industry intervention programme could this be achieved.

Furthermore, the government was mistaken simply to blame increasing imports and falling export income for the balance

> **Devaluation:**
>
> The reduction of the rate at which Australia's currency is exchanged for other currencies.
>
> A devaluation of the A$:
>
> - makes Australia's exports cheaper overseas and hence tends to increase demand for them
> - increases prices for imported goods into Australia and hence tends to reduce demand for imports and encourage demand for locally produced goods

of payments problems and the falling Australian dollar. Of a total current account deficit in 1985/86 of $14.3 billion, only 22.9 percent was attributable to the traded goods (i.e., exports/imports) component. Another 29.7 percent of the current account deficit was directly related to the traded services area, in particular to shipping and insurance costs associated with international trade. An overwhelming 47.4 percent of the deficit, however, was accumulated under the transfer payments component of the current account balance. This covers payments of both interest and principal on foreign loans, together with profits and dividends repatriated by foreign-owned companies (ABS, *Balance of Payments Australia*). While the total foreign debt has rocketed alarmingly, over two-thirds has been generated by the private sector (Budget Paper No. 1, 1987/88). Official figures for private investment income paid overseas show an increase from $2.9 billion in 1982/83 to over $7 billion in 1985/86 (ABS, *Balance of Payments Australia*). One of the largest single contributors to the increased current account deficit has been the dramatic increase in profit repatriation by transnational corporations. The government has not seriously addressed these problems.

THE CRISIS IN INVESTMENT

Quite apart from these externally imposed restraints, one of the major failures of Labor's industry policy has been the continuing low level of business investment in Australia. Whereas investment as a proportion of GDP hovered between 16 and 18 percent during the late 1960s and early 1970s, it dropped to 14.5 percent in the worst recessionary years of 1974/75, 1977/78 and 1982/83. However, the rate of actual investment by business fell even lower during the recovery of 1983/84 and 1984/85. The Hawke/Keating strategy had been to restore the conditions for private capital's profitability in order for business to begin re-investing in industry. But Australian business did not engage in substantial new investment—particularly in manufacturing industry. Increased profitability has never automatically meant that business will increase investment. There are many things that business can choose to do with profits—productive industry investment is merely one. For example, business can choose to use increased profitablity to pay increased dividends, to repatriate increased profits overseas, to increase investment offshore, to takeover other companies or simply to speculate on the share market or the foreign exchange market. In fact, there is evidence that business was engaged in all of these activities rather than in new productive investment. Similarly, while the government has encouraged devaluation as a method of improving the competitiveness and profitability of export oriented production, there is no guarantee that companies already engaged in export industries are going to use their suddenly increased profitability to re-invest in Australian industry. The government has done little to ensure that they do.

THE CONSEQUENCES FOR WOMEN

From women's point of view, Labor's reliance on a fundamentally market based approach to trade and industry policy was particularly inadequate. Not only has the non-interventionist approach applied by Labor failed to produce new investment and an expansion of full-time, permanent jobs from which women could benefit, but the macroeconomic policies used in the attempt have had negative effects for women. Although the intended impact of devaluation to make Australian industry more competitive has been only partially successful, in the process it has substantially increased the prices of imported consumer goods. Low income earners and those dependent upon welfare have particularly felt the impact of this. Similarly, the falling dollar and the need to increase capital inflows to bolster the declining balance of payments has resulted in the government maintaining a high level of interest rates. Consumer debt has rocketed in Australia in recent years as low and middle-income earners have sought to maintain living standards in the context of falling real wages and increasing prices. The high cost of such credit has caused considerable financial hardship for many women and families. High interest rates have also severely increased the cost of housing for both homebuyers and tenants.

The government's market-based approach also acted to increase the pressures forcing Labor to retreat into the increasingly restrictionist budgetary policy which squeezed women, wage earners and the disadvantaged after the 1985/86 Budget. Although a number of factors contributed to force the government in this direction, three of these factors were directly related to the effects of devaluation. Both continuing high interest rates and increasing import prices help to sustain inflation at a level that made a more restrictionist budgetary approach hard to avoid. In addition, devaluation increased the value of Australia's foreign debt in real terms—since it has to pay the interest and principal with a devalued currency. The artificially increased size of the public sector component of the national debt has reduced the government's budgetary flexibility.

There is no doubt about who are the winners and losers from the huge devaluation of the dollar. The winners have been companies already engaged in export oriented production, whose profits have been dramatically increased by devaluation. The losers are those affected by the increasing costs of imports and by high interest rates—including key sectors of local industry, ordinary wage and salary earners and anyone in a vulnerable economic position.

In spite of the basically non-interventionist strategy pursued by the Labor government, it has been pressured into intervening through the implementation of a number of specific industry plans. This form of intervention, however, has been limited in three main ways. Firstly, the Accord conceived of industry policy as providing a degree of government and union influence and control over the process and direction of industrial development. The actual policies implemented under the Minister for Industry, Technology and Commerce, Senator John Button, have been geared towards merely improving the economic framework within which the industry operates and encouraging orderly rationalisation of the industry to allow it to be more competitive. Secondly, industry plans have been developed in only a few specific industries, in particular, in the steel, heavy engineering, motor vehicle and textile, clothing and footwear industries. In all cases government intervention has been in industries that are in serious difficulties, motivated by the government's perception of the need to save them rather than restructure them for the benefit of the workforce and the economy as a whole. Thirdly, the government's intervention

Figure 3.1 The impact of devaluation on budgetary policy

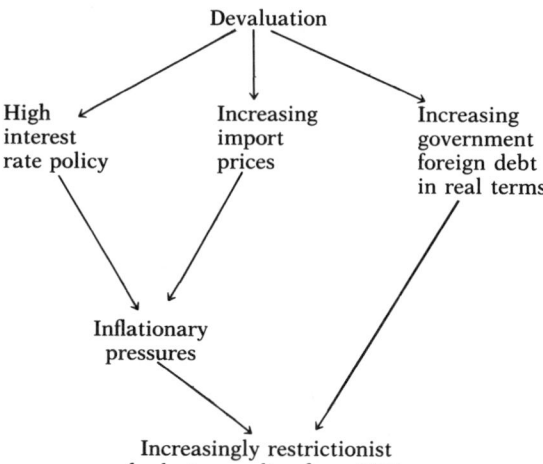

has been limited primarily to industries dominated by male workers. The survival and recovery of the manufacturing sector has been emphasised at the expense of the public and service sectors, where employment is more crucial for women.[7] The exception to this has been the introduction of an industry plan in the textile, clothing and footwear industry, which is dominated by women.

Although industry policy has in practice been male oriented and provided few progressive gains for women, a number of women unionists have continued to argue that women should struggle not only for a more interventionist industry policy but also for utilising industry policy to try to advance the position of women (Jones, 1984). As a result of developments in industry policy and the wage system, unions are entering into negotiations with employers at both industry and enterprise levels over issues not previously discussed. These include work practices, productivity, skill development, industrial health and safety and a range of areas previously considered to be subject to 'management prerogatives'—such as investment policy. It is in the interests of women workers to pressure unions to include women's employment issues on the negotiating agenda. It is critical for women that a strategy for overcoming women's labour market disadvantages be integrated into trade and industry policies.

LESSONS FROM THE LABOR GOVERNMENT

Fundamentally, the Labor government has not been hostile to women's demands for increased economic equality. It has consciously sought women's support electorally (*Times On Sunday* 14 June 1987; *Advertiser* 24 June 1987). It has conducted an extensive survey of women's views and needs through the National Agenda for Women exercise. It has introduced a number of labour market and welfare policies that have deliberately set out to encourage women away from economic dependency on family and the state. Under Labor the state has maintained a significant structure of the bureaucracy devoted to recommending and implementing progressive policies for women.

In spite of this apparent basic sympathy of the government towards improving women's position, however, the results of its policies have provided only limited benefits for women. In fact, some policies have actually worsened women's economic position, particularly for young women, low and middle-income earners, and those in poverty. This illustrates two major problems confronting feminists in attempting to utilise the state to pursue a progressive economic strategy for women.

Firstly, the experience of the Labor government demonstrates how destructive the domination of policymaking by conservative economic theory is for women. The influence of neo-liberal economic theory can be perceived in a wide range of specific policies introduced by Labor that have been negative in their effects on the majority of women. More importantly, however, the application of an overall conservative macroeconomic strategy not only produced economic outcomes that increased inequalities within the economy, but also created a budgetary environment that effectively destroyed the attempts by the government to introduce progressive policies in other specific areas. An economic strategy, even with progressive goals, that primarily relies on the market to distribute resources can only result in continued economic inequality for women.

Secondly, the economic strategy pursued by the Labor government demonstrates how the state tends to respond to the most powerful pressures exerted on it. The state under Labor has faced enormous pressures from powerful business forces to apply policies aimed at overcoming the economic problems of capital but which exacerbate economic inequalities and leave many people, including a great number of women, worse off. The pressures exerted on the state have, of course, not been entirely from capital. Unions have also had a powerful influence on aspects of the economic strategy of the Labor government. However, the concessions and trade-offs won by unions have not only been limited compared to the influence of business, but they have not proportionately benefited women workers.

An alternative economic strategy based on more progressive state intervention to promote increased equality is in the interests not only of the majority of women but the majority of the whole population. A crucially important part of developing a feminist economic strategy, therefore, is constructing strong links with other progressive political movements, such as trade unions, in order to increase the pressure that can be placed upon the state to introduce progressive policies.

In the long term, of course, the achievement of complete economic equality between women and men is incompatible with the unequal market and class systems that are the defining features of capitalism. Therefore, a feminist economic strategy must be integrally linked with a socialist economic strategy. In the shorter term, progress towards significantly increased gender equality within the framework of capitalism must also be linked with a strategy for a far more interventionist role by the state in order to modify and reverse the unequal distributional effects of the market. Feminists need, therefore, to be actively involved in the struggle to develop an 'alternative' economic strategy in Australia.

4 Women and taxation

Taxation is an important economic issue for women. It is also one of the few areas of economic policy debate in Australia in which women have been active participants and have successfully articulated a number of specific concerns. Feminist involvement in taxation policy so far has tended to be restricted to intervention on issues that appear to affect women in specific ways. However, taxation is a central prerequisite of all the state's activities. Therefore, a feminist challenge to the overall role of the capitalist state in relation to women must incorporate also both an analysis of, and a challenge to, the structure of the taxation system as a whole.

WHY TAXATION IS AN IMPORTANT ISSUE FOR WOMEN

Taxation affects women's economic and social well being in a number of ways:

- The taxation system is a major determinant of the amount of revenue that governments have available for those expenditures that benefit women.
- Changes in the mix and the level of taxation affects women's spending capacity both as income earners and as managers of the family household budget.
- Taxation significantly redistributes income and assets between individuals, between different type of families and within families.
- The taxation system significantly affects women's incentives to engage in paid work and their overall opportunities to be economically independent.

REVENUE RAISING

The capacity of the taxation system to raise revenue sets the ultimate parameters of the state's role in relation to women. The taxation system is important, therefore, in determining the amount of revenue available for expenditures on health services, public housing, childcare, income support, education and training and other government programmes and services utilised by women. While women have long recognised the importance of government expenditure, its nexus to the taxation system is less well observed. If women's arguments for an expansion of government expenditures are to be credible the state's capacity to raise revenue must also be examined. Of course, not all the activities of the state benefit women. The state's role in relation to women is ambivalent. Some of its expenditures clearly have a positive impact on women's economic and social status. Others, however, contribute to women's subordination. Nevertheless, in the final analysis, an adequate source of revenue is the lifeblood of the state. Without adequate taxation income the state would be unlikely to perform any role in improving women's economic position.

THE TAXATION MIX

The way in which the state raises its taxation revenue is an important consideration for women. In particular, if women are paying an unduly high proportion of taxation then the overall benefits from any state policies to improve the position of women will be reduced accordingly.

Taxation affects women's living standards both through their personal income tax and through the effect of taxation on the economic position of the family upon which women's status is often dependent. Women now represent nearly 40 percent of individual taxpayers. The proportion of personal income tax paid by women has been rising. Between 1970/71–1981/82 the proportion of female personal income taxpayers increased slightly while women's contribution to individual tax receipts increased by 40 percent (Women's Electoral Lobby, 1985:6). Apart from personal income tax, women are also especially affected by the type and levels of indirect taxes. For example, taxes on clothing, petrol, food and household durables all have an important effect on women's spending capacity as individuals and as household managers.

It is important to note that the amount of taxation women are required to pay is affected not just by those taxes that most obviously affect them (PAYE income tax and taxes on goods and services), but also by the incidence of other taxes that can provide state revenue and thereby reduce the taxation demands placed on women. Women are greatly affected, therefore, by the levels of taxation raised by company profits taxes, wealth taxes and non-PAYE income taxes, even though the majority of women do not themselves pay these forms of taxation. Without adequate revenue from these, the state is likely to be forced to squeeze more revenue from those areas in which the majority of women are taxable.

REDISTRIBUTION OF INCOME AND ASSETS

The taxation system is important to women because it is potentially capable of redistributing the allocation of incomes and assets within society. A progressive taxation system will redistribute incomes and assets downwards from rich to poor and from high-income to low-income earners. While clearly not all women would benefit from such a redistribution, the majority of women would. On the other hand, under a regressive taxation system poorer and lower-income groups pay proportionately more tax than better off groups, which would disadvantage most women.

Redistribution of income and assets between husbands and wives can also be the result of different taxation policies. A shift to joint or married unit taxation increases the tax liability of the spouse with the lower income (usually the woman) and decreases it for the higher earner. Similarly, the use of concessional deductions or rebates for certain types of family expenditures is more likely to increase the disposable income of the man in the family, since his higher income makes it more attractive for him to make the claim on behalf of the family.[1] The actual extent of redistribution of income and assets in the family will depend on how even is the control over family finances between spouses (Edwards, 1983). Taxation policy makers, however, invariably assume that all family resources are shared equitably.

The taxation system can also redistribute income and assets between different types of families. This can result from different tax treatments of children. Taxation rebates for dependent children and childcare lowers the tax liability and increases the disposable income of families with children relative to those without. In Australia the sole parent rebate and the higher dependent spouse rebate are examples of tax relief to particular types of families with children.[2] Support can also be provided to other categories of families through taxation deductions such as rebates for dependent spouses and various family related expenses, such as health care and housing loan interest costs. In Australia the dependent spouse rebate is the main tax device for redistributing income between categories of families. As a result, spouse (women's) dependency rather than the presence of children is the main way in which the tax system differentiates between different types of families.

PAID WORK INCENTIVES

The high effective marginal tax rates that result from the interaction of the taxation and social security systems is one circumstance where economic disincentives exist against women undertaking paid work. The combined impact of taxation on earnings and loss of assistance from means-tested social security is to impose high effective marginal tax rates on social security pensioners and beneficiaries who undertake even meagre forms of paid work. Effective marginal tax rates are frequently higher than the marginal tax rates facing the highest-income earners and can even be greater than 100 percent. The result can be to trap people in poverty and dependency on social security because they can actually be made worse off by undertaking paid work. Loss from paid work also occurs when there are childcare expenses and transport costs. Since there are more than 1.5 million Australian women dependent on social security payments, many of whom live below the poverty line, these circumstances can affect their opportunities to become economically independent. There are other ways in which the taxation system can impact on women's work incentives. For example, the husbands of married women who work lose the tax benefit of the dependent spouse rebate. The wife's income, therefore, may not be considered worth working for. The taxation system can be a powerful mechanism for reinforcing women's economic dependency either on the state or on men.

Finally, it needs to be recognised that while taxation does discriminate against women as a group, changes to the taxation system will have differing effects on women in different class positions. In particular, taxation reforms likely to benefit the majority of women because of their low income will invariably affect wealthy women in a negative way. For example, the introduction of a more progressive income taxation structure or a tax on wealth would benefit the majority of women but would not be welcomed by those who stand to lose. Clearly, this fact does not reduce the importance of taxation policy issues for women. It means, however, that on broad economic policy issues such as taxation the interests of all women will not be identical.

WOMEN AND THE AUSTRALIAN TAXATION SYSTEM

Australia, like most contemporary capitalist countries, has a highly complex system of taxation. However, there are four features of the system that are particularly important influences in determining its impact on women's economic position:

- The overall taxation system is not progressive in its impact on the distribution of income and wealth.
- Almost three-quarters of all taxation revenue in Australia is obtained from the two forms of taxation (PAYE income tax and taxes on goods and services) that most directly affect women.
- The taxation system is highly centralised with the Federal government collecting about 80 percent of total taxation revenue.
- Compared with other industralised countries, Australia has a relatively low overall level of taxation.

THE LACK OF PROGRESSIVITY

Because of the very unequal sexual distribution of income and wealth in Australia, the majority of women would benefit under a taxation system which is progressive in its impact. The precise distribution of Australian taxation is not known. Economists have had neither a strong inclination nor an adequate methodology for analysing the impact of the tax system in practice on the distribution of income and wealth. However, it is widely agreed that the available evidence supports the conclusion that the overall tax system is not progressive.[3] One of the few existing empirical studies, conducted by Neil Warren in 1975/76, concluded that the overall tax system was regressive for lower-income earners and proportional for some 74 percent of households. He found that the only element of progressivity was the high level of taxation paid by very high-income earners. Only personal income tax was progressive in its effect and a number of taxes, particularly taxes on goods and services, were regressive (Warren, 1979:23). For example, petrol excise accounted for 3.4 percent of the income of the poorest income group but only 1.2 percent of that off the top income bracket. Even company tax was regressive, declining from 6.7 percent of lower income households to 4.2 percent of the highest income group (Harding, 1984:42).

Subsequent analyses have been even more pessimistic. One

of Australia's leading tax analysts, Professor Russell Mathews, has consistently drawn attention to the regressive effect of the 'massive' level of tax avoidance by the wealthy in Australia (Mathews 1980, 1985). This effectively undermines the single element of the taxation system that is potentially in any way progressive—the high marginal tax rates for high-income earners. Similarly, in a 1985 paper, the welfare research section of the Brotherhood of St Laurence commented in an overview of the evidence that it believed the tax system had become even less progressive since 1975/76. While in theory the rate structure of the personal tax system remained progressive, the main reason for the regressive nature of the system was increasing avoidance and evasion amongst high-income earners (Brotherhood of St Laurence, 1985:10). The Warren study can also be criticised for underestimating the degree of regressivity of the tax system for women on low incomes. By examining the incidence of taxation only for households as single units, the study ignored the fact that women are almost invariably lower-income earners than their spouses and that the income taxation system is, therefore, likely to be even more regressive for them as individuals.

One of the most important reasons why the Australian taxation system in practice is regressive for women and other low-income earners is the very low or non-existent contribution to tax revenue from company profits, non-PAYE income earners and from the wealthy. In 1986/87 taxes levied on company profits contributed only 10.2 percent of overall taxation revenue (Figure 4.1). While the official company tax rate was 49 percent in that year, in reality companies paid only 19 percent of their overall gross operating surplus in taxes (Aarons, 1987). A number of Australia's largest corporations paid even less by engaging in tax avoidance. The giant investment corporation Industrial Equity Ltd. (IEL) paid only 5.4 percent of its profits in tax (Aarons, 1987). Similarly, non-wage and salary earners, comprising doctors, lawyers, farmers, builders, investors and so on, contributed only 14.3 percent of tax revenue (Figure 4.1).

Australia does not have a general tax on wealth such as an annual net worth tax.[4] At best, therefore, the taxation system can have a redistributive effect only on income. However, women's unequal economic position in Australia is determined more by the gross inequalities in the distribution of wealth than by income inequalities:

- the top 1 percent of individual adult wealth holders hold 25 percent of all net wealth

- the top 5 percent hold over half of all the country's net wealth
- the top 10 percent hold 60 percent of net wealth

In other words, the top 5 percent of wealthy Australians own more wealth than the bottom 90 percent (Raskall, 1987; Piggott, 1987). While there is a lack of firm information about women's wealth it is certain that women hold much less wealth in their own right than men.[5] For example, among the *Business Review Weekly's* list of the 200 wealthiest Australians, only two women gained a place in 1987 (*Business Review Weekly*, 14 August 1987:44) On the other hand, women are over-represented among the poor. Women comprise the great majority of the estimated one-seventh of the Australian population living below the poverty line.

Holders of substantial quantities of wealth and assets clearly have a greater capacity to contribute to government revenue than those without wealth. Consequently, a taxation system that does not require holders of wealth to contribute tax revenue based on their assets is obviously inequitable and regressive. A general tax on wealth containing a reasonable tax threshold would make the tax system more vertically redistributive and would, therefore, benefit the majority of women.

RELIANCE ON PAYE AND GOODS AND SERVICES TAXES

The particular mix of taxes employed significantly affects the overall impact of the system on women. The two most important taxes in the Australian tax system are Paye-As-You-Earn (PAYE) personal income tax and goods and services taxation.

The Australian taxation system relies particularly heavily on PAYE personal income tax paid by wage and salary earners. In 1986/87 personal income taxes contributed nearly 60 percent of Federal government taxation revenue. Almost three-quarters of all personal income taxes were paid by PAYE wage and salary earners. It is often pointed out that Australia has one of the highest proportions of personal income tax amongst the Organisation for Economic Cooperation and Development (OECD) countries. In 1982 Australia ranked third out of 23 OECD countries in terms of the proportion of its total tax revenue coming from personal income tax (Draft White Paper, 1985:22). However, this analysis ignores two important issues. Firstly, as already outlined, it is the PAYE component that contributes the vast majority of personal income taxation revenue. Secondly, Australia is one of the few countries that does not have a

Figure 4.1 Federal government tax mix 1986/87

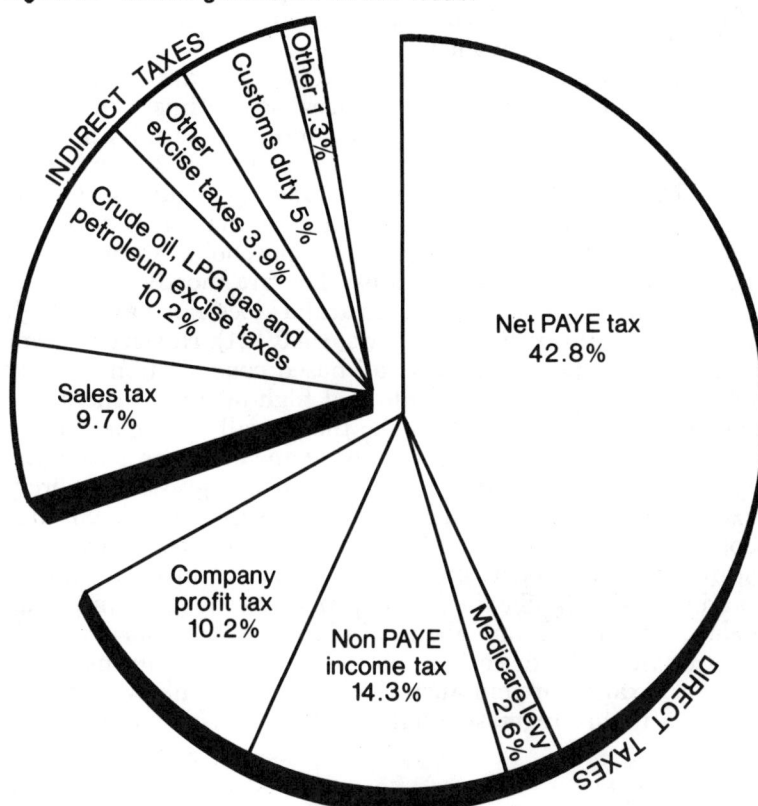

Source: Australian Government Budget Statements 1987/88. Budget paper No. 1 p. 400

social security levy on personal incomes. When this is taken into account Australia's rank position drops to about sixteenth among OECD countries (Indecs Economics, 1988:146). From women's point of view, a taxation system that relies heavily on personal income tax could be seen as positive, since this form of taxation, with its rising marginal tax rate structure, has the capacity to be progressive in its effect. Since many women are not income-earners, and the majority who are earn below average weekly earnings, women could expect personal income taxation to redistribute income in their direction. Unfortunately, the absence of any real degree of progressivity in the operation of the personal income tax structure has undermined this potential benefit. Nevertheless, in strategic terms, support for a reformed progressive income tax structure is certainly in the economic interest of women.

A second feature of the tax mix that is important to women is the role of taxes on goods and services—sometimes referred to as indirect taxes. These taxes (for example, on petrol, imported goods and on consumer purchases) contributed 30 percent of total Federal taxation revenue in 1986/87 (Figure 4.1). This affects women both as consumers and as managers of household budgets. Women in low-income households are adversely affected by indirect taxes because they are mostly regressive. By international comparison, Australia does not have a high level of indirect taxation (Mathews, 1980:121). However, recent New Right proposals for a broad based consumption tax and reduced income tax for middle and high-income earners and companies would certainly make the overall tax system more regressive. In policy terms, it is in women's interest to argue against the introduction of new forms of regressive indirect taxes such as taxes on food and childcare services. There is also scope for women to argue for reform within the structure of indirect taxation itself, since what is taxed is arbitrary and it could be made significantly more progressive (e.g., by imposing higher rates on luxury goods). Unfortunately, from women's point of view, the main item on the agenda for reforms in the indirect taxation area in Australia has been the likely introduction of a highly regressive flat rate broad-based consumption tax.

REVENUE RAISING DOMINANCE OF THE FEDERAL GOVERNMENT

While state and local governments provide crucial services for women such as health care, children's services and welfare, it is at the Federal level that the key decisions about taxation are made. State and local governments together in 1985/86 obtained 43 percent of their revenues from Federal grants and taxation transfers (Moore, 1986:32). Increasing Federal financial stringency towards state and local governments during the 1980s has produced not only cuts in these governments' services but also an increase in regressive state taxes and charges.

A further point about the centralised taxation system in Australia is that in order to change the impact of taxation policies on women, pressure must be primarily exerted on the Federal government. While a decentralised power structure provides feminists with a larger range of 'access points' to affect decision-making, it also tends to produce relatively minor incremental changes to policy. Although a more centralised power structure is more restricting in terms of where political pressure can be applied, it offers the opportunity for more radical changes (Randall, 1982:137). It is notable that the National Taxation Summit in 1985 provided women with a forum to debate taxation reform on a scale never before available in Australia. It also gave women the opportunity to enter into alliances with a range of other powerful interest groups, including trade unions and welfare organisations, on a national level.

AUSTRALIA IS A LOW TAX COUNTRY

In contrast to the strident assertions of some conservative groups, Australia is not a highly taxed nation relative to other industrialised capitalist countries. In terms of total taxation revenue measured as a percentage of GDP, in 1985 Australia was the fifth lowest taxed nation of the 23 OECD countries (Indecs Economics, 1988:147). Moreover, the Scandinavian countries that have had the highest overall levels of taxation have also had very good economic performances. This is particularly significant for women. It means that taxation can be both increased and made more progressive without harming the economy. A higher revenue yield and higher levels of taxation for companies and better-off individuals, therefore, is not only in the interests of women but economically justifiable.

THE TAXATION CRISIS AND ITS IMPACT ON WOMEN

Governments in all Western capitalist countries have over the past two decades been confronted by a major fiscal crisis. This has largely been due to vastly increased demands for state expenditures at a time when the ability of governments to increase their revenues has been restricted. Government budgets have consequently been squeezed from both ends. The results have profoundly affected women because of the resulting cutbacks in certain areas and because of effects on government revenue raising through taxation.

THE FISCAL CRISIS OF THE STATE

The fiscal crisis and the pressures it placed on the taxation system had begun to emerge even prior to the onset of recession. In the early 1970s, James O'Connor developed the argument that long-term changes in the structure of capitalism had combined to produce a vastly greater role for the state. These changes included the concentration of economic ownership into fewer and fewer giant corporations and the transition from competitive to monopoly capitalism (O'Connor, 1973). In response, the state was forced to become more active in assisting capital accumulation for corporations. It also had to involve itself in stabilising the economic system and ensuring the social reproduction of the system as the patriarchal family structure proved increasingly inadequate to carry out this role. James O'Connor argued that vastly increased state spending was required to support the costs of modern private investment projects with the required social and technical infrastructure. These increasing costs related to the state's role in assisting private capital accumulation placed great strains upon the limited financial resources governments could draw upon. Similarly, the increasing involvement of the state in the social reproduction and stabilisation of capitalism as a social system through the growth of the welfare state after World War II completely transformed the size and range of the state's role in the economy.

Naturally the onset of international recession severely exacerbated the fiscal crisis of the capitalist state. On the one hand, the recession placed increasing demands on government expenditures. In Australia, the numbers receiving unemployment benefits rose dramatically from 13 000 in 1970 to 311 000 in 1980. By 1984 the number had reached 585 000. The proportion of the population aged fifteen years and over receiving social welfare had doubled during the period 1970–1984 from 11.7 to 22.2 percent (Kirby Committee Report, 1985:35). Consequently, by the mid-1980s, almost one quarter of the adult population were financially dependent on the state.

On the other hand, the economic recession put further pressure on the sources of government taxation income. Company profitability declined, thereby reducing company tax revenues. Unemployment affected the level of personal income tax collections. To some extent the process of fiscal creep, whereby individual taxpayers paid higher amounts of income tax because of the failure to index the personal tax scales for the effects of inflation, offset the government's taxation revenue shortfalls. Nevertheless, Australian governments, and governments in all capitalist countries, faced rising budget deficits.

The emergence of the fiscal crisis of the state has been accompanied by far-reaching changes in the taxation system that have led to redistribution of the tax burden as well as the benefits conferred by the tax system (termed fiscal welfare).

This has had profound implications for women. Furthermore, the fiscal crisis combined with a growing electoral perception of the redistributive process within the taxation system gave taxation reform a place on the public policy agenda never before achieved in Australia.

TAX EVASION AND AVOIDANCE

During the 1970s and 1980s tax evasion and avoidance became one of the fastest growing 'industries' in Australia. Schemes for avoiding taxation became so common that Professor Russell Mathews, one of Australia's leading tax analysts, argued that paying taxation was in fact voluntary for the rich (*Advertiser* 28 January 1980). The reasons for the increasing degree of tax evasion and avoidance were undoubtedly related to the economic recession and the increasing taxation imposed on taxpayers as a result of governments' failures to index marginal tax rates. Both companies and individuals became increasingly squeezed in the process and many sought techniques to avoid paying their share. From the viewpoint of women, this placed a far heavier share of the overall tax burden on the shoulders of middle and lower-wage earners, including the majority of women workers, who had little or no opportunities to reduce their tax through avoidance or evasion techniques. The implication has been the imposition of higher tax burdens on the majority of working women. In effect, one group's successful evasion or avoidance of tax is another group's increased level of taxation.

The full extent of tax evasion and avoidance in Australia has not been documented. It has certainly been established, however, that it has resulted in major revenue losses. The government's white paper on taxation reform roughly estimated tax evasion as involving a revenue loss of at least $3 billion per year and tax avoidance to run into several billions of dollars (Draft White Paper, 1985:36–7). The opportunities available for certain individuals and companies to evade and avoid tax have mushroomed under a range of structural flaws in the tax system. A number of forms of income have been excluded from the government's definition of taxable income. Income taken in the form of capital gains, gifts and inheritance have been major areas of tax avoidance. In addition, some individuals have been able to take advantage of 'fiscal welfare provisions' to reduce their level of taxation. This is a term coined by Richard Titmuss in 1958 and refers to a range of benefits provided by the state through the taxation system, including measures such as

> **Tax evasion:**
>
> An illegal form of reducing taxation liability through the failure to disclose taxable income
>
> **Tax avoidance:**
>
> A way of reducing taxable income while remaining technically within the law—either by reducing assessable income (payment by fringe benefits; use of trusts, etc.) or by increasing the level of allowable deductions (negative gearing on rented properties, etc.)

the unlimited tax deductability of interest on borrowings by companies, reduced income taxation on lump sum superannuation payments, investment allowances and rebates for dependent spouses. By and large, all of these methods for reducing the amount of taxation paid are available only to the wealthy or high–income earners. They are not generally available to women. Carol Keens and Bettina Cass concluded from an analysis of fiscal welfare that it is welfare for the wealthy and mainly for men (Keens and Cass, 1982:33).

As a result the taxation contribution of those at the top end of the income scale has declined substantially. Over the period 1954/55–1984/85 the personal income contribution of individuals earning more than 160 percent of average weekly earnings decreased from 54 to 21 percent (Draft White Paper, 1985:19). Over the period from 1965/66 to 1982/83 the share of personal income tax paid by non–PAYE income earners, such as professionals, investors and the self–employed, decreased from 33 percent to a low of 18 percent (Australian Government Budget Statements, 1987/88:400). A similar decline also occurred in the proportion of company profit taxes. In 1973/74 company taxes contributed 18 percent of all Federal government revenue. By 1983/84 this had declined to only 9.9 percent (Australian Government Budget Statements, 1987/88:400).

Because of the increased regressivity introduced into the taxation system and the increased tax burden placed upon low-income earners by avoidance and evasion, the elimination of these practices would be of great benefit to the majority of women. Similarly, tax reforms that reduce the system of fiscal welfare and broaden the definition of taxable income could improve the effects of the taxation system on women's economic position.

Figure 4.2 Shares of personal and company taxes in total federal government taxation revenue.

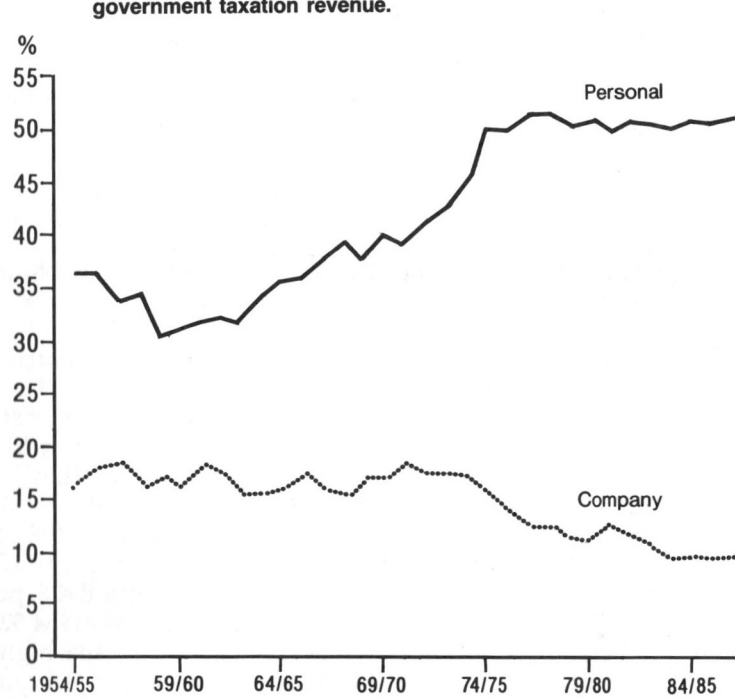

Sources: *Australian Economic Statistics, 1949–50 to 1978–79, Occasional Paper No. 8A* Reserve Bank of Australia, Sydney, 1980
Budget Statements *Budget Paper No. 1, 1986–87* AGPS, Canberra.

THE TAX SQUEEZE ON WAGE AND SALARY EARNERS

The most dramatic change in the structure of the taxation system produced by the fiscal crisis of the state and the recession in Australia has been the increase in tax paid by middle and low-wage and salary earners. As governments have been faced with rising budget deficits and wealthy individuals and companies have increasingly employed tax evasion and avoidance, the tax squeeze on wage and salary earners has increased. Figure 4.2 shows that the personal income tax share of Federal government revenue has risen from around 35 percent in the mid 1950s to over 50 percent in the 1980s. By 1986/87 it had reached 58 percent (Australian Government Budget Statements, 1987/88:400). However, the component of personal income tax that provided the revenue growth was the PAYE tax of wage and salary earners. In 1965/66, net PAYE income tax accounted for 67 percent of all personal income. In 1982/83 this peaked at 82 percent (Mathews, 1980:122; Australian Government Budget Statements, 1987/88:400).

The increased reliance on personal income taxation has been associated with two other changes in the taxation system that have further disadvantaged many women:

- average and marginal rates of personal income tax have increased for low and middle–income earners
- a greater number of social security recipients have found themselves paying income tax

In the first place, since the mid 1970s, average tax contributions from low and middle–income earners has increased faster than from PAYE taxpayers on higher incomes. Two major studies have found that lower–income groups, within which women predominate, have fared substantially worse (Harding, 1982; Harding and Whiteford, 1985). For example, a single lower–income earner ($10770 p.a., expressed in 1981/82 values), paid 21.2 percent more tax in 1981/82 than in 1975/76. A single taxpayer on average earnings ($16654) paid 4.8 percent more. However, a single higher–income taxpayer ($64620) paid 3.5 percent less (Harding, 1982). Therefore, the higher average tax rates that resulted from the increasing squeeze on PAYE taxpayers have affected income earners very unequally. However, not only have many women workers been paying higher average rates of income tax but women with children have especially suffered declines in real disposable incomes relative to single taxpayers. Between 1976/77 and 1984/85 this applied to all families with children (Harding and Whiteford, 1985:15).

As inflation has increased nominal wages and salaries, income earners have found themselves paying substantially higher taxation as a result of governments' failure to index the marginal tax rates. Whereas in the mid 1970s the highest marginal tax rate paid by a middle–income earner would have been 30 percent, by 1984/85 that same person could have been paying 60 percent taxation on a portion of her or his income. In the late 1950s less than 3 percent of taxpayers faced a marginal tax rate of 40 percent or higher on part of their incomes. In 1987/88, however, nearly half of all taxpayers faced the same 40 percent rate (Freebairn et al., 1987:215).

New Right economists have focused a great deal of attention on the negative effects that high marginal tax rates are sup-

economics (Kuttner, 1984:189-90). The increasing levels of taxation on ordinary income earners strengthened calls by the New Right for smaller government and hence reduced taxation. 'Public opinion' was persuaded that the increasing tax burden on PAYE taxpayers was caused by 'big government' rather than by the effects of the economic recession combined with the changing distribution of taxation away from corporations and wealthy individuals.

Political economists James Cronin and Terry Radtke have argued that the more prominent taxation becomes as a political issue, the more conservative are taxation policies (Cronin and Radtke, 1987:264-5). Politically it is much easier to rally support around the benefits of state expenditures than around the benefits of higher or more redistributive taxation policies. Consequently, once taxation itself becomes a political issue the debate is likely to favour the advocates of lower taxation and smaller government. For example, by putting taxation on top of the public policy agenda, the Thatcher and Reagan administrations have been able to place advocates of government intervention, equality and social justice on the defensive. This argument certainly appears to have some relevance to Australia since women's taxation reform proposals have had to struggle against an increasingly influential set of New Right attacks on any progressive taxation policy.

In Australia, the ideas of the New Right have been represented in a range of tax reform packages. The overall direction of these proposals has been to reduce both the progressivity of the taxation system and the amount of revenue raised. Specific proposals presented by the New Right economists have included:

- cuts in the top marginal personal income tax rates
- cuts in company tax rates
- joint husband and wife taxation
- introduction of a broad based consumption tax
- the introduction of a flat rate of income tax
- the introduction of joint income means tested or targeted systems to replace universal transfer systems such as family allowances

The economic assumption behind all these proposals is that taxation, particularly income taxation, has undermined the efficient operation of the market system. By reducing overall levels of taxation, and particularly that of high–income earners and corporations, incentives to work, save and invest will be restored. Any initially adverse distributional effects will be offset later by the 'trickle-down' effect. Viewed from the perspective of women, of course, this assumption is not only false but results in policies that are profoundly inequitable and reduce women's options to become economically independent through paid work.

One of the New Right's taxation policy proposals that has received strong political support in Australia is the introduction of a flat rate of personal income tax.[6] This proposal has been advocated by New Right economists at the Centre of Policy Studies at Monash University. During the 1987 Federal election campaign it was strongly supported by National Party politicians Sir Joh Bjelke-Petersen and John Stone (former Head of the Federal Treasury). The proposal also gained some support within the Liberal Party. While this proposal may appear to be gender neutral in that it advocates an identical level of taxation for all individuals, it can be shown that the introduction of a flat rate of tax would be disastrous for women.

A detailed analysis of the impact of a flat rate tax has been conducted by Patricia Apps (Apps, 1987). She has argued that a crucial feature of the politics of this proposal by the New Right has been to underplay how the tax cuts for higher–income earners are to be paid for. The New Right economists have tended to avoid publicly advocating the policies they have proposed in order to allow the introduction of a flat rate tax. These policies include:

- severe cuts in government expenditures—particularly in 'social wage' areas of importance to women
- increases in other taxes likely to be more regressive for women, for example, consumption taxes
- means-testing of taxation transfers currently of benefit to all women, for example, family allowances

Patricia Apps has also identified a number of ways in which a flat rate tax would directly change the distribution of taxation to the disadvantage of women. She demonstrates that switching from a progressive to a flat rate income tax of 25 percent without altering the overall revenue yield would result in:

- a decrease in the share of tax paid by the top 20 percent of income earners and an increase in the share paid by the bottom 80 percent. The average dollar savings for high–

income earners would be nearly $5000 per annum (1984–85 values)
- a significant decrease in the tax paid by heads of households (mainly men) and an increase in the tax paid by spouses. There would be a $1.96 billion reduction in the tax burden on heads of two–income family units and an increase of $1.15 billion in the amount of tax paid by spouses
- a decrease in the average tax rates of single–income families and an increase in the tax burden for two–income families

Flat rate income tax proposals, therefore, would further disadvantage the majority of women. The majority of women workers, because of their position among the lower range of income earners, would face substantial increases in the proportion of their incomes paid as taxation. Similarly, within the family, married women workers would end up paying a higher proportion of the family's taxation contribution. Patricia Apps has also pointed out that a flat rate tax would result in taxation inefficiencies because of married women's greater labour supply responsiveness to changes in tax rates (Apps, 1987:29–36). She concludes that flat rate tax proposals 'reflect an ethical preference for a greater degree of inequality and discrimination in Australian society, and an indifference towards efficiency costs to the economy' (Apps, 1987:37).

TAX REFORMS UNDER LABOR

A number of changes to the taxation system in Australia were announced by Labor Treasurer Paul Keating on 19 September 1985. These changes were phased in over the following two years. This tax reform package was the outcome of nearly a year of intensive, and unprecendented, public debate on Australia's taxation system.

The debate also provoked an unprecendented involvement by the women's movement in Australia in a major economic policy issue. One of the effects was a spillover of the debate into economic issues in general. As a result, a strong feminist critique of economic policy as a whole began to emerge. The representation of women's groups at the July 1985 National Tax Summit was a marked change from the National Economic Summit held the previous year. To some extent this signalled a public acknowledgement by the Labor government that women's economic concerns justified specific representation. It was also an indication that women themselves had

Table 4.1 Reform of the personal income tax rates 1986–87

Income range (p.a.) $	Marginal tax rate (cents per dollar)		
	Pre-Dec. 1, 1986	Dec. 1, 1986	July 1, 1987
0– 4 595	0	0	0
4 596– 5 100	25	0	0
5 101–12 500	25	24	24
12 501–12 600	30	24	24
12 601–19 500	30	29	29
19 501–28 000	46	43	40
28 001–35 000	48	46	40
35 001 and over	60	55	49

Source: Australian Government, *Budget Statements 1987/88*, Statement No.1

begun to recognise the importance of the state's broader economic policies on their position.

Nevertheless, the gains produced by Labor's taxation 'reforms' have been limited for the majority of women. In part, this result reflects the degree to which the ideas of the New Right have been very influential on the Labor government. Ironically, the greatest gain for women has probably been Treasurer Paul Keating's failure to introduce his preferred Option C. This proposal was distinguished by the inclusion of a broad based consumption tax. Although Option C also attempted to compensate lower–income groups to some degree, it has been demonstrated that such a shift to a broad based consumption tax would hit low–income households hardest (Harding and Whiteford, 1985). Similarly, those with children would be more affected than those without. Furthermore, in practice, it would prove extremely difficult to adequately compensate low–income groups. This would result in a major shift in the tax burden from men to women due to the predominance of women among social security recipients and receivers of child related allowances (Harding and Whiteford, 1985:48). In many cases women would bear the brunt as managers of household budgets. Compensatory adjustments such as cuts in personal income tax marginal rates would go primarily to males. This would have adverse repercussions on the distribution of income in families where income is not pooled (Harding and Whiteford, 1985:48).

The major taxation reform of the Labor government has been the restructuring of the personal income tax scales. Table 4.1 shows the reductions in marginal tax rates for different income

WOMEN AND TAXATION

Table 4.2 Net gains and changes in disposable income for single-income earners from Labor's 1985 tax reforms

comprehensive income [a] ($ p.a.)	taxpayer not affected by base-broadening measures		representative taxpayer	
	net gain ($/week)	change in disposable income (%)	net gain ($/week)	change in disposable income (%)
10 000	3.40	2.0	3.40	2.0
12 500	3.80	1.9	3.70	1.8
17 500	4.90	1.8	4.40	1.6
19 500	5.30	1.8	4.70	1.6
22 500	8.70	2.7	5.80	1.7
27 500	14.50	3.8	9.50	2.4
32 500	22.00[b]	5.1[b]	13.20	3.0
37 500	31.10[b]	6.6[b]	13.60	2.7
45 000	46.90[b]	8.8[b]	11.60	2.0
75 000	110.20[b]	14.5[b]	15.60	1.7
100 000	162.90[b]	17.1[b]	−20.70	−1.6

Notes: a Present taxable income plus income that will become taxable under the proposed base-broadening measures
b It is assumed that there are virtually no taxpayers at these income levels who would not be affected by the base-broadening measures
Columns 2 and 3 assume that individuals are not affected by the introduction of tax evasion and avoidance reforms such as capital gains and fringe benefits taxation.
Columns 4 and 5 are assumed to be more representative of the experience of taxpayers at different income levels on the basis of Tax Office data on the value of tax avoidance practices by income level.

Source: Statement by the Treasurer, The Hon. Paul Keating, *Reform of the Australian Taxation System*, Canberra: AGPS, p. 80.

levels. The benefits for women were extremely limited. It was mainly those women in higher–income households who benefited from this reform. Some pensioners and welfare beneficiaries whose incomes were close to the tax threshold also benefited.[7] However, most pensioners and welfare recipients received no benefit. Similarly, few working women benefited. The vast majority of women workers earn below the average male earnings above which the income tax cuts were concentrated. Women's relative economic position has declined as a result of this taxation reform because the gap between those below average weekly earnings and those above has widened.

Furthermore, the government's own estimated distributional impact of its personal income tax reforms confirm that the absolute and relative income gap between lower and higher–income groups has dramatically increased. As table 4.2 col-

Table 4.3 Tax reforms under Labor 1985-87

Reform	date of introduction	estimated change in revenue 1986/87 $M	1987/88 $M
restructuring personal income tax scales (see Table 4.1)	1/9/86 & 1/7/87	−1435	−4560 (full year)
Fringe Benefits tax	1/7/86	+ 535	+ 750
Capital Gains tax	20/9/85	-	+ 50–100
substantiation requirements for employment related expense claims	1/7/86	-	+ 190–200
rationalisation wholesale sales tax	20/9/85	-	+ 110
Prescribed Payments System	1/7/86	+ 150	+ 50
quarterly provisional tax	1/7/87	-	+ 70–140
company imputation system	1/7/87	− 350	− 50–300
tax free threshold applied pro-rata	1/7/86	+ 85	+ 85
tax shelters (net) (e.g., Pitt Street farmers, film concessions, water conservation, foreign income, negative gearing rental properties)	20/9/85	+ 196	+ 197
non-deductibility of entertainment expenses	19/9/85	+ 310	+ 330
increase in Medicare levy (0.25%)		+ 175	+ 325
Medicare levy exemption for low-income households		− 10	− 10
poverty traps	1/11/87	− 140	− 195

Sources: Australian Government Budget Statements, Budget Paper No. 1, Canberra: AGPS 1986/87 and 1987/88.
Statement by the Treasurer, *Reform of the Australian Tax System,* Canberra: AGPS, 1985.

umns 4 and 5 show, the only real element of progressivity suggested by the government's own figures is that the relative gap between very high-income groups (over $100 000 p.a.) and all other income groups appears to decrease. Even here, however, the effectiveness of the government's reforms will depend on its ability to close off tax evasion and avoidance avenues currently available to high-income earners.

Labor's tax reforms in the interests of women were of a much smaller scale in terms of revenue. Table 4.3 indicates the relative revenue importance of the various tax reforms. Reforms such as the introduction of fringe benefits tax and capital gains taxation were certainly of benefit to women. These taxes broadened the income tax base, increased the progressivity of the taxation system and helped to reduce tax avoidance and evasion. A range of additional measures were also designed to reduce the latter, including the elimination of a number of tax shelters, requirements to increase the substantiation of tax deductions and the extension of the prescribed payments system.[8]

However, while the government has argued that its crackdown on tax avoidance and evasion will increase the progressivity of the tax system, some doubt exists about the effectiveness of these measures. For example, Daryl Dixon has argued that in spite of the government's reforms, significant tax shelters remain that will involve annual revenue losses in excess of $6 billion (Dixon, 1987a:14–6). Consequently, the gap between very high–income earners and other income groups will remain.

One of the major areas of taxation reform that had been advocated by women's groups concerned the elimination of a number of discriminatory effects for women resulting from the interaction between the social security and taxation systems. In its reform package, the Labor government did introduce a number of measures to reduce the effects of poverty traps. It also allowed increased exemptions of the Medicare levy for low–income households. These reforms were relatively minor ones, although they undoubtedly will be of benefit to some women. Women's groups had also argued strongly for an overall reduction in subsidies and benefits provided under the taxation system (fiscal welfare). Since women are largely excluded from fiscal welfare because of their labour market position and their relatively lower incomes, it was argued that a fairer tax system could be achieved by reducing the distribution of government benefits through the taxation system.[9] Although the government again made some adjustments to the fiscal welfare area it generally ignored women's groups' calls for reform in this area. Tax concessions for superannuation, estimated to involve a revenue cost between $6 and 12 billion in 1987/88 (Dixon, 1987b:41), and the dependent spouse rebate, costing about $1 billion in 1987/88, are examples of fiscal welfare mainly of benefit to men that remained untouched in the government's reform package. The main form of fiscal welfare that benefits women and is vertically redistributive is the sole parent rebate. No increases were made to these benefits.

A number of other tax reforms important for improving women's relative economic position were largely ignored by the government. In particular, the dependent spouse rebate was not cashed out to women themselves. It remains effectively a subsidy to men for women's continued dependency in the home. In certain situations, a woman who chooses to engage in paid work will not only have to pay tax herself but will cause her husband to lose his dependent spouse taxation rebate. The high effective marginal tax rate thereby imposed on the couple's joint earnings may severely reduce her incentive to engage in paid work.

Part of Labor's tax reform package has been to offset the tax cuts to middle and upper–income groups with a system of joint income means-tested family allowances. In the process, there has been a further redistribution of the tax burden towards women. From October 1987 the previous universal system of family allowances primarily paid to women began to be phased out for those families on combined husband and wife incomes over $50 000. In the first instance this might appear to comply with the objective of vertical redistribution. However, a family with two children, a husband earning $40 000 per annum and a wife earning $11 000 per annum does not necessarily have a greater ability to pay tax than another family with a single income of $48 000 with the wife providing childcare and other household services. Nevertheless, the latter family would keep their family allowance while the former would not. In any case, in both the two–income and single–income family examples it is the man who would receive the tax cuts while the woman in the two–income family loses the family allowance.

This particular aspect of Labor's tax reform has shifted the tax burden from husbands to wives and from one income to two–income families (Savage, 1987:8). Such a policy response is hardly an adequate means of redressing the decline in the position of families with children relative to those without. Instead, it has tended to worsen women's relative economic position.

Business taxation is another area in which Labor's taxation reforms have been negative for women. The main feature of company taxation in Australia over recent years has been its declining contribution to total taxation revenue, mainly due to tax avoidance. As a consequence, the share of taxation revenue paid by other groups, including women, has been higher. Also, tax avoidance practices have contributed to economic inefficiency by tying up resources in activities that have done little to increase Australia's productive resource base and by creating a climate of opinion that honest endeavours do not pay. While the company tax rate was raised in the government's 1985 tax reform package, there remains an enormous

Table 4.4 Tax paid as a percentage of pre-tax profits by 16 Australian companies 1987/88

	%
Adelaide Steamship	0.18
Equiticorp Tasman	0.71
Overseas Strategic Investment	4.04
IEL	4.08
Westfield Capital Corp	4.24
Northern Star	4.40
Linter	4.43
Southern Farmers	5.60
Ariadme	8.16
AFP	8.75
Bond corp	8.95
Kern Corp	9.17
Bell Group	10.46
Elders IXL	10.48
Hooker	11.56
News	12.22

Source: Colleen Ryan, 'Why We Desperately Need the Government's Tax Review', *Sydney Morning Herald's* second annual survey of tax paid (carried out by the Stock Exchange Research Service), 31 October 1987.

gap between the official rate of 49 percent and what companies actually pay. Table 4.4 shows that some of Australia's largest companies are in fact the lowest taxpayers.

Apart from continuing access to significant areas of fiscal welfare (e.g., unlimited deductibility of interest on loans, exemptions for gold miners and friendly societies, accelerated depreciation, etc.), the corporate sector has engaged in practices such as use of tax havens and transfer-pricing schemes to avoid tax. Profit shifting to offshore tax shelters and transfer pricing alone are estimated to reduce taxation revenues by $3–4 billion each year (Fell, 1988:20). The Auditor-General's Report has pointed out that 40 000 corporations engaging in international trade worth $20 billion per year are in a position to shift profits offshore to tax havens. Therefore, it is not as if this is a practice unknown to the government (Fell, 1988:20). Nevertheless, very little has been done. The major 1985 tax reform for the corporate sector was the introduction of the company imputation system, representing a further step in the direction of a lower tax revenue contribution from the corporate sector.[10] To the extent that reforms such as capital gains taxation, fringe benefits taxation and the closing off of some tax shelters has increased the contribution of business taxation, it has probably been non-PAYE individual taxpayers or small businesses that have paid more tax. Such business tax reforms fall well short of increasing the progressivity of the income tax system.

The reasons for the disappointing effects of Labor's tax policies on women are clear. Vertical redistribution was not the main objective of the government's taxation reform exercise. As Treasurer Keating put it, 'from the outset a major objective of tax reform has been to substantially lighten the heavy hand of high marginal tax rates on honest taxpayers in this country' (Statement by the Treasurer, 1985:3). In other words, restoring equity between the higher–income PAYE taxpayers and higher–income non-PAYE taxpayers, who had been able to lower their tax liability through tax evasion and avoidance, was the central (horizontal) equity objective. Neither did Labor's approach incorporate any recognition of women's specific economic and social position. Both of these missing components are essential to any worthwhile taxation reform package for women. Furthermore, the Hawke government's taxation policies were unlikely to be progressive for women in view of its overall economic strategy and the increasing strength of New Right economic ideas.

FEMINIST CRITIQUES

Economists have traditionally used the criteria of equity, efficiency and simplicity to evaluate taxation systems. By and large these criteria have been readily accepted by the community also—as illustrated in the Australian tax reform debates in 1985. The acceptance of the economists' framework is an indicator of the strength of the hold economists exert in the taxation policy area. Unfortunately, women's concerns have been largely ignored within the framework of mainstream economics and taxation has been no exception. While these taxation criteria may appear to be gender neutral in principle, their application does not always accord with a taxation system that is equitable, efficient and simple in practice for women. One important reason for this is that taxation analysts frequently use these criteria in conjunction with traditional economic assumptions. The result being taxation policies which adversely impact on women.

However, within the framework of mainstream economics a number of substantial critiques of traditional taxation analyses and policies exist that could form the basis of a feminist critique (Apps, 1981, 1983 and 1987; Savage, 1984, 1985 and 1987; Edwards, 1980, 1984 and 1985). These analyses have demonstrated that by employing more appropriate assumptions about women, a taxation policy aimed at achieving equity, efficiency and simplicity would look very different from economists' more conventional policy conclusions. They have used the strategy, therefore, of demonstrating that, even using economists' own criteria, taxation policies can be used to improve women's position. They have effectively criticised economists' use of their own taxation criteria on a number of grounds:

- Economists have failed to recognise that policies that have discriminated against women have also been, according to their own criteria, inefficient for the economy.
- The criterion of taxation equity has been defined in ways that have resulted in the inequitable treatment of women.
- In practice, economists have given higher priority to efficiency than to equity goals as a result of their own value judgements.
- Tax policies that appear to be gender neutral can discriminate against women because of their existing disadvantaged position.

EFFICIENCY

An economically efficient tax is one which minimises its impact on economic decisions or the choices people make. That is, the tax should not alter an individual's choices between what goods and services they buy or what work (paid and unpaid), leisure, savings and investment activities they undertake. If a tax changes economic behaviour it is presumed that waste will be incurred (because the revenue raised for expenditures is not considered to be enough to compensate the taxpayers). The underlying assumption here is that individuals and businesses left to their own devices will make choices in their own best interests. Economic analysis recognises that some of these choices preferred by an individual or business may not be the best for society as a whole. Therefore, taxation also has a role to play in deliberatively altering economic behaviour as markets can fail in efficiently allocating resources (e.g., taxing polluting agents). Consequently, a taxation policy is deemed to have an efficiency cost if it changes the economic behaviour of people unintentionally.

However, taxation is thought to inevitably distort economic behaviour. For example, taxation reduces income available for spending. Similarly, a lack of neutrality (and hence efficiency) is inevitable insofar as some activities are taxed and others are not. For example, unpaid work and leisure are not taxed. The result tends to be an increase in these activities in comparison to paid work—an inefficient outcome. The extent to which taxation distorts paid and unpaid work activities is, therefore, increased if unpaid work is subsidised by the taxation system such as through the dependent spouse rebate.

Feminist analyses have criticised traditional taxation theory in Australia for ignoring the efficiency effects of taxation on women's choices between paid and unpaid work. That is, they have argued that economists have supported taxation policies that are inefficient even according to mainstream economics. In part, economists have assumed these effects to be negligible. However, evidence has now accumulated that women's paid work choices are much more sensitive than men's to changes in tax rates (Edwards, 1985:59; Apps, 1987:29). For example, a study by Glenn Jones and Elizabeth Savage found that Australian females were approximately three times more likely than males to reduce their labour participation with increased tax rates (Jones and Savage, 1986).

Given the emphasis economists place on efficiency, these critiques have given women's taxation concerns a place in economic analysis. Equity arguments alone have rarely been seen by economists as justifying changes in taxation policy. However, a number of economists have combined 'equity for women' arguments with 'efficiency for the economy' arguments to criticise a range of taxation policies, including the dependent spouse rebate, joint taxation of husbands and wives (income splitting) and the New Right's proposals for a flat rate of personal income tax (Apps, 1987; Savage, 1984; Apps, Jones and Savage, 1981; Edwards, 1985, 1983 and 1980).

EQUITY

Feminist economists have argued that mainstream economists have applied the criterion of equity in ways that have not produced genuine equity within the taxation system for women. In particular, they have argued that economists have:

- emphasised horizontal rather than vertical equity
- not been concerned with the equity effects of taxation policies within the family
- excluded key elements relevant to women in determining ability to pay taxation

The equity criterion refers to the fairness of the taxation system. There are two dimensions of equity that the taxation system is supposed to fulfil—horizontal and vertical. Horizontal equity is the notion that people in the same circumstances pay the same amount of tax. Vertical equity requires those in different circumstances to pay different amounts of tax—those able to pay more are taxed more. While few openly dispute that the taxation system should be equitable, in practice economists have often defined equity in a way that disadvantages women. They have also given a lower priority to vertical equity.

Of the two, horizontal equity is considered by economists to be more objective than vertical equity. The implementation of horizontal equity will not improve women's relative position because it is essentially about preserving the existing income distribution. The reforms of the Hawke/Keating Labor Government with their emphasis on the objective of horizontal equity provides an excellent example. Historically the taxation system has never been about vertically downward redistribution. To the extent that governments have intended any degree of income redistribution downwards, they have preferred to use the social welfare system.

Feminist analyses have also pointed out that mainstream taxation analyses have usually failed to include any examination of the impact of taxation policies within the family as part of their equity concerns. Traditional taxation analyses conveniently assume that family income is pooled. Genuine taxation equity, as Meridith Edwards has pointed out, should be 'based on less impressionistic judgements and more on facts' (Edwards, 1985:62). Her research has shown that women often have less control over family income than their husbands (Edwards, 1983).

Feminist critiques have argued that an equitable tax system for women must take into account the value of goods and services produced in the home, the value of leisure, the presence of dependent children and the control each spouse has over family income. Within the public finance tradition, which is the dominant theoretical influence on the Australian taxation debate, these factors are either completely excluded or inadequately considered. One reason for this is that money income is traditionally taken as the sole indicator of a person's ability to pay tax. For example, taxation policies have assumed that a dependent spouse reduces a single–income family's ability to pay tax and offers the breadwinner a taxation concession. Other economists, however, have argued that, on the contrary, having a dependent spouse available to produce home based goods and services enhances the breadwinner's 'ability to pay' tax. The effect of using the mainstream economists' definition of 'ability to pay' has been policies that firstly discourage married women from working and secondly discriminate against those that do work (Apps, 1987; Savage, 1984).

ECONOMISTS' IDEOLOGY

Economists and policymakers do not give equal weight to the different criteria they apply to evaluate taxation policies. Efficiency invariably is awarded priority over equity and policies that fulfil horizontal equity goals are ranked above vertical redistribution. Simplicity, which refers both to the ease with which taxpayers are able to understand the system as well as to the costs of administration and compliance, is not used as a criterion by itself to justify a particular tax policy. Although 'lack of simplicity' is often used as a reason why vertically distributive policies should not be implemented. Conservative economists often oppose the introduction of a wealth tax on this basis.

One reason for the lower priority give to equity is that efficiency is deemed more objective. But, it is also the case that economists often find the concept of equity at odds with their own more subtle set of value judgements. In particular, the goal of vertical equity is explicitly rejected by those economists who operate within a neo-liberal 'free market' framework. Vertical redistribution implies involvement of the state at a level of intervention and planning that is seen as destructive to the effective workings of the market (George and Wilding, 1985: 23–6).

Moreover, economists often hold their own value judgements that are incompatible with women's goals of economic independence and equality. For example, Queensland economists Alan Duhs and Alan Lougheed have argued in favour of income–splitting for spouses—a policy that discriminates against married women—on the grounds 'that more is involved than the social desirability of encouraging more married women to pursue careers'. In their view married women's careers have resulted in an as yet unmeasured social cost, involving 'a contribution to increased youth unemployment rates, juvenile crime rates, drug dependence, child abuse, incidence of no income families and perhaps family break-up rates and amorphous changes in attitudes to work and authority' (Duhs and Lougheed, 1985:196). Paramount here is an ethical judgement about the home based role of women and the breadwinning role of men.

UNEQUAL OPPORTUNITIES

Feminists have pointed out that even in cases where the state's taxation policies are intended by policymakers to be gender neutral they can actually be disadvantageous to women. Taxation policies frequently fail to take into account women's specific position in the economy. Since this position is often a disadvantaged one, such policies can inadvertently act to reinforce or worsen that disadvantage. For example, a policy of reduced marginal tax rates for income earners on average weekly earnings and above will disadvantage women relative to men. As Sheila Shaver has pointed out, while the tax system is sex neutral in the sense that it treats both men and women as equal tax units, it affects them very differently because of their already existing inequalities (Shaver, 1983:160). Therefore, a reduction of tax for middle and upper–income earners, by primarily benefiting men relative to women, is not gender neutral in practice.

A FEMINIST TAXATION STRATEGY

While some strands of neo–classical economics may be used by feminists to produce policy conclusions that do not discriminate against women, the framework of mainstream economic theory can provide only incrementalist reforms to a fundamentally inequitable taxation system. The state cannot achieve significant advances towards overcoming women's unequal economic position by means of marginal adjustments within the existing taxation system. If the tax system is to be used by feminists to improve significantly the level of equality, a more fundamental restructuring of its goals and structure is required.

This raises the question of whether such a fundamental restructuring of the taxation system is possible within the restrictive framework under which the capitalist state operates. In spite of Joseph Chamberlain's view that taxation was the ransom paid by the rich in order to maintain their riches, historically the taxation systems of capitalist states have basically not been the means for real progressive income and wealth redistribution (Miliband, 1969:78). Redistribution downwards has been done via the social welfare system rather than the taxation system (Harding, 1984; Kakwani, 1983). Therefore, it may be unlikely that taxation reforms are themselves going to be the vanguard of positive changes for women. Nevertheless, taxation policy is an essential part of any feminist strategy to challenge the power of capital and men over the state's policies in other areas.

The first important principle of a feminist taxation strategy is to argue for a system that yields adequate revenue to finance state activities to benefit women and is at the same time progressively redistributive. A reform strategy that would be progressive for the majority of women in both these senses would include the following specific changes:

- *Tax evasion and avoidance*: a major crackdown on tax evasion and avoidance by high PAYE income earners and non-PAYE income earners to make the nominally progressive income tax system genuinely progressive and to substantually increase revenue.
- *Wealth tax*: the introduction of a general tax on wealth to significantly increase the progressivity of the overall tax system, to increase revenue, and to help reduce the current extreme inequalities in wealth distribution.
- *Company taxation*: a substantial increase in the current very low level of revenue yield from taxes on company profits combined with a crackdown on tax evasion and avoidance by corporations.
- *Capital gains tax*: an expansion of the current very mild capital gains tax, which continues to provide incentives for tax avoidance. Without an effective capital gains tax, income is simply converted into capital gains by the wealthy and is taxed at a lower rate than other income.
- *Fiscal welfare*: the elimination or severe restriction of government taxation benefits and concessions that primarily benefit wealthy males, increase the regressivity of the overall tax system and produce enormous, and largely unscrutinised, losses to state revenue.

In addition, a feminist programme for taxation reform should also be based on the principles that the system should not re-inforce women's dependency on men but should allow, and encourage, them to be economically independent. Neither should the taxation system assume that family income is pooled. Rather, it should recognise women as individuals in their own right. However, it should also recognise the particular social and economic position of women, for example by acknowledging that the rearing of children is both a private and community responsibility. In order to encourage women's economic independence the state should not provide taxation disincentives to women's workforce participation. It should also ensure that state welfare benefits women but does not trap them into increased dependency on the state.

A key element in any feminist strategy for taxation reform is the recognition that although taxation debates are generally conducted in the language and framework of economics, ultimately taxation policies, like all the activities of the state, are decided politically. It is important for feminists to understand the mainstream economists' debates and to use economic arguments to 'beat them at their own game' where possible, but substantive reforms will only be achieved if feminists develop a very clear set of political goals and principles for the taxation system and a political strategy to defeat the vested interests that currently defend the existing inequitable system.

5 Women and superannuation

During the 1980s occupational (i.e., employment related) superannuation was firmly placed on the public policy agenda in Australia.[1] Traditionally, superannuation has been a 'fringe benefit' available to a selected minority of the workforce. Under the Hawke Government it has received increased emphasis in Labor's retirement income, taxation and wages policies, becoming a major economic policy issue affecting all in the community.

Superannuation, however, has never been seen as a women's issue. Policymakers have not perceived women's low participation in superannuation schemes and their inferior access to the benefits of the schemes they have belonged to, as warranting detailed analysis or a prominent place in policy debates. Women themselves have not participated widely in superannuation policy debates. They have not regarded it as an important working condition, like childcare. Superannuation negotiations between government, trade unions and employers have been silent on the implications for women and have taken place with a virtual absence of female representation.

WHY SUPERANNUATION IS AN IMPORTANT ISSUE FOR WOMEN

The widespread perception that superannuation is basically irrelevant to women's economic interests is fundamentally wrong. Superannuation should be seen as an economic issue of major concern to women. Occupational superannuation is about worker retirement incomes. Women now make up over 40 percent of the Australian labour force and nearly 60 percent of the aged. Projections indicate further increases in these percentages. Women's need for an independent retirement income is certainly no less than men's. Women live on average six years longer, they retire earlier from the workforce and have to stretch savings and assets over a longer period of retirement. Most women live the last years of their life alone without the option of male financial support. One in three marriages ends in divorce and divorced or separated women have little access to former husbands' superannuation as a source of retirement income. Increasing numbers of women are never marrying, so they need to provide for themselves in retirement as well as during their working lives. Women are also more likely to head single-parent households and need to be able to insure against loss of earnings in the event of death or invalidity. Women's lack of alternative retirement income provision has resulted in them comprising the majority of aged persons dependent on the state and therefore being more vulnerable to poverty.

The benefits which superannuation could provide for women are considerable. Superannuation provides a wide range of benefits to recipients, including:

- an independent, and superior, source of retirement income in addition to the state's aged pension
- generous taxation benefits and concessions during one's working life
- income protection for dependents through insurance against death
- income insurance against invalidity
- a highly attractive form of savings through deferred pay

In practice, a two-tiered retirement income system has evolved in Australia—the state's aged pension and state or private superannuation schemes. Clearly, superannuation schemes provide superior benefits. Furthermore, many of the elite group with access to superannuation have also been able to double-dip into the state's aged pension benefit as well. While the trade union leadership has recently sought to include superannuation as part of the social wage benefiting the community as a whole, in reality it is part of the occupational welfare system. As such, it automatically benefits women less because of women's position in the workforce. Women have had a far lower level of direct participation in superannuation schemes than men. Nearly three–quarters of all members of superannuation schemes are men (ABS, *Employment Benefits Australia* 1987). Furthermore, women who do have superannuation coverage are likely to receive far lower benefits from the system than men.

The state has played an important role in the development of superannuation in Australia. Governments, the Arbitration Commission and other state institutions have facilitated the development of occupational superannuation in ways that have perpetuated the economic inequalities between women and men. Australia is now on a path whereby occupational superannuation is expected to become a greater component of retirement incomes. Superannuation is also expected to play a more important role in remunerating labour. Clearly, without specific strategies to address the needs of women, occupational superannuation will be an important mechanism for extending existing economic inequalities into retirement.

WOMEN'S UNEQUAL ACCESS TO SUPERANNUATION

Those women who are beneficiaries of superannuation income, either on their own account as retired workers or as the surviving spouse of a superannuant, also receive lower benefits on average than men. As a result superannuation contributes less to women's total retirement income than it does to men's. One in four working women are members of an occupational superannuation scheme compared to one in two working men (ABS, *Employment Benefits Australia* 1987). In every category of ABS survey data (by sector, income, industry, occupation, hours worked and age), women workers have a lower rate of superannuation scheme membership than men. Therefore women's unequal participation cannot be explained simply in terms of their labour force segmentation (Hancock, 1977). Nor is it merely a result of women's relatively lower participation in the labour force. The fact is, women in paid work are less likely to be members of an occupational superannuation scheme than their male counterparts for all sectors, industries, occupations, incomes, hours worked and age groups.

If the lack of superannuation among women not in the paid workforce is taken into account as well, women's participation in occupational superannuation is extremely low. In 1986 about 11 percent of all women compared with 32 percent of all men aged 15–64 years were members of a superannuation scheme (ABS, *Employment Benefits Australia* 1986; ABS, *Census Australia* 1986). Although more women than men receive a superannuation retirement benefit as the surviving spouse of a member, this does little to close the gap between the sexes. Spouse benefits are, with few exceptions, less than a member's benefit. Not all women have spouses and, given the high rate of divorce, spouse benefits are not a certain source of retirement income for individual women. Also, not all schemes have provision for spouse benefits.

Women's relatively low superannuation coverage needs to be seen in the context of the overall proportion of the Australian population that are contributors or beneficiaries of super-

> **Some facts on women's superannuation coverage in Australia**
>
> - In 1986, 25 percent of women workers were members of a superannuation scheme compared to 49 percent of men workers.
> - In 1986, 11 percent of all women aged 16–64 years were members of a superannuation scheme compared to 32 percent of all men aged 16–64 years.
> - In 1986, only 4 percent of part-time workers were members of a superannuation scheme. Women comprise 80 percent of all part-time workers.
> - Between 1974 and 1987 both men's and women's membership of superannuation schemes increased by about 8 percent.
> - Low income working women have the lowest level of superannuation coverage. In 1986, 60 percent of women with incomes over $520 per week had superannuation compared to only 11 percent of women earning less than $280.
> - In all industries women have less superannuation coverage than men.
> - In every major occupational group women are less likely than men to have superannuation.
> - Public sector employees are twice as likely to have superannuation than private sector employees. But women in the public sector have significantly lower coverage than male employees. Women in the private sector have the lowest coverage of all.
> - Women's coverage decreases after the mid-twenties and recovers after 45 years but at a lower rate. In contrast, the rate of superannuation coverage increases with age for the male labour force.
>
> *Sources:*
>
> ABS, *Superannuation Australia* February 1974, Catalogue Number 6319.0
> ABS, *Employment Benefits Australia* August 1986, Catalogue Number 6334.0
> ABS, *Types & Conditions of Part-time Work, South Australia* October 1986, Catalogue Number 6203.4

annuation. In 1987 40 percent of employees were members of a scheme. Since 1974 coverage has increased steadily from about 30 percent and is expected to continue to increase. In March 1985 the executive of the ACTU endorsed a strategy for securing universal superannuation coverage for the Australian workforce. This strategy was initially heralded by the ACTU as likely to quickly extend superannuation to all workers. However, universal coverage is no longer expected in the short term. One estimate is an improvement to around 50 percent of the workforce with a maximum possible coverage of about 60 percent (McCallum and Shaver, 1986:8).

Increases in women's superannuation coverage have occurred recently, although they have not been dramatic. Between 1979 and 1986 the superannuation coverage of female wage and salary earners (working 20 hours or more per week) rose from 26.3 to 30.4 percent. The comparable figures for men were 50.0 and 50.6 percent (ABS, *Employment Benefits* 1979; ABS, *Employment Benefits* 1986). However, these figures do not cover part-time work where most of the employment growth has been for women. The majority of part-time workers do not have access to employer-sponsored superannuation schemes. An ABS survey of part-time workers in 1986 showed that only 4 percent were members of an employer-sponsored superannuation scheme (ABS, *Type & Conditions of Part-time Employment South Australia*, 1986).

Women who do belong to superannuation schemes have been shown to be less likely than men to collect a benefit by remaining in the scheme until retirement (Rosenman and Leeds, 1984:6–13). They are more likely than men to withdraw before retirement age (Human Rights Commission, 1986:78).

Furthermore, resignation payments often include neither the employer's contribution nor a commercial interest return on their own contributions. Consequently, women who join superannuation schemes but do not ultimately claim a retirement benefit effectively subsidise those (mostly male) members who do. Even when women do claim a retirement benefit they on average receive a much smaller benefit than men (Rosenman and Leeds, 1984:34).

WHY WOMEN DO NOT JOIN SUPERANNUATION SCHEMES

Women do not join superannuation schemes for a wide range of reasons, which include:

- they are not in the paid workforce and therefore are not eligible
- as workers, they are not eligible to join because some schemes directly discriminate against women
- they lack access to a scheme in their occupation or industry
- they make an economic choice not to join because of a scheme's lack of benefits for women

WOMEN OUTSIDE THE WORKFORCE

Superannuation is a form of occupational welfare only available to those in the paid workforce. Also, schemes generally do not have provisions that allow people to move in and out of the paid workforce and retain any superannuation benefits accrued while in paid employment. Consequently, unemployed women and women engaged in unpaid activities in the home on a full-time basis are automatically excluded from membership.

OVERT DISCRIMINATION

Historically many women in paid work have also been ineligible to join a scheme. In some instances this has been a result of direct discrimination whereby they were excluded because they were women or because they were married. In 1982–83, 34 private and public sector funds were identified in a survey as still practising direct discrimination against women joining their scheme (ABS, *Census of Superannuation Funds Australia*, 1985). In addition, some schemes restrict the membership of married women. For example, a woman may not be able to join a scheme if her husband is already a member (ACTU, 1986:17). Until the 1970s, women in Federal and State government schemes had to resign upon marriage because married women could not have permanent jobs in the public service.

LABOUR FORCE SEGMENTATION

A more enduring reason for women being ineligible to join an existing employer-sponsored superannuation scheme is because of the types of jobs they typically occupy. Women workers, being segregated into a narrow range of industries, are much more likely than men to be in jobs where there is no employer-sponsored superannuation. For example, the two industry categories wholesale and retail trade and recreation, personnel and other services, which together account for one third of all women workers, had superannuation coverage rates of 16.7 and 8.8 percent respectively. Only mining and agriculture, accounting for 9 percent of all male workers, had lower coverage (6.8 and 4.7 percent). Another 28 percent of women workers are in the industry category community services, which had only half the rate of superannuation membership (37 percent) of the highest covered industries of communication (87 percent) and electricity, gas and water (75 percent). (ABS, *Employment Benefits Australia* 1987; ABS, *Labour Force Australia* 1987). Similarly, women's ineligibility for superannuation membership can be restricted by their occupation. The 1982-83 ABS Census of Superannuation Funds showed over 800 funds restricted membership on the basis of managerial status.

Part-time and casual workers have generally not been eligible to join superannuation schemes and women form some 80 percent of this group of workers. The Human Rights Commission Inquiry into superannuation expressed particular concern over the practice whereby predominantly women workers are classified as 'temporary' employees while in fact they frequently have continuous employment with a single employer for more than a year (Human Rights Commission, 1986:75-6) This suggests that many women are not eligible simply because of arbitrary employment practices.

ECONOMIC REASONS

Even women workers who are eligible to join a superannuation scheme often do not do so. In some cases this may be simply because they are unaware of the existence of a scheme or of its benefits for them. In other cases, however, it is clear that women do not join because it does not appear economically rational to do so.

Undoubtedly, some women may unwisely perceive that their husband's superannuation is the best way to provide for retirement income. However, in a study of the New South Wales State superannuation scheme, less than 9 percent of female employees gave their husband's superannuation coverage as their main reason for not joining the scheme (Rosenman and Leeds, 1984:57). A more important reason is likely to be the lack of information directed specifically at women workers. Part-time and casual employees particularly seem to lack information to make an active decision whether or not to join. An ABS survey revealed that nearly one-third of such employees did not know if an employer-sponsored scheme was available (ABS, *Type and Conditions of Part-time Employment, South Australia* 1986).

While lack of information or unwise judgements may explain the failure of some women to take advantage of an available superannuation scheme, in other cases the financial benefits simply are outweighed by either the costs involved or the barriers placed in the way of obtaining the full benefits of the scheme. One important factor in reducing the attractiveness of superannuation for women is its lack of integration with the state's aged pension.

Superannuation pension schemes may simply cut low-income women out of the income-tested aged pension. Another negative factor is that women's relatively low earnings can make it difficult for them to allocate part of their income to retirement savings. However, the most important factor undoubtedly is the fact that superannuation schemes have generally been discriminatory against women. Consequently, many women have quite correctly perceived that their chances of obtaining the full benefits of a superannuation scheme are limited.

HOW SUPERANNUATION SCHEMES DISCRIMINATE AGAINST WOMEN MEMBERS

Women who join a superannuation scheme are likely to benefit from it to a far lesser extent than men. Either they do not remain in the schemes long enough or, if they do, are likely to receive less than the full retirement benefit that most men receive. Mainstream economists writing about superannuation have not observed, let alone analysed, this phenomenon (for example, see Norman, 1986). Should they be asked to explain women's unequal treatment, mainstream economists frequently contend that it derives from the individual choices women make about their marginal participation in the labour market.

From a feminist perspective, however, the real reasons can be related to the many forms of sexual discrimination imbedded in the structures of almost all superannuation schemes in Australia. Superannuation scheme provisions have been shaped by the assumption that a male work pattern is the norm. This male model of a working life is a traditional one of unbroken, full time employment with a single employer until retirement at age 65. In contrast, women's employment is characterised by a broken workforce pattern, including possibly changes in employment status from full time to part-time work.[2]

Superannuation provisions which favour, or even require, a full-time and continuous, work pattern clearly discriminate against women. Such provisions can both make women workers ineligible for membership and lower the benefits they obtain from superannuation coverage relative to men. They also mean that it is not economically rational for women to be members of an occupational superannuation scheme. Moreover, women members who join but are unable to remain in schemes until retirement effectively subsidise the benefits of the (largely male) retirement beneficiaries.

Superannuation schemes have discriminated against women because they have failed to provide adequate terms and conditions in four areas essential to women. These are:

- preservation provisions
- portability provisions
- vesting provisions
- maternity and parenting leave provisions

PRESERVATION

Preservation provisions are the single most important element of a superannuation scheme for women. Without preservation the majority of women who take time out of the workforce are forced also to resign from the employer-sponsored fund and accept a limited payout. As a result, these women subsidise the benefits of those fortunate enough to remain in the scheme until retirement. In addition, women who rejoin a superannuation scheme when they return to paid employment after child bearing and rearing (in some cases the same employer and scheme) usually face a significantly lowered retirement benefit because they cannot fulfil the scheme's requirements for obtaining a maximum benefit.[3]

Preservation enables employees to defer their accrued superannuation benefits until retirement age in the event of resignation (or retrenchment). If they return to the same employer (or industry in the case of industry–based funds) they simply take up their membership from when they left it. Preservation also allows a person to put their accumulated entitlements into 'cold storage' while on leave without pay, maternity and parental leave or if they change from full-time to part-time work. It therefore allows a person to move in and out of the workforce and change their working arrangements without loss of superannuation benefits. Traditionally, few superannuation schemes have actually provided a preservation provision.

Preservation provisions can vary considerably between funds. Key issues for women are whether the employer contribution is preserved as well as their own and whether there are requirements that must be met before an employee is entitled to the option of preservation. An appropriate preservation option for women would involve deferring until retirement age any benefits arising out of both the employer contribution as well as any of their own. Preserving the employer contribution is called non-cash vesting (see below) and without it the value of the superannuation benefits is severely reduced.[4] Preservation options commonly require a minimum period of membership before employees may preserve their entitlements. Preservation from the date of joining is essential if women are to have the same opportunity as most men in obtaining a retirement benefit in proportion to their years in the paid workforce. Satisfactory preservation arrangements are therefore central if superannuation is to be seen as a condition of employment equally adapted to the working patterns of both women and men. Significantly, it is also an essential element of a retirement income policy that aims to make superannuation a larger component of retirement incomes.

PORTABILITY

Portability is the ability to transfer one's accrued benefits to another employer and/or fund when changing jobs. For members of industry-wide or public-sector schemes portability can mean remaining in the same scheme but having transferability between employers. Portability is in effect the ultimate form of preservation, requiring not only storage arrangements for members accrued benefits but also agreements between superannuation funds about the transfer value and age for paying benefits. Portability provisions are therefore even less common than preservation provisions.

Undoubtedly portability, in addition to preservation, would assist superannuation schemes to better match with women's workforce pattern. However, while women would benefit from its inclusion, the lack of portability is probably somewhat less important to women than it would be to men. While men tend to resign from their employment to move to another job, women tend to resign and temporarily withdraw from the labour market.[5]

Discrimination can also occur in those few schemes that have portability arrangements with different values being calculated for the amount of benefit to be transferred for women and men members. Transfer values may be based on statistical data that is often used to justify different benefits for women and men (Human Rights Commission 1986:85–7).

VESTING

Vesting refers to the worker's right to all or part of the employer's contribution where membership is terminated before retirement age. If a benefit is fully vested it means the whole accrued employer contribution is 'owned' by the employee.

Vesting can also take the form of a cash benefit payable directly to the worker or it can refer to a preserved (or deferred) benefit.

The majority of superannuation schemes have had poor vesting provisions. Benefits have not generally been fully vested until completion of fifteen years service, although partial vesting may have begun by five years (Human Rights Commission, 1986:78). In addition, full vesting in the form of a preserved benefit held in the fund is generally fixed in money terms. Even 'full vesting' in these circumstances is a problem for people with a broken work pattern because the benefit is eroded by inflation.

Since women are extremely likely to break the continuity of their employment with any particular employer they are especially disadvantaged by the absence of adequate vesting provisions. An analysis of the Commonwealth Superannuation Scheme (which has compulsory membership) shows that the rate at which women left the scheme was higher than men for all age groups and length of employment. Women employees in the 25–29 age group had over five times the leaving rate of men (Human Rights Commission, 1986:79). Given that full vesting is traditionally only provided after fifteen years of service and rarely before five years of service women who break service for child bearing and rearing are indirectly discriminated against.

Cash vesting does pose a dilemma for women. Increasing the value of resignation payments through cash vesting could put pressure on women to take their superannuation benefits when they resign and use them to supplement family finances. This can raise the standard of living of low–income families, but it does not assist in increasing women's opportunities to have an independent source of retirement income. Without vesting, preservation and portability provisions would be of less value because benefits before retirement age may only include the employee's contributions plus interest minus administration costs. In this situation the average employer's contribution per worker can be lowered significantly. Thus full vesting is necessary for effective preservation and portability, and vice versa.

MATERNITY AND PARENTING LEAVE

Most superannuation schemes do not make provision for accouchment, maternity or parenting leave. However, the bearing and rearing of children shapes the majority of women's working lives. These activities distinguish women's work pattern from the work pattern of the majority of men. Yet 74 percent of government funds and 82 percent of private funds have no maternity leave provisions (ASFA, 1980:44). In practice, this means such leave is characterised by inflexible arrangements. Choice does not exist for a person to cease contributions, continue contributions, obtain death and disability cover and so on. In short, the treatment of maternity leave does not constitute a recognition that it is a legitimate episode in a woman's working life.

In Australia the majority of maternity leave is unpaid. Some funds penalise women for having children by requiring them to maintain superannuation contributions while not earning an income. They may also be denied the employer's contributions for the period of leave or may even be required to themselves contribute the employer's share. Such provisions are discriminatory. Birth and confinement constitutes an enforced period of leave that only applies to women. A period of breast-feeding could be argued to extend the time women's biological differences keep them out of the workforce. Women's social role in being responsible for children extends this time-out even further. Being required to maintain contributions while on unpaid leave can cause hardship. Not allowing women to contribute also penalises them for their biological and social role. It does this by reducing their retirement benefit and denies them entitlements such as death and disability cover while on maternity leave. Even provisions for unpaid leave can offer more flexibility than maternity leave with employees often having a choice whether or not to pay their contributions.

Treating maternity leave equivalent to, or inferior to, any other unpaid leave means that women workers are required to bear the full cost of their biological and social role. Underlying this is economists' assumption of free personal choice. That is, women choose to have a broken work pattern by having babies and looking after children. By contrast, other social practices have been legitimated as a 'social benefit' by superannuation schemes by being ascribed favourable terms and conditions. For example, soldiers who served overseas during the Vietnam War while on leave without pay from positions in the South Australian Public sector had their own contributions, as well as the employer's contributions, paid by the South Australian government (Sharp, 1985:11).

While refusing to acknowledge the legitimacy of maternity leave, superannuation funds do legitimate women's dependency in some cases by paying spouse (dependent or not) and dependent children's benefits in the event of death of a member. As a result, the differential benefit has been estimated to be up to 30 percent more received by married members than by single members (Owen, 1984:368). Recognising maternity leave by ascribing it favourable terms and conditions as a socially legitimate practice for working women is unlikely to be as costly. At the very least, accouchment, maternity and parenting leave provisions should be flexible, so they do not constitute a barrier to retirement savings.

OTHER DISCRIMINATORY FEATURES

In addition, women are discriminated against because of a number of other features of superannuation schemes:

- in superannuation schemes providing a lump sum pay-out that is converted into regular income payments from an annuity, the monthly income provided for males is greater than for females (based on statistical data that women live longer than men)
- women invariably receive lower retirement benefits since the final benefits paid are earnings related
- women who benefit indirectly from superannuation through the death of a spouse receive a reduced and insecure benefit.

Use of actuarial data
Statistical, or actuarial data on mortality, morbidity, resignation rates and so on, is used as the basis for determining the contributions of employees and the benefits payable by an employer. It is also used to calculate the weekly income an annuity pays—a tax–favoured insurance policy lump sum superannuation beneficiaries can purchase to roll over their lump sum into a stream of income payments. Different superannuation contributions, benefits and annuities for women and men have been legitimated by the use of actuarial data. As one overseas analyst has observed, in practice the only factor that accounts for differences in superannuation calculations is the sex of the beneficiary (Laurent, 1986:681). While there are very marked differences in the life expectancy of various categories of male workers for example, this factor is generally not taken into account in actuarial calculations. It is somewhat curious that it remains permitted solely in the case of women workers. Linda Rosenman argues that the small number of women receiving benefits on retirement has meant little attention has

been focused on sex discrimination in the use of actuarial data. As a result annuities purchased from lump sums can pay a higher monthly income to men than to women (Rosenman, 1986:256). Consequently, women's relatively lower superannuation benefits are lowered even further.

Superannuation benefits are earnings related
Employer contributions are usually calculated as a proportion of the employee's wage or salary. Consequently, the higher the member's income, the greater the amount the employer contributes. In addition, the income tax laws limit the amount that a beneficiary can be paid as a lump sum from non-government schemes and still receive the applicable taxation concessions. In 1987 this limit was seven times salary. This provision clearly discriminates against low income non-government superannuation scheme members, particularly women. Seven times a small salary does not give the same level of benefit as seven times a large salary. Women's low earnings is a major factor in reducing the benefit they gain from superannuation relative to men.

Limited and insecure spouse benefits
The main means by which women have benefited from superannuation has been through sharing in their spouse's superannuation retirement income. Some schemes also pay a spouse benefit to a widow (and less often a widower) in the event of a member's or retiree's death. Thus superannuation, like other areas of economic importance to women, has been primarily available to women on the basis of their dependency on men. This is summed up by Linda Rosenman's argument that the system of spouse benefits, while not necessarily bad in itself, is based on beliefs about marriage and superannuation that ultimately limit the access of women and in fact all workers to superannuation as a right (Rosenman, 1986:259).

Even the payment of a spouse benefit is not treated as a right by many superannuation schemes, as many do not pay this benefit, and if they do the trustees have considerable discretion in deciding who receives the benefit. The increased trend towards lump sum superannuation benefits rather than pension benefits means reduced availability of spouse payments. In short, there is no guaranteed superannuation entitlement of a spouse upon death, divorce or retirement of a beneficiary. Consequently, women find themselves without equal or secure access to the benefits of superannuation whether they be workers in their own right or the dependents of men.

THE ROLE OF THE STATE

The state has played an important role in the development of occupational superannuation in most industrial capitalist economies. While the nature of state intervention in the area of superannuation has varied considerably from one country to another, the three main forms it has taken have been:

- the provision of superannuation coverage for the state's own employees
- the provision of a national superannuation fund for all workers in some countries
- state monitoring, supervision and regulation over private superannuation schemes

In Australia, the state has tended to be less directly involved in superannuation than it has in many other capitalist countries. While the Australian state, both at a Federal and local State levels, has over a long period provided superannuation coverage for its own employees, it has not developed a national superannuation scheme. Nor has it been very active in regulating the terms under which private schemes operate compared to other countries (Tamburi and Mouton, 1986:136). One of the main reasons for this is undoubtedly the fact that the Australian state very early this century introduced its own means-tested aged pension, which became the principal means of retirement income support. However, since the election of the Hawke Labor government in 1983 superannuation has become a far more important focus for government intervention.

EARLY DEVELOPMENT

As we have seen, superannuation schemes in Australia have developed in ways that have been highly discriminatory towards women. The state has participated in and has been partially responsible for this discrimination, primarily as a result of the operations of its own schemes. In Australia, occupational superannuation dates back to the mid–nineteenth century. The earliest superannuation schemes were established by banks and by the state for their own employees. The South Australian Civil Servant Scheme (1854) and the Bank of New South Wales Scheme (1862) were two of the earliest schemes in the colonies (Knox, 1986:23). Initially, therefore, the main means by which the state influenced the development of superannuation was through the establishment of schemes for its own employees. In this way the state has also indirectly had an effect in determining the terms under which superannuation has been provided—including who is eligible for coverage. This influence continues to be reflected in the structures of present day schemes.

The objectives of the early superannuation schemes, whether public or private, were similar—to provide gentlemanly retirement as an incentive and a reward for long and faithful service. Initially very much employer initiated, the early schemes sought to provide an incentive for highly valued, usually professional, employees to stay with the organisation. Thus superannuation effectively developed as a mechanism for maintaining continuity of class lifestyle in retirement (McCallum and Shaver, 1986:7). These objectives of superannuation were clearly articulated by the Attorney-General, Mr L.E. Groom, when he introduced the Commonwealth Superannuation Bill in 1922:

> The object of the scheme now submitted is to provide payments for those who have given a life-long service to the State, so that when they reach the age limit for retirement they will not find themselves in a position of pecuniary embarrassment. Moreover, should they, during their term of service, become permanently incapacitated, they will not be altogether without means of support, neither will their widows, or dependants, should death overtake the breadwinners, be penniless. The Commonwealth should have an efficient, capable, and contented Public Service, and should be able to retain in its ranks the best men obtainable.
> (*Commonwealth Parliamentary Debates* 19 September 1922:2364)

For many decades the eligibility requirements of superannuation schemes were alone sufficient to exclude women. Few women occupied jobs in either the public or private sector that would have allowed them to be considered for superannuation in their own right. If they were in such occupations, different terms and conditions were usually applied. For example, in the Commonwealth Superannuation Scheme, which was established in 1922, membership was only available to (and in fact was also compulsory for) permanent employees. This discriminated against women since their permanent status in the public service was taken away upon marriage and they were forced to resign from the superannuation scheme. Until the Commonwealth Public Service Act was amended in 1966, women who were permanent public servants and later married were, in effect, forced to subsidise the retirement benefits of others.[6] Single women who were eligible to join usually contributed to the scheme at a lower rate, received lower retirement benefits and were not eligible for children's benefits to be provided in the event of their death. Government schemes have continued to apply different terms and conditions to women members well into the 1980s. The Victorian State government, for example, operated a separate married women's superannuation scheme with significantly lower benefits until 1984.

A minority of women benefited indirectly from the early superannuation schemes, through their spouses' participation. In schemes such as the Commonwealth and New South Wales Government's, the family unit was used as the basis for insurance cover (Commonwealth Superannuation Board, 1973:1). As a result, married women benefited through their husbands' superannuation cover. Apart from such benefits being indirect and therefore less secure, they were also of lower value, being a fraction of the contributor's benefit. Therefore, in its early years of development, superannuation benefited women largely as a function of the occupational status of their husbands and their own economic dependency.

The state's role in the provision of retirement incomes was dramatically increased with the introduction of the Commonwealth aged pension in 1909. The introduction of a welfare provision for the aged provided the basis for a far more equal treatment of men and women in the state's retirement incomes policy. However, the levelling potential of the aged pension was limited in its early years (McCallum and Shaver, 1986:7) Being means tested, it was seen as being charity rather than a right. In contrast, superannuation was seen as a form of deferred pay. The means-tested aged pension, operating alongside occupational superannuation, put in place a two-tier retirement income system, under which the latter provided an independent source of retirement income for a select group of salaried males. Women were seen as receiving preferential treatment in the welfare retirement system established by the state because they could collect the aged pension at an earlier retirement age (60 years) than men (65 years) (Jones, 1983:188). However, such a conclusion was usually reached without reference to women's discriminatory treatment under the more prized superannuation system. Not only was the state instrumental in the establishment of a two-tier retirement income system, but it has treated women differently to men under each system.

POST-WAR EXPANSION

After World War II, superannuation was extended to broader groups of employees. Trade unions began to recognise superannuation as a valuable fringe benefit for workers and were successful in broadening coverage among their members. Blue-collar workers began to receive occupational superannuation, although the benefits were usually of a lower level. Often they were designed to be a supplement to the means-tested aged pension. The importance of superannuation as a component in salaried employees' renumeration packages increased. Employers continued to use superannuation to attract and retain such employees.

The expansion of occupational superannuation coverage in the post-war period was facilitated also by generous Federal government taxation concessions. The main concessions available until modified by the Labor government in 1983 were:

- employee's contributions to superannuation funds were tax deductible
- employer contributions to a superannuation fund were tax deductible business expenses
- superannuation fund earnings were not subject to tax as long as the fund invested 60 percent of its funds in government securities
- only 5 percent of the benefits paid were assessed for taxation at ordinary personal income tax rates

These taxation concessions were regressive, since higher–income earners gained greater tax savings as a proportion of their income than lower-income earners. Also, unless superannuation was paid as a pension, where it was subject to ordinary income tax, the taxation concessions virtually made superannuation benefits tax free (Albon, 1986:62). One taxation lawyer described this system as an upside-down subsidy providing the greatest assistance to the wealthy and nothing to the poorest (Krever, 1987:16). Women taxpayers, being less likely to receive superannuation retirement income, and lower-income earners generally, were in effect providing a significant retirement income subsidy to superannuation members.

EXPLAINING THE STATE'S ROLE

The state's significant historical role in the development of discriminatory superannuation schemes seems to have been the result of a combination of influences from class and patriarchal pressures. Initially, the state established its own schemes largely to attract and retain high quality male employees. These schemes were extended and their discrimination retained as a result of pressures from trade unions in male–dominated areas of employment. The further expansion of the role of the state through the provision of taxation concessions that primarily benefited high-income men was undoubtedly also linked to class-based policies. These policies were aimed to appeal to the affluent and middle class electorate that provided the power base for the long-serving conservative government in Australia during the 1950s and 1960s. Furthermore, there was a lack of any organised pressure group activity from women themselves on the issue of superannuation. It was simply not perceived as an issue relevant to women's interests.

Also of crucial importance in explaining the state's discriminatory treatment of women through its superannuation policies are the dominant mainstream economic assumptions about women. That they are assumed to have a breadwinning husband is explicitly reflected in superannuation schemes provision of women's coverage and benefits that are lower than men's. Similarly, the withdrawal of a widow's benefit upon remarriage clarifies the assumption that the woman's entitlement was based on her position as a dependent in a family rather than as an individual in her own right.

In its superannuation policies the state has ignored the different work patterns of women. It has never acknowledged that women's domestic and childcaring responsibilities have prevented them as workers from participating equally in superannuation. The state has perceived superannuation exclusively as a work-related benefit. Since it has seen work in the domestic sphere as separate from legitimate employment, it has never perceived superannuation rights as applicable to non-waged women, even those who are only temporarily outside the paid workforce.

Finally, the state in Australia has historically perceived superannuation as making a very specific contribution towards its own general task of facilitating the social reproduction of the capitalist economy. The capitalist state in most countries has taken actions designed to maintain a minimal level of social consensus and support for the economic system. Providing care for the aged has been one important example of the state's role in this area. Another dimension to the state's role in the social reproduction of capitalist society has been intervention to maintain the existing class structure and class relations.

The role that superannuation has played in the state's performance of these responsibilities in Australia has indirectly resulted in the development of a system to which women have had little access.

In Australia, the role of maintaining the aged in retirement has been primarily allotted to the patriarchal family and the state's aged pension. In other societies, the break-down in the ability of the family to care adequately for the aged was a major impetus for the state to take an active role in the development of superannuation. In Australia, this role was left to the welfare system producing, as we have noted, a basic welfare for all the aged. Superannuation, on the other hand, served primarily to maintain the class position of the better-off into their retirement. Although some women, because of their class position, benefited from the elite superannuation system, the vast majority has been confined to the inferior income retirement system provided by the state's aged pension.

THE HAWKE LABOR GOVERNMENT

Under the Hawke Labor government occupational superannuation has become incorporated more directly into the state's broader economic strategy. The government has initiated changes to the superannuation system that will dramatically transform both its coverage and its role within the Australian economy. These changes could significantly affect the economic welfare of all the population—including women. At this stage, however, it appears more than likely that women will continue to miss out on the potential benefits. Consequently, these initiatives will further exacerbate women's unequal position unless the reasons why women have been historically discriminated against are recognised and challenged.

The changes to the structure of superannuation introduced by the Labor government have been primarily aimed at integrating superannuation into two main areas of the state's economic policy and role. Firstly, superannuation is now perceived by the government as playing a more important part in the provision of adequate retirement incomes for the aged. In this sense, Labor appears to be seeking to transfer part of the state's established role in the social reproduction of capitalist society to the private sector. Secondly, the Labor government has sought to incorporate superannuation more formally into the framework of its wages policy. In this sense, the Labor government appears to be attempting to incorporate superannuation into the state's broader role of intervening in the process of capital accumulation within the economy.

SUPERANNUATION AND RETIREMENT INCOMES POLICY

The attempt to make superannuation a more integral part of the state's retirement incomes policy is the result of increasing concern among policy-makers about the reliance on, and cost of, the aged pension. Since the 1970s the state's fiscal crisis has made governments more concerned about the escalating costs of welfare. This concern has been further strengthened by New Right attacks on government expenditures in the welfare and social wage areas. Neo-liberal economists have a strong ideological preference also for a retirement incomes policy based more on individual savings that on a taxation–funded welfare system. Additionally, the ageing of the Australian population has raised concern about the ability of the state to finance the aged pension in the future. It has been estimated that the proportion of aged persons to the taxation paying population could increase from 17.2 to 30.5 percent over the period 1981–2031 (Ford, 1986:2).

The result of these concerns is that the Labor government no longer perceives occupational superannuation as merely a fringe benefit for a relatively small group of elite workers. Increasingly the state will attempt to encourage workers to provide for their own retirement incomes through occupational superannuation. Signalling this change of approach, the Labor government has already begun to reduce the universal availability of the aged pension. An income and assets test was re-imposed on the aged pension in the Hawke Government's May and August 1983 budgets. The income test for over 70-year-olds, abolished by the Whitlam Labor Government in 1972, was re-introduced. The test is not indexed for inflation so the number of pensioners affected will increase over time. An assets test for all aged pensioners, which the Fraser Liberal/National Coalition abolished in 1976, was re-imposed. Pensions were reduced for home-owning pensioners with assets (excluding their home) in excess of $70 000 (single) and $100 000 (couples). The assets test is also important in preventing people avoiding the income test by rearranging their financial holdings. At the same time, taxation concessions on superannuation payments taken as lump sums have been considerably reduced. The government's intention was primarily to encourage the taking of superannuation retirement benefits in a pension form.

What effect is this shift likely to have on women? In the first place, it is unlikely that the government's continued use of the taxation system to encourage greater superannuation coverage and to reduce aged pension budget allocations will increase women's access to superannuation. Women have historically gained little benefit from superannuation taxation concessions, which have primarily benefited high income-earning males. A study by the Department of Social Security shows clearly that the value of the reformed tax concessions provided by the Labor government to high–income (primarily male) earners is far in excess of the total benefit provided to an aged pension recipient:

> For example, (given current pension indexation arrangements, and average life expectancy of males at age 65), a male employee retiring at age 65 without any private source of retirement income could expect to receive a maximum single rate pension totalling $62 500 in real terms over 14 years. This compares with the estimated Government subsidy of $124 500 to a lump sum recipient who on average receive AWE (average weekly earnings) during his working life. (Donald, 1984:42)

Although the examples quoted in this study are male (and females live slightly longer), there can be no doubt about the highly regressive nature of the overall effect of these taxation concessions on women's position.

Secondly, however, Labor's policies are not likely to reduce the pressures on the state's budget but will most likely increase the future pressure for further cut-backs to welfare areas. Labor's taxation changes leave superannuation as an untaxed fringe benefit still regarded by tax experts as the best tax investment shelter available (Dixon, 1987a:15). Julian Disney of the Australian Council of Social Service has estimated that these taxation concessions now cost the government $12 billion each year in revenue. A more conservative estimate has been made by tax expert Daryl Dixon, who contends that the cost of this tax shelter could not be less than $5 billion at the moment but will increase annually (Dixon, 1987:15). Some perspective can be gained on this cost to state revenue by comparing it with the total overall cost of state social security and welfare expenditures. In 1986/87 these amounted to $20.5 billion (Budget Statements, 1987/88:392–3). That is, the current loss of revenues to the state caused by superannuation tax concessions represents between 24–58 percent (depending upon different estimates) of all existing state expenditures in the welfare area. This enormous potential loss of revenue to the state must increase the pressure for restrictionist budgetary policies. Conversely, of course, the removal of these concessions would offer the opportunity for solving the state's budget deficit problem by a progressive rather than a regressive method. It would also permit a degree of expansion in the areas of the state's budget that most affect women.[7]

In summary, the Labor government's initiatives to include superannuation as a more integral component of the state's retirement incomes policy appears likely to be disastrous for women. It is unlikely that increased numbers of women will gain access to the more highly lucrative superannuation system. Rather, this policy direction is likely to make the two-tiered retirement incomes system even more unequal, with women being the majority of those in the aged pension or poverty alleviation system. Furthermore, the increasing drain on the state's revenue from the generous tax concessions to those fortunate enough to have access to superannuation is going to mean continually increasing pressures on the state's budget and further cut-backs of expenditures in areas of particular importance to women.

SUPERANNUATION AND WAGES POLICY

Under the Hawke Labor government occupational superannuation has also become part of the state's wages policy. Superannuation in fact became the lynchpin of the re-negotiated Prices and Incomes Accord between the government and the ACTU in September 1985. Central to this agreement was the ACTU's agreement to forgo its entitlement to a 2 percent wage increase for all workers in the April 1986 National Wage Case. In return the government agreed to:

- support the ACTU's case before the Conciliation and Arbitration Commission for a national productivity payment of 3 percent of wages to be made in the form of a superannuation payment
- legislate before the next Federal election (scheduled in 1988 but held in July 1987) to establish a national safety net for those employees not covered by an existing superannuation scheme
- provide regulations on vesting, preservation and portability standards applicable to the 3 percent productivity payment into superannuation

Clearly, this agreement was constructed as part of the government's overall economic strategy to restrain wages and assist the rate of capital accumulation and investment by business (see Chapter 3). However, the ACTU heralded the agreement as a 'great leap forward' in this country's superannuation arrangements (Weaven, 1986:119). What effect, then is the incorporation of occupational superannuation within the wages system likely to have on women's economic position?

Several criticisms of this strategy in relation to women can be made. Firstly it is debatable whether foregoing a wage indexation increase in return for a superannuation payment is the best outcome for women. Any reduction in real wages lowers the standard of living of those without wealth to buffer the decline in purchasing power through inflation. For low-income families the gap between their incomes and the poverty line only needs to be narrowed marginally to cause serious hardship. A retirement benefit in the future may have less value than maintaining an adequate standard of living now. Married women not in the paid workforce have no direct or secure right to the superannuation benefit. Yet, as managers of household budgets and dependent on their spouses' incomes, they will personally experience declines in living standards from real wage declines. In short, present income will tend to be redistributed from women and children now to benefit men at a future time.

Secondly, the re-negotiated Accord Agreement locks the retirement income system into a more hierarchical structure. That is, retirement income will closely reflect one's position within the income hierarchy during one's working life (Ingles, 1986:21). Women cannot share equally with men in any form of earnings–related superannuation even if the obvious forms of direct and indirect discrimination are eliminated.

Thirdly, a number of aspects of the way in which the re–negotiated Accord has developed in practice have made the arrangements even less attractive to women:

- the failure of the Arbitration Commission to award the 3 percent superannuation payment to all workers
- the failure of the government to implement a national safety-net scheme
- the existence of serious loopholes in the minimum vesting, preservation and portability standards applied by the government

The 3 percent productivity payment
The re-negotiated Accord agreement was subject to the endorsement of the Arbitration Commission. In its June 1986 National Wage decision the Commission pulled back from

awarding a 3 percent productivity payment in the form of superannuation to all workers. Instead it simply agreed to ratify union-employer negotiated superannuation agreements to the value of 3 percent of ordinary time earnings of employees. The decision simply gave unions the right to negotiate with employers on a union by union, industry by industry basis. The weaker female-dominated unions are less likely to successfully negotiate agreements. Clearly, such women workers would have been better off with a wage indexation increase.

National safety–net scheme
It now appears that the government does not intend to proceed with the national safety-net scheme (*Advertiser*, 1 February 1988:17). The scheme was initially intended to provide for those without access to an industry scheme. Clearly, women workers would be the largest losers from the government's failure to fulfil its promise. Potentially, however, the scheme is a key element of the strategy to ensure universal superannuation coverage of the workforce. As overseas observers have commented, it would place Australia among a limited number of OECD countries that for reasons of equity have made supplementary protection compulsory for all employees while maintaining a private system of superannuation (Tamburi and Mouton, 1986:136).

Minimum standards
The application of minimum vesting, preservation and portability standards for the 3 percent productivity payment has manifested loopholes that potentially disadvantage women workers. In December 1985 the Labor Government released a set of draft guidelines that formed the basis of the operational standards for superannuation funds issued by the Treasurer in June 1986. In respect of any negotiated 3 percent productivity payments, the standards require that the amount be fully vested (i.e., owned) by the employee and preserved until age 55, death or disablement or permanent departure overseas. However, problems arise in the implementation of these important standards. There is considerable flexibility allowed for the use of the 3 percent productivity payment and, in practice, the payment is frequently being used to improve existing schemes or establish new ones. It becomes quite possible for women workers in particular to miss out on any negotiated 3 percent. For example, if the 3 percent is incorporated into a new superannuation scheme it may be used to provide preservation from, say, year five for all entitlements. However, a high proportion of women leave within five years. In doing so,

they lose their accrued benefits including their 3 percent. In the case of existing schemes the 3 percent has been applied to improve the early retirement benefit instead of providing improvements that allow women to collect retirement benefits. Furthermore, many women employed on a casual basis miss out on negotiated productivity payments simply because it is considered administratively complex to include them.

The government has also made it clear that it is not prepared to take a strong line against direct and indirect discrimination against women. It has been slow to respond to the Human Rights Commission Report recommendation in 1986 that the exempted Section 41(1) of the Sex Discrimination Act be repealed. Until this section of the Act is repealed it remains legal for superannuation funds to discriminate against women. The Government's Operational Standards provided it with an additional opportunity to reduce discrimination arising from the lack of appropriate standards on vesting, preservation, portability, maternity leave and spouse benefits. Apart from the requirement that employee contributions be fully vested in the employee compulsory standards in relation to existing (nearly 200 000 in 1985) funds, terms and conditions were not set. This is both inconsistent with women's interests and the state's own policy, which seeks to make occupational superannuation a greater component of retirement income support.

The introduction of vesting, preservation, portability and maternity leave provisions is obviously controversial. Employers' organisations such as the Confederation of Australian Industry are strongly opposed to it (Nolan, 1986:66). However, the rationality and importance for ensuring equity of these provisions has been stressed by various reports over a number of years—including the 1977 Hancock Inquiry and the 1983 Report of the Commonwealth Task Force on Superannuation (Gruen, 1985:618). The Labor government has clearly capitulated to powerful vested interests, running counter even to its own proposed reforms.

A FEMINIST STRATEGY ON SUPERANNUATION

A strategy to achieve sexual equality in the area of superannuation will need to be developed around a package of short-term reforms to existing schemes combined with long-term proposals for the restructuring of the superannuation system itself.

In the shorter term, by introducing a number of specific,

achievable reforms, the state could significantly increase women's access to, and share of, the benefits of superannuation. These reforms could easily be introduced, even given the policy directions of the Hawke Labor government. These reform measures would include state intervention to:

- establish compulsory vesting, preservation and portability provisions for all schemes that take into account women's broken work patterns
- require superannuation schemes to permit parents to retain membership rights during maternity and parental leave
- establish the right of all employees, including part-time, casual and home workers, to join an existing employer-sponsored scheme
- establish a safety-net scheme for workers without access to an employer-sponsored scheme
- integrate the aged pension system more equitably with the superannuation system so that lower–income groups are not denied adequate retirement incomes
- promote the use of flexible and nil employee contribution rates
- eliminate the use of statistical data that results in women receiving lower weekly pensions and payment from annuities simply on the basis of their average longer life expectancy
- establish dependent women's rights to spouses' superannuation benefits on the basis of their unpaid domestic contribution
- pay superannuation payments awarded through the wages system at a flat rate (instead of a percentage rate, which gives a greater dollar amount to higher-income groups)
- ensure women's equal representation on all superannuation policy-making bodies and negotiations. Current male domination of all aspects of superannuation means that the concerns of women are almost always overlooked

These reform measures are dependent upon the complete removal of the exemption for superannuation in the Commonwealth Sex Discrimination Act 1984. Anything less than the full repeal of the Act's exemption will make universal access of working women to superannuation unrealisable. Sex discrimination legislation is a crucial, though insufficient, step for establishing the right of women to superannuation as a condition of employment.

A further reform of enormous benefit to the majority of

women would be the elimination of regressive superannuation taxation concessions. The savings from the abolition of this drain on state revenue should be directed specifically towards upgrading the retirement incomes of those without access to superannuation.

While these specific reform proposals could significantly improve the access women have to the benefits of occupational superannuation in the short term, they would still leave them a long way short of equality with men in their retirement incomes. As superannuation is a work-related benefit, women will only benefit equally with men when they occupy an equal position in the workforce. This, of course, requires far-reaching changes to break down labour market segmentation, to ensure equal pay and to provide the social infrastructure (childcare, changes in the domestic division of labour and so on) to allow women to achieve equality in the workforce.

A realistic alternative option for women to push for in the medium term, however, is for women to lobby the state to build its retirement incomes policy around a national superannuation strategy that is not directly earnings-related. Union schemes such as the one established for building workers (BUS scheme) is an example whereby earnings differences between members does not translate into different superannuation benefits. This scheme is industry-based, does not require any employee contributions and the employer contribution is the same for all workers. However, only a national superannuation scheme, based on progressive contribution rates, has the capacity to produce substantially more equitable retirement incomes to all men and women at a level well above the present aged pension's inadequate levels. Such a scheme could also provide an opportunity to break the inequitable relationship between class, gender and the benefits provided under the state's retirement incomes policy. Its success in this regard would depend very much on its design (Rosenman, 1986:257). While many countries have national superannuation schemes, their various structures result in very different results for women. Some, for instance, still assume dependency by women on men (Rosenman, 1986:258). Similarly, the Hancock Committee recommended a national superannuation scheme in which contributors received a pension at retirement that was broadly based on their prior contributions (Hancock, 1977). Clearly, the closer retirement incomes are linked to career earnings the more discriminatory the scheme will be for women.

It is in women's economic interests to argue for a progressive scheme that serves to promote equality and social justice in the retirement incomes of all men and women. Obviously this would meet strong opposition from both male high-income earners and from the private superannuation industry itself. This industry is dominated by a small number of giant life insurance offices and is currently worth $35 000 million. Industry estimates suggest that the changes introduced by the Hawke Labor government will increase the total value to more than $60 000 million within ten to twenty years (*Age* 13 December 1985:17). The magnitude of the industry can be illustrated by a simple comparison to the total 1986/87 Federal budget, which stood at $73 000 million.

While opponents of a reduction of private control over these vast superannuation funds would undoubtedly portray a national superannuation scheme as merely another form of taxation, their opposition would be based on self-interest. The beneficiaries of such a reform would include the majority of women and other currently disadvantaged groups. However, the benefits of a national superannuation scheme could also be attractive to a far wider section of the population as a result of the huge potential source of funds it could provide to the state from the retirement savings of workers. With union and worker participation in the control of the scheme, there is an enormous potential for influencing the overall direction and conditions of capital investment in Australia. This influence could ensure a major increase in social investment from which women could benefit far more than they do from current private investment strategies. A proposal for a national superannuation scheme based on joint government/union control could, therefore, bring the full weight of the union movement behind a strategy from which women would be major beneficiaries. Of course, a greatly increased role for women within trade unions is an essential prerequisite to the success of such a strategy.

III

CONCLUSION

6 From theory to strategy

We have attempted in this book to identify the framework within which the economic policies of the capitalist state are constructed and how they serve to reinforce and exacerbate women's economic inequality. We have argued that the gender and class bias of neo–classical economics as well as the nature of the state itself serve as major constraints to improving women's economic position. Of course, this is not to say that the state is not capable of pursuing economic policies and strategies that may improve women's position. However, more active involvement by feminists in influencing economic policymaking is critical to achieving increased economic equality. If women are to utilise the state and economic policy effectively as part of a feminist strategy, then existing approaches must be broadened in a number of ways.

EXPANDING THE PROGRESSIVE ROLE OF THE STATE

Existing feminist theories of the state as yet do not form an adequate basis for feminist political action. A telling comment by Sara Dowse, former head of the Australian government's Office of Women's Affairs, aptly illustrates the inadequacy of existing feminist theories of the state to act as a guide to feminist strategy:

> What has intrigued me, however, throughout my life as a feminist is the fact that, despite my scepticism about the so-called democratic process of government and my philosophical abhorrence of the modern capitalist state, when I want something done I look to just that arena. My expectations are low, but my directions are clear. I look to the public sector. And despite all claims to the contrary so do most of my feminist sisters, even the most radical among them. (Dowse, 1984:139)

Ideally, of course, theory and strategy should go hand in hand and be equally important in building an understanding of society and the ways to make it a better one. However, as Sara

Dowse has suggested, a substantive gap exists between feminist theories of the state and the strategies being employed in practice by feminists of all types. While some of these strategies may actually be ineffective or counter-productive, the theory of the state is itself inadequate in a number of ways and needs to be extended in order to ensure that feminist strategies utilise the state to the maximum extent possible.

The inadequacies of feminist theories of the state can be summarised under four headings. Firstly, most feminist theories have tended to address only a very limited range of the state's activities that affect women. As we have attempted to demonstrate in the case studies considered earlier, the state's economic policies and strategies in many different areas profoundly affect women.

Secondly, liberal theories of the state have failed to adequately understand the role played by the state in preserving the existing class and patriarchal power structures. The overall economic strategies pursued by the Hawke Labor government and the role of the state in relation to both taxation and superannuation clearly illustrate that the state can be expected to generally act to maintain existing gender inequalities. The pressures upon the state to do so are enormous. As our case studies have shown, the two major pressures are the ability of the dominant forces within society to influence the state and the critical role played by conservative economic theory.

Thirdly, however, while socialist and radical feminist theories of the state *have* focused on the role of the state in maintaining women's subordination, they have paid relatively little attention to those activities that potentially benefit them. The complexity of the state's tasks invariably cause its role to be ambiguous. In many cases, for example, it is forced to intervene in the economy to soften the harsh inequalities produced by 'market forces'. Furthermore, the state can also be forced to introduce progressive policies when pressures to do so are greater than those opposed.

Fourthly, these theories have also tended to see the state as playing merely a functional role in serving the needs of the established systems of capitalism and patriarchy rather than itself being an arena within which conflict and struggle occur.

These conclusions have clear implications for the strategies that might be employed by feminists in relation to the state:

- A feminist strategy needs to greatly expand the areas of public policy within which pressure is brought to bear on the state. Women's economic position is profoundly influenced, not only by policies pursued by the state in relation to the labour market and welfare, but also by the state's taxation and expenditure policies and its overall macroeconomic strategy. Women cannot afford to allow state policies in these areas to remain uncontested. The majority of women share a common interest in the state adopting wide-ranging policies that promote increased equality and progressive economic redistribution.

- State intervention in specific policy areas has historically provided only limited gains for women since they are often cancelled out by the quite contradictory role of the state in other areas. For example, policies to provide increased training and retraining opportunities for women workers can have only limited success if the state's macroeconomic strategy is simultaneously restricting overall employment growth. A feminist economic strategy therefore needs to be comprehensive, coherent and integrated. It should not be focused solely on specific policy issues that may appear to most affect women.
- A feminist economic strategy needs also to address the structural relationship between women's dual economic roles in the household and in the paid workforce. State policies that recognise and seek to challenge patriarchal family structures and women's dependency (both on men and on the state) are crucial to women's economic equality and independence. Feminists, therefore, need to develop an economic strategy that recognises childcare and the democratisation of the sexual division of labour in the home as crucial economic issues.
- The state tends to be more politically and ideologically inclined to promote reforms that primarily benefit individual higher-income women. Significant changes that benefit the majority of women can only be achieved by structural economic reforms. Feminists, working inside the state, in community groups, and in trade unions, need to apply more pressure for changes that benefit working class women and women as a whole rather than a narrow range of elite women workers.

CHALLENGING MAINSTREAM ECONOMICS

An understanding of the weaknesses of neo–classical economics in relation to women is a first step in developing a feminist economic strategy. A strategy for change needs to determine the ways in which mainstream economics can be challenged and modified. As well as seeking alternative frameworks of economic analysis, it also needs to assess the ultimate limitations mainstream economic theories and policies pose.

There should exist little doubt that the ideas of neo–classical economics have played a considerable role in shaping the public policies of the capitalist state. Over the past two decades in Australia, as in other industrialised countries, economic issues have dominated the agendas of governments. Neo–classical economic ideas have almost totally dominated and shaped these debates. John Maynard Keynes once warned of the intellectual influence of economic ideas:

> ...the ideas of economists and political philosophers, both when they are right and when they are wrong, are more powerful than is commonly understood. Indeed the world is ruled by little else. Practical men, who believe themselves to be quite exempt from any intellectual influences, are usually the slaves of some defunct economist. (Keynes, 1936)

From women's perspective, it is not only 'defunct' economic ideas that are a problem but current ones also.

To the extent that neo–classical economics acts in a class and ideological role to develop and legitimate policies to benefit capitalism, it will never be likely to play a positive role for women in reducing structural inequalities within capitalism. In reality, its market-oriented ideology is more likely to result in women's already unequal position being worsened. Furthermore, the methodological framework of neo–classical economics provides only a limited basis for incorporating an understanding of women's important but unequal role in the economy. It, therefore, provides a fundamentally inadequate basis for developing progressive policies for change.

Our analysis has suggested that the ideological and methodological framework of neo–classical economics ultimately limits the ability of mainstream economic theories and policies to act as a mechanism for achieving economic equality for women. In an important address to a feminist conference in 1984 Margaret Power remarked on these difficulties. Nevertheless, she expressed some optimism about the effects that feminism might have on mainstream economics:

> ...the economists and policy makers who have written women out of the economy will not easily write them back in. Inequality between women and men is embedded in all the institutions of the economy. If women can, however, succeed in their struggle to get into the mainstream, the mainstream itself will be transformed. (Power et al., 1984:41)

A feminist economic strategy should seek to obtain the best possible outcome for women working within the framework of mainstream economics. Specifically, such a feminist strategy should seek to modify economic analysis in the following areas:

- A concerted attempt needs to be made to ensure that women's specific and often disadvantaged position is taken into account in economic analyses and policies. Feminists need to continually attack the myth of economic policies being gender (and class) neutral in their impact.
- Economic analyses and policies reflecting and reinforcing a split between the paid and the unpaid economic spheres should be challenged. Also, the true economic contribution of women's paid and unpaid work needs to be assessed and appropriately reflected in policies.
- The assumptions of economic analyses and policies should be scrutinised for their appropriateness in promoting women's economic independence and equality.
- The ideology of the New Right and neo-liberal economic theories need to be challenged. If women are going to benefit from mainstream economic policies at all, it will only be as a result of reducing the increasing domination of this ultra-conservative strand of economic theory.
- Feminists need to concern themselves with a broader range of economic issues—from the state's overall macroeconomic strategy to individual economic policies such as taxation and wages policies. Also, issues such as childcare, normally assigned to social policy, need to be incorporated into economic policies.
- Feminists need to utilise the state in a positive role in redistributing resources to create a more equal society. While the state's intervention in the economy has historically not always benefited women, allowing the market mechanism to allocate resources will never increase the degree of economic equality in society.

Finally, feminists should also be actively engaged in the struggle to develop alternative economic strategies that challenge and seek to change the existing distribution of power, wealth and income in society. Alternative economic theories will not themselves be sufficient to achieve the introduction of policies to end inequalities within the framework of a capitalist economy. However, the development of alternative theories and strategies is a crucial part of the long-term ideological struggle to develop economic alternatives to our existing unequal system.

TOWARDS AN ALTERNATIVE ECONOMIC STRATEGY

In the United Kingdom, proposals for an alternative economic strategy have been strongly criticised by feminists. The strategy has been perceived as primarily aimed at restoring full employment in male areas of the workforce. As Anne Phillips has argued, 'Why should women support a strategy that says so little about their needs and experience?' (Phillips, 1983:35) The strategy was also criticised for its false assumption that capitalism, with increased intervention by the state, can provide prosperity and equality for all (Phillips, 1983:36). To date, alternative proposals in Australia can be subjected to similar criticisms. The Accord (insofar as it can in any way be construed as an 'alternative' strategy) and the proposals outlined in the ACTU's *Australia Reconstructed* are both vulnerable to such criticisms.

Unfortunately, therefore, little effective progress has been made in Australia towards the development of a more highly interventionist 'alternative strategy'. The most detailed attempt made so far has been a package of radical reform proposals developed by Australian political economist Frank Stilwell. This strategy presents a range of policies that include:

- an interventionist trade and industry policy
- an expansionary budgetary policy based on increased expenditure on the social wage
- progressive tax reform
- increased democratic control over the economy through state intervention in increased public ownership, national and regional economic planning, regulation of the finance sector, control of foreign investment, and control of monopoly pricing
- expanded labour market programmes for technology and retraining
- the introduction of industrial democracy—particularly within the state itself

Frank Stilwell's strategy is superior to that of the Accord and *Australia Reconstructed* because it does not operate on the false assumption that an economic strategy introduced by the state can resolve the conflicting needs of different class group within capitalism. It is genuinely conceived as a transitional strategy 'of a socialist character' (Stilwell, 1986:123). On the other hand, while they avoid the tendency of other strategies to focus solely on creating jobs in male areas of employment, Frank

Stilwell's proposals, to a significant extent, fail to recognise the particular economic situation of women. Consequently, while this programme seems to offer an appropriate starting point for a feminist economic strategy, it would need to be extended in a number of ways to adequately include the economic interests of women:

- While it is vitally important for women that highly interventionist trade and industry policies be developed within an expansionary macroeconomic framework, it is also crucial that these policies are aimed specifically at expanding areas of women's employment. As Anne Phillips has pointed out. 'Unless we discuss explicitly what any strategy means for women, we fall unthinkingly into policies for men' (Phillips, 1983:34).
- Any expansionary economic strategy must be accompanied not only by progressive taxation reforms but also by reforms that produce an adequate source of revenue. Without adequate revenue the state's expenditure programmes that most benefit women are likely to be continually under budgetary pressures.
- Expanded social wage expenditures are important to women, but it is crucial for women's economic independence that welfare policies be integrated with labour market policies. Genuine equality for women can never be achieved simply by creating a bigger welfare state, which locks them into continued economic dependence.
- Labour market strategies to benefit women should go beyond proposals that are limited to expanded training and re-training schemes. They should also include the introduction of universally available childcare, the introduction of genuine equal pay, and the re-definition of skill to include women's areas of employment.
- Strategies to change the economic division of labour in the home are also a relevant and important part of an overall economic strategy to increase women's equal participation in the economy. Without such changes, attempts to create increased opportunities for women to participate equally in the wider economy can have only limited success.

IMPLEMENTING A FEMINIST ECONOMIC STRATEGY

Sexual equality cannot be achieved by means of minor economic reforms or simply by 'including women' in existing economic strategies. In order to achieve genuine economic equality, dramatic changes are required in the present highly inequitable distribution of income and resources in society.

Clearly, the process of transforming our society into a just one requires us to 'think big'. It requires that we think beyond equal opportunity programmes, increased welfare expenditures and taxation reforms—important as each of these are. The achievement of equality will require extensive and radical changes to our economic structures. The state can play an important role in achieving these changes, but we need to understand clearly that it will do so only under certain circumstances:

- Progressive policies will only be introduced by the state under enormous pressure for reform from progressive organisations outside the state. The development of alternative policies to benefit women will almost certainly be ineffective without the mobilisation of considerable political pressure in support of change. The pressures applied to the state from capital and patriarchy *against* progressive changes are formidable.
- To utilise the state in a more progressive role for women strategies are needed to break down the authoritarian structures of the bureaucracy and to make the state as a whole more democratically accountable. The internal structures of the capitalist state have inclined it to introduce policies in support of capital and patriarchy. The less democratic the structures and processes of the state, the more likely that its policies will be directed to serving the vested interests of capital and patriarchy.
- While internal pressure for change from 'femocrats' can be important in the struggle to use the state as part of a feminist strategy, this is unlikely to be effective without strong pressure for progressive policies from outside the state. Femocrats also are subjected to pressures from within and outside the state not to 'rock the boat'. The motivation and capacity of feminist bureaucrats to push for more radical policies are likely to be greatly increased by the application of organised pressure from outside.
- Historically the state has been receptive to organised pressure from trade unions—representing the collective power of (primarily male) workers. It is strongly in the interests of women to work within the structures of trade unions in order to gain more effective representation of women's interests. Because of their disadvantaged economic position,

the majority of women do not have a great deal of political power. However, women's political influence can be greatly enhanced through increased involvement in trade unions, since they share a common interest with many male workers in the development of policies that promote increased equality.

A feminist economic strategy needs to recognise that while women as a whole share many economic interests, their economic position is also influenced by their class position. Consequently, while all women stand to gain in one sense from the principle of equality being adopted by the state, policies which improve the economic position of the majority of women will inevitably go against the economic interests of some groups of women.

Finally, while the state can be utilised as part of a feminist strategy for change, it is important to distinguish between the short-term reforms for women that are possible within the framework of the state and the long-term strategies required to end the exploitation and subordination of women in capitalist society. Inevitably, the achievement of equality for women is incompatible with a capitalist economy that is built upon the principles of economic competition and inequality. Of course, the transition to a socialist economic framework does not automatically guarantee sexual equality. However, a socialist society based on the principles of equality and socially useful production makes sexual equality possible.

Notes

1 Women and the state

1 Needless to say, the categories of liberal, radical and socialist feminism used here to describe the various strands of feminist thought are useful only as generalisations. While most feminists might be located basically within one framework, many individuals obviously adopt elements of more than one of these political tendencies in their thinking.
2 Amongst socialist feminists, Michele Barrett has perhaps gone furthest in explaining why a major feminist assault on the state is essential and should not be regarded as reformist. In the first place she argues that simply because the state plays a considerable political and ideological role in women's oppression, a systematic attack on this aspect of the state's role is warranted. Secondly, however, the state is not simply an instrument of oppression, but also a site of struggle. The state's role in relation to women is to some extent contradictory or ambivalent. For example, the state has been the major employer of women over the past decades. It has also provided essential support for a great number of women in difficult circumstances. Therefore, while not endorsing the liberal feminist assumption that pressuring the state can itself bring women's liberation, Barrett sees the state as to some extent responsive to concerted pressure. Thirdly, the failure by women to engage in struggles over the determination of state policies can result in a deterioration in women's economic position. Pressures on the state from conservative forces have the potential to increase women's dependency on men as a result of the current economic recession. Feminist intervention in the arena of the state, therefore, becomes an important part of an overall strategy for liberation (Barrett, 1980:243).
3 There exists also a small number of socialist feminists who, in theory, reject any form of reformism and adhere to a belief in a strictly revolutionary strategy. These are located primarily in the socialist 'splinter' parties.
4 The question that arises at this point is why the state, with its liberal-democratic structures, should remain a capitalist state—serving the interests primarily of the minority dominant class. There has been a stormy debate about this question. Ralph Miliband originally tended to stress two factors. One was the class and ideological background of the state elite. The other was the political power of the dominant class as a pressure group resulting from its ownership and control of the economy. However, a third

and more important factor identified by other writers such as Nicos Poulantzas and Ian Gough (and ultimately Miliband himself) is that the capitalist economy itself has an overwhelmingly dominant effect over the government and the state (Poulantzas, 1973; Gough, 1979; Miliband, 1977). It has its own rationale to which any government must sooner or later submit, and usually sooner. Any government, in other words, that loses the confidence of capital (as in the case of the Whitlam Labor government in Australia) invariably finds itself subjected to the most extreme pressures—not only from within the local economic system but potentially from the forces of international capital as well.

5 The most explicit expression of this theory was developed by Veronica Beechey (Beechey, 1977:56-60). She argued that capital always requires a flexible population of fringe workers who are available to be brought into and expelled from industry as production needs change. Capital doubly benefits from this since the reserve army can also act as a competitive force—depressing wages and forcing other workers to accept higher levels of exploitation. However, although women are particularly attractive to both capital and the state, there is no intrinsic reason why they alone should make up the reserve army. In fact, any group of workers in a vulnerable position are useable. Beechey suggests that women are attractive from capital's point of view because they are likely to be dependent upon sources of income other than their own wage—either their husbands' wages or state welfare. Thus they can be persuaded to accept wages below the level required to maintain themselves at the prevailing standard of living and they can disappear back into the domestic sphere when no longer required.

6 We are conscious that in pursuing our task we have simplified and compressed numerous layers of complex arguments. As Sara Dowse exclaimed in her extremely clear-headed analysis of the role of the state: 'Yet the subject remains a conceptual maze' (Dowse, 1984:139).

7 For example, Mary McIntosh concludes her analysis of the role of the state by acknowledging that her approach has been overly functionalist. She acknowledges the contradictions that emerge in the process by which the state's policies are constructed and the degree to which policy outcomes are contested (McIntosh, 1978:281-5).

2 Women and economics

1 Adam Smith is regarded as the founder of modern economics. His book *An Inquiry Into the Nature and Causes of the Wealth of Nations* was published in 1776.
2 For a more detailed explanation of the nature of, and differences between, these strands of neo–classical economic theory and their policy implications see Grant and Nath, 1984; Sawer, ed., 1982; Smith, 1987; Whitwell, 1986.

3 Keynes' influential book *The General Theory of Employment Interest and Money* was published in 1936.
4 There were 506 women economists recorded in the ABS 1986 Census, Australia. This represented 27 percent of all employed economists in 1986 compared to 18 percent in the 1981 Census.
5 The classical economists, for example, used the labour theory of value to justify private property, whereas Marx had used it as the basis for his theory of exploitation. When Marx destroyed the usefulness of the labour theory of value in the ideology of capitalism it was discarded and replaced by a 'new' marginal utility theory of value, which could both support the theory of free markets and ward off the Marxist attack (Fusfeld, 1986:94–5).
6 The neo–classical theory of income distribution—the theory of marginal productivity—concludes that workers are paid a wage equal to the value of the last unit of output they produce. That is, workers receive what they earn, no more, no less. Highly skilled and productive workers earn higher wages because they produce more at the margin.
7 Methodological individualism is the term given to this principle. It is the opposite to 'methodological holism', whereby social wholes (e.g., the state) have functions that cannot be reduced to the beliefs and actions of the individuals who make them up. See Blaug, 1980:49–52 for a discussion of the role of methodological individualism in neo–classical economics.
8 See McClelland, 1987 for a discussion of the factors that affect the equity/efficiency choice. In particular, full employment can be argued to both transform the supposed equity/efficiency conflict and also be an essential condition for maximising equity and efficiency.
9 Logical positivism is a philosophical approach to knowledge that developed in the twentieth century. It advocates the universality of scientific method (i.e., the method of the natural sciences). A fundamental principle of logical positivism is that all scientific statements and theories must be verifiable. Metaphysical statements, value judgements or ethical statements are not verifiable. Therefore, by definition, an economics that adopts this approach is 'value free'. This methodology was purported to underlie 'positive economics'—an approach that achieved wide consensus amongst economists in the post-war period. Milton Friedman and Richard Lipsey have been two of its strongest proponents. Positive economics, while maintaining that it is 'value free', only requires that something of the theory (e.g., assumptions or predictions but not both) is testable or falsifiable (not verifiable) to fulfil the criteria of scientific method. See Katouzian, 1980:10–84 for an excellent insider's discussion of these methodological issues.
10 Subsequent editions have removed the sexist language from this definition of economics.
11 The concept of the basic (male) family wage has been significant

historically in extending both these assumptions to economic policies in Australia.

3 Women and the Hawke Labor government

1   Estimates of the numbers of Australians who are homeless vary from 40 000 (*Australian Society* August 1985:35) to 100 000 (Paris, 1987).
2   A 1985 study found that 62 percent of single parents living in private rental housing were in poverty (Wettenhall, 1987:26–7).
3   The banks claimed that increased interest rates would allow them to release more money for housing loans. However, the decline in housing construction commencements that followed suggested that the main effect was to further retard the growth of the housing sector.
4   The main beneficiaries were those already well enough off to have gained access to the home ownership market. The primary benefit for people in poverty was the government's decision to raise weekly rental assistance by a maximum of $10 for poor private tenants. However, the government policy most beneficial to women in hardship would have been a dramatic increase in the provision of public housing. While the government has substantially increased grants and loans to the states for public housing purposes, this has not resulted in a major increase in public housing activity. In part, this is because CSHA grants are partially used by the states to fund rental subsidies. In part also this is because a far greater commitment of funds is required to lift the proportion of public sector houses above the 1987/88 level of about 6.5 percent. While this figure represents a slight improvement on the figure of 6.1 percent in 1983/84, it is long way short of Labor's earlier goal of doubling the proportion of public housing in the rental market.
5   Between June 1977 and June 1987 the total number of adult women in Australia dependent upon government pensions or benefits increased by 30 percent (Department of Social Security, 1987).
6   A Bureau of Labour Market Research study has concluded that, contrary to the previous assumptions of economists (Lewis, 1985), sex segmentation in the Australian workforce is increasing, not decreasing (Karmel and MacLachlan, 1986).
7   To some extent, of course, the blame for this trend should be directed at the union movement itself since the government has tended to initiate action on industry policy only in those areas where unions have applied most pressure.

4 Women and taxation

1   Since 1975–76 in Australia personal income taxation rebates have replaced concessional deductions. This has been a more equitable policy as the value of the latter rose with the marginal tax rate and therefore favoured higher–income groups. Furthermore, rebates for family expenditures have been substantially reduced since 1985–86, when the concessional expenditure rebate

for superannuation, medical expenses, education expenses and land tax was abolished. As these items were only rebateable above a threshold amount it was easier for a couple to reach that figure if such expenditures were consolidated to the higher (usually the husband) income earner. As Sheila Shaver describes it, 'the state collects taxes from individuals and returns part of women's income to men as tax relief in respect of family living costs, thereby reconstructing the family as breadwinner and dependent spouse' (Shaver, 1983:159).

2 In May 1976 the Liberal-National Party coalition government replaced the taxation rebates for dependent children (and the existing child endowment) with a system of family allowances. Family allowances are a cash payment to the primary care-giver and are therefore generally identified as part of the state's social welfare expenditure. However, because family allowances were historically designed to achieve a degree of horizontal equity between families with and without children they can also be conceptualised as a taxation measure. In any case, family allowances highlight the need to consider the taxation and social security system together.

3 There have been two major studies of the incidence of taxation in Australia. Bentley, Collins and Drane undertook a commissioned study for the Asprey Taxation Review Committee in 1975. Their study used 1966–67 data. The more recent major study is that of Neil Warren, which used 1975–76 Household Expenditure Survey data. For details of other tax incidence studies see Harding, 1984:26–51. A critique of tax incidence studies is provided in Groenwegen (ed.), 1987, Part two. The inappropriateness of tax incidence analysis in relation to women is raised by Savage, 1984.

4 It is frequently emphasised by conservative economists that Australia has a high level of property taxation compared to other OECD countries. However, the main existing property tax is local government rates. Generally the tax is a flat rate levied on the unimproved capital or site value of the land. As a result only a proportion of the value of the asset is being taxed. Furthermore, the monies are spent by local councils in providing services and facilities to the residents of the council area. To the extent that more affluent local government areas have better services and facilities, local government property taxes are not redistributive of wealth.

5 The only official wealth study in Australia was undertaken in 1915 and it explicitly only surveyed the wealth of men. Phillip Raskall using 1970 data showed that women had about half the wealth of men for wealth holdings $15 000 and above. Women's wealth holdings were particularly low in the 20–29 age group, falling to one-fifth of men's. Raskall concludes, 'These results clearly emphasise the economic disadvantage of women both in terms of occupational status and the social arrangements within marriage, and possibly also through initial inheritance' (father

passing the business on to his son) (Raskall, 1978). During 1987 sections of the community (ALP left, welfare groups and others) sought to place a wealth inquiry on the political agenda. The attempt was squashed with the October stock market crash since the government assumed that there were now less wealthy Australians. In fact, there had occurred merely a redistribution of wealth amongst the well-off, which has often historically been the case.

6 Interestingly, some liberal taxation economists and policymakers have also argued for a flat–rate personal income tax and/or a broad based consumption tax. However, the assumptions underpinning their arguments are very different from those of the New Right economists. For example, Professor Russell Mathews has argued that a flat rate income tax might be the only way of overcoming tax avoidance. Similarly, given the regressive nature of income tax in practice as a result of avoidance and evasion, he argues that a broad based consumption tax might be less regressive. In contrast to the New Right economists, however, Russell Mathews argues also for the inclusion of wealth and capital gains taxes in order to make the overall tax system progressive (Mathews, 1985).

7 The extent of the gain for women is determined even here by the financial arrangements prevailing within the family.

8 The main legislative attack on tax evasion has been the introduction of the Prescribed Payments System (PPS) in 1983. It provides for tax deductions at source from payments for work in industries such as the building industry. In its first year of operation $400 million was raised under the PPS, of which $200 million was estimated to be tax previously evaded (Draft White Paper, 1985:38).

9 The lack of access to fiscal welfare in general by women was a key reason why the tax deductibility of childcare was not widely pursued by women's groups.

10 The company imputation system provides tax relief to shareholders. Dividends paid to shareholders by companies that have paid the full profits taxation receive a tax credit. Effectively, refunds of company taxes are made to individual shareholders when dividends are paid. Consequently, total company tax collections can be expected to decline as share ownership increases (Dixon, 1987a:16).

5 Women and superannuation

1 Occupational superannuation is a work related means of savings for retirement. The Commonwealth Income Tax Assessment Act (1936) determines what constitutes superannuation for tax exemption purposes under Section 23 (ja), 23 (jaa), 23 F and 23 FB. Hence, in practice, superannuation is largely defined by the Income Tax Act. Occupational Superannuation can be employer-sponsored or a personal policy taken out with an insurance

company. In Australia, the first superannuation schemes were employer-sponsored and the great majority of superannuation involves an employer contribution.

2 Historical data is not available to provide a clear picture of women's work patterns over time. Some perspective is gained by examining data for the population at points in time (cross sectional data). By plotting the percentage of employed women in each age group an M-shaped pattern is indicated. The pattern is shaped by high rates of labour force participation for young (20–24 age) women, which then decline for women of child bearing age (25–34) and rise again, but at a lower rate, for women in the 34–44 year age group. The employment patterns of male workers is different. It rises steadily to the age of 35–44 and falls off sharply after the age of 60. The M-shaped labour force participation pattern of women reflects the fact that many women leave the labour force after the birth of their first child and return after the youngest child enters school. For the 25–34 age group, 55.4 percent of married women were not in the labour force compared to 13.6 percent of married men (ABS, *Labour Force Experience Australia* 1985). Hence women's employment is characterised by a broken workforce pattern whereas men's workforce pattern is characterised by continuity. Women's broken workforce pattern also reflects breaks between full-time and part-time employment status. The incidence of part-time work among women almost doubles during women's peak childbearing and rearing ages of 25–34 years.

3 It is common for superannuation schemes to specify the number of years of membership necessary to qualify for a maximum retirement pension or lump sum. A typical example would be 35 years membership in order to obtain a benefit equal to seven times salary. The Human Rights Commission reported that Commonwealth Superannuation fund data showed that women bearing and caring for children are likely to leave the workforce for seven to sixteen years. If all the years of a woman's fund membership are not counted for the calculation of benefits then it is extremely unlikely the majority of women would qualify for maximum benefits.

4 Preservation in this sense is defined as the retention of vested benefits until a specified retirement age. This concept of preservation is essential for women.

5 Research on labour market turnover does not distinguish between the relative rates of job change as opposed to taking time out of the labour force between women and men. However, recent research suggests differences in quit rates for women and men have been overstated with aggregate data (Office of the Status of Women, 1985a; Chapman and Prior, 1986). Given that cross-sectional data indicate women are more likely to take time out of the workforce, changing jobs would seem to be a relatively more important factor in men's quit rates. This is consistent with the long held importance male workers have placed on portability provisions in super-

annuation schemes. In effect, the lack of portability is probably less important as a source of discrimination than the lack of preservation arrangements for women workers.

6 Although married women may have been eligible for a resignation pay-out, because of the lack of vesting this payment was invariably lower than if they had invested their money elsewhere. The effects of this type of discrimination will continue to be borne by women workers for many decades because opportunities to 'catch-up' on past service have not been offered by superannuation funds.

7 The redistributive impact of reducing superannuation taxation concessions depends on what the government does with the revenue. If, for example, it is used to reduce company tax rates, then the majority of women are unlikely to be better off, and those who are scheme members will be worse off. Moreover, the inequitable nature of the taxation concessions lies in the fact that the value of the concession increases with income. If this aspect was redressed and scheme discrimination against women removed, then some superannuation taxation concessions would be consistent with equity.

Bibliography

Aarons, Laurie (1987) 'Corporate profits soar–tax payout drops' *Tribune* 7 October
Advertiser, The 24 June 1987, 1 February 1988
Age, The 13 December 1985:17
Albon, Robert (1986) *Taxation Policy in the Eighties* Sydney: Allen & Unwin
Amsden, Alice (ed.) (1980) *The Economics of Women and Work* Harmondsworth: Penguin
Anand, Anita (1983) 'Rethinking women and development' *Women in Development* Geneva: Women's International Information and Communication Service
Apps, Patricia, Glenn Jones and Elizabeth Savage (1981) 'Tax discrimination by dependent spouse rebates or joint taxation' *Australian Quarterly* 53 (3) Spring, pp. 262–79
Apps, Patricia (1987) *Tax and Social Security Reform: An Analysis of Equity and Disincentive Effects* Occasional Paper No. 2, Sydney: Australian Tax Research Foundation
——(1983) 'The tax unit: An Australian perspective' in Head, John (ed.) *Taxation Issues of the 1980's* Sydney: Australian Tax Research Foundation
——(1981) *A Theory of Inequality and Taxation* Cambridge: Cambridge University Press
Arrow, Kenneth (1973) 'The theory of discrimination' in Ashenfelter, O and A. Rees (ed.) *Discrimination in Labour Markets* Princeton: Princeton University Press
Association of Superannuation Funds of Australia (1980) *Survey of Superannuation Funds* (issued by the ASFA)
Australian Bureau of Statistics (1987) *Labour Force Australia* November, Catalogue Number 6203.0
——(1987) *Employed Wage and Salary Earners Australia*, June, Catelogue Number 6248.0
——(1987) *Employment Benefits Australia*, August, Catalogue Number 6332.0
——(1986) *Type and Conditions of Part-Time Employment South Australia*, October, Catalogue Number 6203.4
——(1986) Census of population and housing: Small area data (preliminary data)
——(1986) *Employment Benefits Australia*, August, Catalogue Number 6334.0
——(1985–86) *Balance of Payments Australia*, Catalogue Number 5301.6

BIBLIOGRAPHY

——(1982–83) *Census of Superannuation Funds Australia*, Catalogue Number 5636.0
——(1979) *Employment Benefits Australia* February to May, Catalogue No. 6334.0
Australian Council of Trade Unions and the Trade Development Council (1987) *Australia Reconstructed: A Report by the Mission members to the Australia Council of Trade Unions and the Trade Development Council* Melbourne: ACTU/TDC
Australian Council of Trade Unions (1986) *Superannuation and Women* Melbourne: ACTU
Australian Financial Review, 14 May and 16 September 1987
Australian Government (1987/88) *Budget Statements*, Canberra: AGPS
Baldock, Cora V. and Bettina Cass (1983) *Women, Social Welfare and the State* Sydney: Allen & Unwin
Barrett, Michele (1980) *Women's Oppression Today: Problems in Marxist Feminist Analysis* London: Verso
Bascand, G.M., J.P. Cox and M.G. Porter (1985) 'Through the tax reform maze' *Institute of Public Affairs Review* pp. 10–2
Becker, Gary (1973) 'A theory of marriage' *Journal of Political Economy* 81, pp. 813–46
——(1971) *The Economics of Discrimination* Chicago: University of Chicago Press
Beechey, Veronica (1978) 'Women and production: A critical analysis of some sociological theories of women's work' in Annette Kuhn and Ann Marie Wolpe, (eds) *Feminism and Materialism: Women and Modes of Production* London: Routledge and Kegan Paul
——(1977) 'Some notes on female wage labour in capitalist production' *Capital and Class* 3, pp. 45–66
Bennett, Laura (1984) 'Legal intervention and the female workforce: the Conciliation and Arbitration Court 1907–21' *International Journal of the Sociology of Law* 12 (1), February, pp. 23–36
Blackman, Danny (1984) 'Women and the Accord' in *Australian Left Review* 89, Spring, pp. 17–23
Blaug, Mark (1980) *The Methodology of Economics: or How Economists Explain* Cambridge: Cambridge University Press
Boserup, Ester (1970) *Women's Role in Economic Development* New York: St Martin's Press
Botsman, Peter (1987) 'The need for Labor research' *Labor Forum* December, pp. 18–20
Brain, Peter and Barry Gray (1986) 'We've found the J-curve, but does it matter?' *Australian Society* May, pp. 24–6
Brennan, Deborah (1986) 'Rights—At a price' *Australian Society* June, pp. 38–40
Brennan, Theresa (1977) 'Women and work' *Australian Journal of Political Economy* 1, pp. 34–52
Broomhill, Ray (1978) 'The meaning of Fraser's economic strategy' *Journal of Australian Political Economy* 2, pp. 38–45
Brotherhood of St. Laurence (1985) *Tax Reform, Jobs and Justice* (Unpublished submission to E.P.A.C.) January
Brown, Carol (1981) 'Mothers, fathers and children: From private to

public patriarchy' in Sargent, Lydia (ed.) *Women and Revolution* Boston: South End Press

Bryson, Lois (1984) 'The welfare state 1984' in Eastwood Jill, John Reeves and John Ryan (eds) *Labor Essays 1984* Victoria: Drummond

Buechler, Steve (1984) 'Sex and class: A critical overview of some recent theoretical work and some modest proposals' *The Insurgent Sociologist* 12 (3), Summer, pp. 19–32

Burton, Clare (1985) *Subordination: Feminism and Social Theory* Sydney: Allen & Unwin

Business Review Weekly 14 August 1987

Cass, Bettina (1986a) *The Case for Review of Aspects of the Australian Social Security System* Background/Discussion paper No. 1 for the Social Security Review, Canberra: A.G.P.S.

——(1986b) *Income Support for Families with Children* Issues Paper No. 1 for the Social Security Review, Canberra: A.G.P.S.

——(1985) 'The changing face of poverty in Australia: 1972–1982' *Australian Feminist Studies* 1, Summer, pp. 67–90

Chapman, Bruce and Heather Prior, (1986) 'Sex differences in labour turnover in the Australian Public Service' *The Economic Record* December, pp. 497–505

Cockburn, Cynthia (1983) *Brothers: Male Dominance and Technological Change* London: Pluto Press

Cohen, Marjorie (1985) 'The razor's edge invisible: feminism's effect of economics' *International Journal of Women's Studies* May–June, pp. 286–98

Commonwealth Superannuation Board (1973) *Fiftieth Annual Report 1971–72* Canberra: A.G.P.S.

Coote, Anna (1981) 'The AES: A new starting point' *New Socialist* 2

Council of Action for Equal Pay (1984) 'Shame Labor shame' *Scarlet Woman* 19, Spring, pp. 32–3

Cronin, James and Terry Radtke (1987) 'The old and the new politics of taxation: Thatcher and Reagan in historical perspective' in Miliband, Ralph, et al. *The Socialist Register 1987* London: Merlin Press

Curthoys, Ann (1984) 'The women's movement and social justice' in Broom, Dorothy H. (ed.) *Unfinished Business: Social Justice for Women in Australia* Sydney: Allen & Unwin

——(1986) 'The sexual division of labour: Theoretical arguments' in Grieve, Norma and Ailsa Burns (eds) *Australian Women: New Feminist Perspectives* Melbourne: Oxford University Press

Dale, Jennifer and Peggy Foster (1986) *Feminists and State Welfare* London: Routledge and Kegan Paul

Delphy, Christine (1984) 'The main enemy' in *Close to Home: A Materialist Analysis of Women's Oppression* London: Hutchinson

Department of Social Security (1987) *Six-Monthly Statistical Bulletin* Canberra: Department of Social Security, June

Dex, Shirley (1985) *The Sexual Division of Work: Conceptual Revolutions in the Social Sciences* Brighton: Wheatsheaf Books

Dixon, Daryl (1987a) 'Tax shelters—the $6 billion story' *Australian Society* October.

——(1987b) 'How new tax could change the system' *Business Review Weekly* 16 October
Dolan, Edwin and Roy Vogt (1981) *Basic Economics* Toronto: Rineharts and Winson
Donald, Owen (1984) *Government Support of Retirement Incomes in Australia* Research Paper No. 24, Department of Social Security, April
Dowse, Sara (1984) 'The bureaucrat as usurer' in Broom, Dorothy, H (ed.) *Unfinished Business: Social Justice for Women in Australia* Sydney: Allen & Unwin
Draft White Paper (1985) *Reform of the Australian Tax System* Canberra: AGPS
Duhs, Allan and Allan Lougheed 'Family income splitting and Australian tax reform' *Economic Analysis and Policy* 15 (2), September, pp. 190–201
Eccles, Sandra (1984) 'Women in the Australian labour force' in Broom, Dorothy (ed.) *Unfinished Business: Social Justice for Women in Australia* Sydney: Allen & Unwin
Edwards, Meredith (1985) 'Relevance of economic analysis for feminists' *Australian Feminist Studies* 1, Summer, pp. 55–66
——(1984) 'The distribution of income within households' in Broom, Dorothy (ed.) *Unfinished Business: Social Justice for Women in Australia* Sydney: Allen & Unwin
——(1983) *The Income Unit in the Australian Tax and Social Security Systems* (PhD Thesis), A.N.U.
——(1980) 'Social effects of taxation' in Wilkes, John (ed.) *The Politics of Taxation* Sydney: Hodder and Stoughton
Eisenstein, Hester (1985) 'The gender of bureaucracy: Reflections on feminism and the state' in Goodman, Jacqueline and Carole Pateman (eds) *Women, Social Science and Public Policy* Sydney: Allen & Unwin
Eisenstein, Zillah (ed.) (1979) *Capitalist Patriarchy and the Case for Socialist Feminism* New York: Monthly Review Press
Elliot, Anthony (1986) 'The Hawke government and social policy' *Australian Quarterly*, Winter, pp. 134–45
Fell, Liz (1988) 'Tax reform: ACOSS takes the running' *Australian Society* February
Ferguson, Kathy (1984) *The Feminist Case Against Bureaucracy* Philadelphia: Temple University Press
Ford, John (1986) 'Demography and the future cost of pensions' in Mendelsohn, Ronald (ed.) *Finance of Old Age* Canberra: Centre for Research on Federal Financial Relations
Franzway, Suzanne (1986) 'With problems of their own: Femocrats and the welfare state' *Australian Feminist Studies* 3, Summer, pp. 45–57
Freebairn, John, Michael Porter and Cliff Walsh (1987) *Spending and Taxing: Australian Reform Options* Sydney: Allen & Unwin
Fusfeld, Daniel. R (1986) *The Age of the Economist* Illinois: Scott, Foresman and Company

Galbraith, John Kenneth (1973) *Economics and the Public Purpose* London: Andre Deutsch

Game, Ann and Rosemary Pringle (1984) 'Production and consumption: Public versus private' in Broom, Dorothy. H. (ed) *Unfinished Business: Social Justice for Women in Australia* Sydney: Allen & Unwin

Gardiner, Jean and Sheila Smith (1982) 'Feminism and the alternative economic strategy' *Socialist Economic Review 1982* London: Merlin Press

George, Vic and Paul Wilding (1985) *Ideology and Social Welfare* London: Routledge and Kegan Paul

Gilman, Charlotte Perkins (1966) *Women and Economics* New York: Harper and Row

Gough, Ian (1979) *The Political Economy of the Welfare State* London: MacMillan

Grant, Wyn and Nath, Shiv (1984) *The Politics of Economic Policymaking* Oxford: Basil Blackwell

Gregory, R.G. et al. (1986) *A Tale of Two Countries: Equal Pay for Women in Australia and Britain* Canberra: ANU Centre for Economic Policy Research

Groenewegen, Peter (ed.) (1987) *Australian Taxation Policy* (second edition) Melbourne: Longman Cheshire

——(1984) *Public Finance in Australia: Theory and Practice* (second edition) Sydney: Prentice–Hall

Gruen, Fred (1985) 'Australian government policy on retirement incomes' *The Economic Record* September, pp. 613–621

Hall, Phillipa (1983) 'The Accord: What's in it for women' *Scarlet Woman* 17, Spring, p. 17

Hancock, Keith (Chairperson) National Superannuation Committee of Inquiry (1977) *Occupational Superannuation in Australia* Canberra: AGPS

Harding, Ann and Peter Whiteford (1985) *Equity, Tax Reform and Redistribution* Department of Social Security Research, Paper No. 28

Harding, Ann (1984) *Who Benefits? The Australian Welfare State & Redistribution* University of New South Wales Social Welfare Research Centre, April

——(1982) 'Unequal burdens–Personal income tax changes since 1985' *Current Affairs Bulletin* July

Hartmann, Heidi (1981) 'The unhappy marriage of Marxism and feminism: Towards a more progressive union' in Sargent, Lydia (ed.) *Women and Revolution* London: South End Press

Head, John (ed.) (1986) *Changing the Tax Mix* Sydney: Australian Tax Research Foundation

Henderson, Ronald F. (1975) *Poverty in Australia*, 1, Canberra: Australian Government Publishing Service

Hicks, A., R. Friedland and E. Johnson (1978) 'Class, power and state policy' *American Sociological Review*, 43, June

Holmstrom, Nancy (1981) 'Women's work, the family and capitalism' *Science and Society*, 45, pp. 186–211

BIBLIOGRAPHY

Hughes, Barry (1980) *Exit Full Employment* Melbourne: Angus & Robertson

Human Rights Commission (1986) *Inquiry into Superannuation & Insurance & the Sex Discrimination Act 1984* Part 1—Superannuation, Canberra: AGPS

Humphries, Jane (1977) 'The working class family, women's liberation and class struggle: The case of nineteenth century British history' *Review of Radical Political Economics*, 9, pp. 25–41

Indecs Economics, (1986) *State of Play 4: The Australian Economy Up-to-date* Sydney: Allen & Unwin

Indecs Economics (1988) *State of Play 5* Sydney: Allen & Unwin

Ingles, David (1986) 'Dividing up the nest eggs' *Australian Society* March

Jackson, John and Campbell McConnell (1980) *Economics: Australian Edition* Sydney: McGraw Hill

Jackson, Sue (1986) 'According to some' in *Scarlet Woman*, 22, Spring, pp. 10–12

Jones, Glen and Elizabeth Savage (1986) 'Modelling household labour supplies and commodity demands for tax analysis' (Paper presented at the Analytic Economics Workshop) Canberra, ANU, February

Jones, Michael (1983) *The Australian Welfare State* Sydney: Allen & Unwin

Jones, Suzie (1984), 'Mainstreaming women's employment: Women and industry policy' *From Margin to Mainstream: A National Conference about Women and Employment* Melbourne: Ministry & Employment and Training

Kakwani, Nanak (1983) *Redistribution Effects of Income Tax and Cash Benefits in Australia* Centre for Applied Economic Research, Working Paper No. 26, August

Kaluzynska, Eva (1981) 'Wiping the floor with theory—A survey of writings on housework' *Feminist Review*, 6, pp. 27–54

Karl, Marilee (1983) 'Women and rural development: An overview' in ISIS *Women & Development* Geneva: Women's International Information & Communication Service

Karmel, T and M. MacLachlan (1986) *Sex Segregation—Increasing or Decreasing?* Canberra: Bureau of Labour Market Research

Katouzian, Homa (1980) *Ideology & Method in Economics* London: MacMillan

Keens, Carol and Bettina Cass, (1982) *Fiscal Welfare: Some aspects of Australian Tax Policy—Class and Gender Considerations* Social Welfare Research Centre, Report No. 24

Keynes, John Maynard (1936) *The General Theory of Employment Interest and Money* London: MacMillan

Kirby, Peter (1985) *Report of the Committee of Inquiry into Labour Market Programs* Canberra: AGPS

Knox, David (1986) 'Occupational superannuation in Australia: Present and future' in Mendelsohn, Ronald (ed.) *Finance of Old Age* Canberra: Centre for Research on Federal Financial Relations

Kramer, Robin (1983) 'Economic theory and the sexual segregation of the labour market' *Australian Quarterly*, Summer, pp. 388–404

Krever, Rick (1987) 'Super: the upside-down subsidy' *Australian Society* October
Kronemann, Michaela (1981) 'Modern feminist theory' in Grieve, Norma and Patricia Grimshaw (eds) *Australian Women: Feminist Perspectives* Melbourne: Oxford University Press
Kuttner, Robert (1984) *The Economic Illusion* Boston: Houghton-Mifflin
Lamaro, Ana (1985) 'Labor taxes labour: Low income women bear the cost' *Scarlet Woman* 20, Spring, pp. 21–6
Land, Hilary (1975) 'The introduction of family allowances: An act of historic justice?' in Hall, P. et. al. *Change, Choice and Conflict in Social Policy* London: Heinemann
Laurent, Andre (1986) 'The elimination of sex discrimination in occupational social security schemes in the EEC' *International Labour Review*, 125 (6), November–December
Lawrence, Geoffrey (1987) *Capitalism and the Countryside: The Rural Crisis in Australia* Leichhardt NSW: Pluto Press
Leonard Barker, Diana (1978) 'The regulation of marriage: Repressive benevolence' in Littlejohn, G. et. al. *Power and the State* London: Croom Helm
Lewis, D.E. (1985) 'The sources of change in the occupational segregation of Australian women' *Economic Record*, 61, pp. 719–36
Lipsey, Richard (1963) *Introduction to Positive Economics* London: Weidenfield & Nicholson
Lovenduski, Joni (1986) *Women and European Politics: Contemporary Feminism and Public Policy* London: Wheatsheaf
McCallum, John and Sheila Shaver (1986) 'Industry superannuation: A great leap forward?' *Australian Social Welfare Impact* October, pp. 6–8
McClelland, Alison (1987) 'The economics of equity' in Coghill, Ken (ed.) *The New Right's Australian Fantasy* Ringwood: Penguin
McIntosh, Mary (1981) 'Feminism and social policy' *Critical Social Policy*, 1 (1), Summer, pp. 32–42
——(1978) 'The state and the oppression of women' in Kuhn, Annette and Ann Marie Wolpe (eds) *Feminism and Materialism* London: Routledge & Kegan Paul
MacKinnon, Catherine (1983) 'Feminism, Marxism, method and the state: Toward feminist jurisprudence' *Signs* 8
Manning, Ian (1985) *Incomes & Policy* Sydney: Allen & Unwin
Mathews, Russell (1985) 'The mythology of taxation' *Economic Papers*, 4, March
——(1985) *Distributional Equity, Tax Neutrality and Tax Effectiveness: Issues in Tax Reform* (Keynote address at conference on major issues in Australian tax reform, April 30) Sydney: Committee for Economic Development of Australia and the Australian Tax Research Foundation
——(1980) The Structure of Taxation' in Wilkes, John (ed.) *The Politics of Taxation* Sydney: Hodder and Stoughton
Miliband, Ralph (1977) *Marxism and Politics* Oxford: Oxford University Press

——(1969) *The State in Capitalist Society* London: Weidenfeld and Nicholson

Mincer, Jacob and Soloman Polacheck (1974) 'Family investments in human capital: Earnings of women' *Journal of Political Economy*, 82 (2) March/April, pp. S76–S108

Monthly Review (1977) 'Keynesianism: Illusions and delusions' (editorial article) 28 (11) April, pp. 1–9

Moore, Des (1986) *Developments in Commonwealth–State Financial Relations* Canberra: Centre for Research on Federal Financial Relations (Reprint Series 73)

Nolan, David (1986) 'Superannuation from the employers' viewpoint' in Mendelsohn, Ronald (ed) *Finance of Old Age* Canberra: Centre for Research on Federal Financial Relations, ANU

Norman, Neville (1986) 'Superannuation in Australia: An economist's view' in Mendelsohn, Ronald (ed.) *Finance of Old Age* Canberra: Centre for Research on Federal Financial Relations, ANU

O'Donnell, Carol (1984a) *The Basis of the Bargain: Gender, Schooling and Jobs* Sydney: Allen & Unwin

——(1984b) 'Major theories of the labour market and women's place within it' *Journal of Industrial Relations*, June, pp. 147–65

Office of the Status of Women (1985a) *Comparative Quit Rates for Female and Male Employees* Canberra: Department of the Prime Minister and Cabinet

——(1985b) *What Women Think: A Survey of Mothers' Attitudes to the Family Allowance, the Dependent Spouse Rebate and Family Finances* Canberra: Department of the Prime Minister and Cabinet

Owen, Mary (1984) 'Superannuation was not meant for women' *Australian Quarterly*, 56 (4), Summer, pp. 363–73

Pala, Achola (1977) 'Definitions of women and development: An African perspective' *Signs* 3 (1), Autumn

Palmer, Ingrid (1979) 'new official ideas on women and development' *IDS Bulletin* 10 (3) April

Paris, Chris (1987) 'Housing under Hawke: Promise and performance' *Journal of Australian Political Economy* 21, May, pp. 3–24

Peattie, Lisa and Martin Rein (1983) *Women's Claims: A Study in Political Economy* Oxford: Oxford University Press

Peetz, David (1985) *The Accord and Low Income Earners* Canberra: Department of Employment and Industrial Relations, Paper No. 7 (Wages and incomes policy research)

Phelps, Edmund (1972) 'A statistical theory of racism and sexism' *American Economic Review* 62 (4) September

Philips, Anne and Barbara Taylor (1986) 'Sex and skill' Feminist Review (ed.) *Waged Work: A Reader* London: Virago

Phillips, Anne (1987) *Divided Loyalties: Dilemmas of Sex and Class* London: Virago

——(1983) *Hidden Hands: Women and Economic Policies* London: Pluto Press

Piggott, John (1984) 'The distribution of wealth in Australia: A survey' *Economic Record* September

Pocock, Barbara (1988) *Demanding Skill* Sydney: Allen & Unwin

Porter, Michael and G.M. Bascand (1986) 'Taxes and incentives—The leaky bucket' in Head, John (ed.) *Changing the Tax Mix* Sydney: Australian Tax Research Foundation, pp. 355–74

Poulantzas, Nicos (1973) *Political Power and Social Classes* London: New Left Books

Power, Margaret, Sue Outhwaite, Stuart Rosewarne, Joan Templeman and Christine Wallace (1984) 'Writing women out of the economy: Economic theory and its effects' in *From Margin to Mainstream: A National Conference About Women & Employment* Melbourne: Ministry of Employment and Training

Power, Margaret (1980) 'Women and economic crises: The great depression and the present crisis' in Windschuttle, Elizabeth (ed.) *Women, Class and History* Melbourne: Fontana

——(1974) 'The wages of sex' *Australian Quarterly* 46, pp. 2 –14

——(1975) 'Women's work is never done by men: a socio-economic model of sex typing in occupations' *Journal of Industrial Relations* September 17 (3), pp. 225–39

Power, Marilyn (1983) 'From home production to wage labour: Women as a reserve army of labor' *Review of Radical Political Economics*, 15 (1), pp. 71–91

Prendergast, Helen (1986) 'The 'other' workers: Women and work in Australia over the past 20 years' *Lilith: A Feminist History Journal*, 3, Winter, pp. 4–25

Randall, Vicki (1982) *Women and Politics* London: MacMillan

Raskall, Phil (1987) 'Wealth: who's got it? Who needs it?' *Australian Society*, May, pp. 21–4

——(1986) 'Wealth: Who's got it? Who needs it?' *Australian Society*, March, pp. 12–5

——(1978) 'Who's got what in Australia: The distribution of wealth' *Journal of Australian Political Economy*, 2, pp. 3–16

Robinson, Joan (1962) *Economic Philosophy* Harmondsworth: Penguin

Roe, Jill (1976) *Social Policy in Australia* Melbourne: Cassell Australia

Rogers, Barbara (1980) *The Domestication of Women: Discrimination in Developing Societies* London: Tavistock

Rose, Hilary (1978) 'In practice supported, in theory denied' *International Journal of Urban and Regional Research*, 2 (3), pp. 521–37

Rosenman, Linda and Marilyn Leeds (1986) *Women & the Australian Retirement Age Income System* Sydney: Social Welfare Research Centre, University of New South Wales

Rosenman, Linda (1986) 'Women and retirement age income security' in Mendelsohn, R. (ed). *Finance of Old Age* Canberra: Centre for Research on Federal Financial Relations, ANU

Rossiter, Chris, Joan Vipond and Neil Warren (1985) 'Housing costs in relation to incomes: How women are affected' (Unpublished paper) Adelaide: Women's Housing Action Conference 1–3 March

Rowbotham, Sheila (1973) *Woman's Consciousness, Man's World* Harmondsworth: Penguin

Rubery, Jill (1980) 'Structured labour markets, worker organisation and low pay' in Amsden, Alice (ed.) *The Economics of Women and Work* Harmondsworth: Penguin

Ryan, Edna and Anne Conlon (1975) *Gentle Invaders: Australian Women at Work 1788–1974* Melbourne: Nelson

Sawer, Marian (ed.) (1982) *Australia and the New Right* Sydney: Allen & Unwin

Saunders, Peter and Peter Whiteford (1987) 'Pricing the poverty pledge' in *Australian Society* September: pp. 22–4

Savage, Elizabeth (1987) 'The tax debate—Catchcries don't tell the story' *Australian Social Welfare Impact* April, pp. 6–8

——(1985) 'Tax reform and the end of the 1980's' *Labor Forum*, 7 (2), June, pp. 5–9

——(1984) 'Discrimination and public policy: The role of traditional economic theory' Canberra: Keynote address to Inter–Section symposium: Women and Economics 54th ANZAAS Congress, ANU, May 14–16

Sawhill, Isabel (1980) 'Economic perspectives on the family' in Amsden, Alice (ed.) *The Economics of Women and Work* Harmondsworth: Penguin

Schultz, Theodore, (1974) *Economics of the Family: Marriage, Children & Human Capital* Chicago: University of Chicago

Scott, Hilda (1984) *Working Your Way to the Bottom: The Feminization of Poverty* London: Pandora Press

Sharp, Rhonda (1987) 'Perils for part-timers' *Australian Society*, November, pp. 37–8

——(1985) 'Women and the South Australian Superannuation Fund', Submission by the Women's Adviser's Office, Department to the Premier & Cabinet to the Committee of Inquiry into South Australian Public Sector Superannuation

Shaver, Sheila (1983) 'Sex and money in the welfare state' in Baldock, V. Cora and Bettina Cass (eds) *Women, Social Welfare and the State* Sydney: Allen & Unwin

Short, Christine (1986) 'Equal pay—what happened?' *Journal of Industrial Relations* 28 (3), September, pp. 315–33

Simms, Marian (1981) 'The Australian feminist experience' in Grieve, Norma and Patricia Grimshaw (eds) *Australian Women: Feminist Perspectives* Melbourne: Oxford University Press

Smith, David (1987) *The Rise and Fall of Monetarism: The Theory and Politics of an Economic Experiment* Harmondsworth: Penguin

Statement by the Treasurer, The Hon. Paul Keating (1985) *Reform of the Australian Taxation System* Canberra: AGPS

Stigler, G.G. and Gary Becker (1977) 'De Gustibus Non Est Disputandum' *American Economic Review* 67 (2)

Stilwell, Frank (1986) *The Accord and Beyond: The Political Economy of the Labor Government* Leichhardt N.S.W: Pluto Press

Summers, Anne (1986) 'Mandarins or missionaries: Women in the federal bureaucracy' in Grieve, Norma and Ailsa Burns (eds) *Australian Women: New Feminist Perspectives* Melbourne: Oxford University Press

Tamburi, Giovanni and Pierre Mouton (1986) 'The uncertain frontier between private and public pension schemes' *International Labour Review*, 125 (2), March–April, pp. 127–40

Taxation Institute (1979) *Taxation & the Family Unit* (Report of Proceedings of a Public Seminar) Sydney: Taxation Institute Research and Education Trust

Taylor, Debbie (1985) 'Women: An analysis' in New Internationalist, *Women: A World Report* London: Methuen

Times on Sunday 14 June and 1 November 1987

Titmuss, Richard (1958) 'The social division of welfare: Some reflections on the search for equity' *Essays on the Welfare State* London: Allen & Unwin

Vipond, Joan (1986) 'The changing face of poverty' *Australian Society* February, pp. 19–21

Wajcman, Judy and Stuart Rosewarne (1986) 'The 'feminisation' of work' in *Australian Society* September, pp. 15–7

Warren, Neil (1979) 'Australian tax incidence in 1975–76: Some preliminary result's *Australian Economic Review* Third quarter

Weaven, Gary (1986) 'Superannuation: The great leap forward' in Mendelsohn, Ronald (ed.) *Finance of Old Age* Canberra: ANU

Wettenhall, Gib (1987) 'Housing: What happened to the great Australian dream?' *Australian Society* August, pp. 25–40

Whitwell, Greg (1986) *The Treasury Line* Sydney: Allen & Unwin

Wilkes, John (ed.) (1980) *The Politics of Taxation* Sydney: Hodder & Stoughton

Williams, Ross (1983) 'Ownership of wealth and personal dwellings in Australia' *Australian Economic Review* June

Wilson, Elizabeth (1977) *Women and the Welfare State* London: Tavistock

Windsor, Kim (1987) 'Who's being flexible' *Australian Society* February, pp. 20 and 46

Women's Budget Program (1986/87) *An Assessment of the Impact on Women of the 1986–87 Budget* Canberra: AGPS, August

Women's Budget Statement (1987–88) *An Assessment of the Impact on Women of the 1987–88 Budget* Canberra: AGPS, September

Women's Bureau (1987) *Women at Work* Canberra: Department of Employment and Industrial Relations

——(1984) *Women and Labour Market Programs*, (Submission to the Committee of Inquiry into Labour Market Programs) Canberra: Department of Employment & Industrial Relations

Women's Electoral Lobby (1985) *Women & Tax Reform* (Submission to EPAC)

Yanz, Lynda and David Smith (1983) 'Women as a reserve army of labour: A critique' *Review of Radical Political Economics* 15 (1), pp. 92–106

Zaretsky, Eli (1976) *Capitalism, the Family and Personal Life* London: Pluto Press

Subject Index

advertising, 6
alternative economic strategies, x, 32, 95, 165, 166–9
Australia Reconstructed, 88, 166
Australian Council of Social Service (ACOSS), 151
Australian Council of Trade Unions, 64, 74, 80, 88, 133, 152–3
Australian Financial Review, 69, 71

balance of payments, 64, 65, 71, 88–90, 91
Bjelke-Petersen, Sir Joh, 114
budget deficit, 65, 66, 68, 69, 77, 106, 109, 152
business (capital), 13, 24, 28, 29, 48, 54, 55, 64–5, 66, 70–1, 90–1, 92, 94–5, 101, 120, 128
  investment, 65, 66, 70, 90–1, 106, 152–3, 158
  profits, 34, 65, 66, 90, 92, 101, 106, 121
  taxation, 101, 104, 105, 106, 108, 113, 120, 122, 128
Business Review Weekly, xi, 102
Button, Senator John, 92

capital accumulation, 13, 17, 48, 70, 106, 150, 152, 158
capitalism, 4, 7, 9, 10–11, 13, 14, 15, 21, 27, 28–9, 34, 35, 39–40, 41, 42–3, 47, 48, 54, 55, 57, 61, 63, 95, 105–6, 144, 148, 149, 162, 166, 168–9
Centre of Policy Studies, 114
childcare, xiv, 3, 10, 22, 36, 51, 62, 68, 73, 82, 86–7, 97, 98, 99, 112, 120, 130, 157, 163, 165
class, 8, 9, 11, 19, 37, 41, 43, 46, 53, 54, 78, 95, 99, 145, 148, 149, 162, 164, 165, 166, 169
  bourgeoisie (capitalist), 12–13, 26, 28, 29, 30, 56, 74
  conflict, 14, 24, 30, 64
  feudal aristocracy, 12
  'middle', xv, 79, 148
  and women, xiv–xv, 26–7, 46, 53, 98, 99, 163, 169
  working, 10, 19, 23, 28, 73, 163
clothing industry, 56, 92–3
Commonwealth–State Housing Agreement, 79
Community Employment Program, 47, 69, 85
comparable worth, 73
Confederation of Australian Industry, 155
consumption, 48

debt, 90, 91–3
deskilling, 22, 23
devaluation, 65, 88–90, 91–3
divorce, xv, 52, 126, 130
domestic labour, xiv, 13, 16, 21, 23, 25, 36, 43, 45, 47–51, 124, 135, 148, 156
domestic labour debate, the, 13, 16–17

economic efficiency, 37, 40–1, 43–4, 115, 120, 122, 123–4
economic equity, 43–4, 66, 80, 82, 86, 114, 122, 123, 124–6, 154
economic growth, 34, 38, 62, 63, 67, 68
  private-sector led, 64–5, 69
  public-sector led, 66–7, 68, 69, 71, 73
economic recovery, 55, 62, 63, 65, 66

189

economic redistribution, 25–6, 35, 53, 55, 66, 70, 71, 72, 73, 76, 80, 96, 98–9, 101–4, 106, 113, 119, 122, 125, 126, 127, 128, 163, 165
economic restructuring, 66, 74, 87–8, 92–3, 105–6
economics,
 assumptions, 31, 34, 37, 39–41, 49, 51–3, 70, 98, 114, 115, 122–3, 126, 137, 141, 148, 165, 166
 and class bias, 37, 54, 94–5, 148, 161, 164
 conservative nature of, ix, 31, 44, 53–7, 61, 94, 163–5
 'crowding out' theory, 70
 expansionist school, 55, 63–4
 feminist critiques, 36–8, 39–53
 gender blindness, x, 33, 45–6
 gender neutrality, x, 31, 33, 46, 53, 114, 122, 123, 127, 165
 human capital theory, 49–50, 86
 as ideology of capitalism, 39–41, 48, 55, 69–70, 164
 Keynesianism, 33, 34–5, 40, 41, 54, 55, 61, 64
 mainstream, 31–2, 33–6, 38, 39–53, 57, 70, 94, 122, 124, 126, 127, 129, 148, 163, 164–5
 methodology, 33, 34, 35, 39, 41–7, 49, 100, 111, 164
 neo-classical, 33, 34–5, 39–53, 57, 127, 161, 163
 neo-liberal, 33–4, 35, 53–7, 61, 64, 68, 94, 112, 126, 150, 165
 New Right, 31–2, 53–7, 61, 104, 110–11, 112–15, 116, 122, 124, 150, 165
 patriarchal bias, 41, 51–3, 126
 'positive', 44
 progressive role for women, 33, 35, 38, 95, 127–9, 164
 public finance school, 125
 public/private split, 47–51, 53, 148, 165
restrictionist school, 63–4
theory of state's role, 34–5, 41, 43
and women's subordination, ix, 31–2, 33, 35, 36–7, 38, 39, 41, 43, 44–5, 46, 47, 51–3, 164
education, 14, 18, 22, 50, 51, 70, 73
employment,
 apprenticeships, 47, 86
 casual, xiii, 46, 55, 83, 155, 156
 discrimination, 5, 47
 growth, 65, 82, 91
 health and safety, 93
 job creation, 47, 85
 legislative reforms, 84–5
 male/female work patterns, xii–xiv, 46–53, 137, 139–42, 148, 156
 occupational welfare, 26, 131
 outworkers, xiii, 56, 74, 156
 part-time, xiii, 46, 54, 73–4, 83, 133, 134, 135, 136, 138, 156
 private sector, 83, 133
 protective legislation, 21, 24
 public sector, 61, 68, 75, 83, 88, 133
 training, 47, 50, 51, 73, 85–6, 97, 163
 wages, xii, 21, 23, 25, 36, 49–50, 54–5, 56, 61, 64, 65, 71–2, 73–4, 91
 working conditions, xii, 21, 55, 56, 83, 130
equal opportunities, 3, 5, 73, 84–5, 168
equal pay, xii, 10, 23, 73, 74, 157, 167
equality,
 as a goal, ix, xv, 35, 36, 41, 45, 61, 66, 80, 81, 82, 86, 95, 113, 122, 126, 155, 157–8, 163, 164, 167–8, 169

family, the, xv
 and capitalism, 13, 16, 17–18, 106

SUBJECT INDEX

economic analysis of, 49
economic inadequacies, 17–18
income distribution within, xii–xiv, 52–3, 98, 116, 125–6
and New Right, 15, 57
and patriarchy, 14, 15, 16, 23, 29, 149
and poverty, xii, 52
and the state, 15–20
women's economic role in, xiii–xiv, 16, 36, 43, 46, 47–51, 96, 104, 116, 163, 165
and women's subordination, xiii–xiv, 8, 10, 15–17, 23, 36, 46, 47–53
family allowances, xiv, 53, 62, 69, 80–1, 114, 120
family wage, 21, 23, 31
feminist economic strategies, 3–6, 7, 8, 10, 24–32, 35–6, 45, 57, 94–5, 96, 127–9, 155–8, 161–9
feminist economists, 6, 33, 36–8, 42, 48, 122–7
femocrats, 6, 11, 168
feudalism, 12, 29
'fight inflation first' strategy, 54, 63
finance industry, 64, 79
financial deregulation, 56, 64, 66, 79
First Home Owners Scheme, 78–9
fiscal welfare, 26, 37, 106, 107–8, 119, 121, 128
Fraser government (1975–1983), 54, 55, 61, 63–4, 73, 76–7, 85, 86, 150
Friedman, Milton, 35
full employment, as a goal, 40, 54, 64, 82, 166
functionalism, 4, 9, 13, 16, 20, 24, 25, 28–31, 162

government economic policy, alternative economic policies, x, 32, 95, 165, 166–9
budgetary (fiscal), 25, 26, 27, 34, 50–1, 63, 65, 66–71, 75, 77, 80, 92, 96–7, 163, 166–7
and class bias, 54–5, 78, 95, 148
education, 51, 70, 72, 76, 97
expansionist, 55, 63–4, 65, 67, 68, 70, 71, 75, 97, 166–7
health, 26, 54, 68, 75, 76, 96–7
housing, 26, 54, 63, 70, 76, 78–80, 97
interventionist, x, 26, 34, 35, 41, 43–4, 46, 54, 61, 63, 64, 66, 71, 72, 87, 89, 92–3, 96, 113, 126, 144, 148, 150, 162, 166–7
labour market, 25, 47, 50, 61, 62, 63, 73–4, 82–7, 94, 99, 110–11, 125–6, 128, 166–7
macroeconomic, x, 26, 62–6, 68, 70, 79, 83, 88, 91, 94, 163, 165
monetary, 25, 34, 64, 79
non-interventionist, 26, 35, 41, 43–4, 54, 83, 87, 91, 92, 126
prices, 64, 71–2, 73, 166
restrictionist, 63–4, 65, 70–1, 75, 76, 77, 80, 92, 151
social wage, 54, 55, 56, 72, 73, 75–82, 114, 150, 166–7
superannuation, x, 26, 51, 130–58, 162
taxation, x, 20–1, 25, 26, 27, 31, 36–7, 51, 52, 53, 56, 62, 64, 67, 68, 72, 73, 77, 96–129, 130, 150–1, 152, 162, 163, 165, 166–7, 168
trade and industry, 10, 63, 66, 71–2, 87–95, 166–7
wages, 54, 55, 63, 64, 67, 71–5, 130, 149, 152–5, 165
welfare, 20–1, 25, 26, 27, 31, 52, 54, 56, 62, 63, 67, 68, 70, 72, 75, 76, 80–2, 94, 150, 163, 167, 168
Great Depression, 34
Gross Domestic Product, 67, 68, 90, 105
Gross National Product (US), 48

Hawke, Bob, 68, 69
Hawke Labor government, 47, 53, 55–6, 61–95, 112, 115–22, 130, 149–55, 158, 162
Hayden, Bill, 69
Hayek, Friedrich von, 35
Howe, Brian, 82

ideology, 55, 56, 61
 of capitalism, 13, 14, 17, 39–41, 42–3
 economics as an, 39–41, 48, 55, 69–70, 126, 150, 164–5
 of patriarchy, 15, 19, 22, 28–9, 31
income distribution, x–xi, xiv, 25, 26, 38, 41, 100, 153, 165, 168
 in the family, xiii–xiv, 52–3, 98
individualism, 10, 32, 35, 42–3, 57
industrial democracy, 158, 166
Industry Equity Ltd (IEL), 101
inflation, 35, 54, 55, 63, 64, 69, 73, 106, 110, 140, 150, 153
interest rates, 26, 79, 88, 91–3

J-curve, the, 89
JOBSTART, 85

Keating, Paul, 69, 87, 89, 116, 122
Keynes, John Maynard, 34, 41, 164

labour market,
 deregulation, 56
 government economic policy, 25, 47, 50–1, 62–3, 82–7, 99, 110–11, 125–6, 128
 sex segmentation, xii–xiii, 10, 20–1, 37, 83, 85–6, 88, 132, 135–6, 157
 women's participation rates, xii–xiii, 22, 85, 130, 132
 women's position, 37, 45, 46, 49–50, 55, 56, 87, 131
legislative reform,
 affirmative action (AA), 62, 84–5

equal opportunities (EEO), 84–5
 sex discrimination, 62, 84–5, 156
liberal feminists, 5–7, 10, 14, 17, 19–20, 32, 162
liberalism, 39–40
logical positivism, 44

male domination, 8–9, 23, 31, 128, 148, 156
manufacturing industry, 73, 88–9, 90–1, 92–3
market (capitalist), 34, 35, 40–1, 42, 43–4, 47–9, 56–7, 61, 63, 64, 66, 79, 87, 89, 94, 95, 113, 126, 162, 164
 ideology of the, 40, 69–70, 164
 international money, 66, 70
Marx, Karl, 12, 39, 40
Marxism, 4, 12–14, 16
Medicare, 76, 119

National Agenda for Women, 94
National Tax Summit (1985), 115
neo-Marxism, 12–15
New Right,
 economics of, 31–2, 53–7
 and the family, 15, 57
 and Hawke government, 55–6, 61, 150
 moral conservatism, 56–7
 and superannuation, 150
 taxation policies, 56, 104, 110–11, 112–15, 116, 122, 124

Office of the Status of Women, 53
Organisation for Economic Cooperation and Development (OECD), 102, 103, 105, 154

patriarchy, 4, 7, 8, 9, 10–11, 15, 18, 22–4, 27, 28–9, 30, 31, 32, 41, 73, 106, 148, 149, 162, 168
pluralism, 4, 6–7, 19
political parties, 3, 55
 Australian Democrats, 6

SUBJECT INDEX

Australian Labor Party, 6, 11, 64, 69, 80
Liberal Party, 6, 114
National Party, 114
poverty, xi–xii, 38, 41, 46, 52, 53, 76, 78–9, 81, 82, 99, 102, 112, 130, 152, 153
Prices and Incomes Accord, the, 64, 71–5, 77, 80, 88, 92, 152–3, 166
privatisation, 56

race, 8, 9, 41
 aboriginal women, 55
 migrant women, 55
radical feminists, 3, 7, 8–9, 14, 15, 18, 32, 162
rape crisis centres, 3
Razor gang, 77
Reagan, Ronald, 53–4, 113
recession, 50, 55, 61, 70–2, 76, 83, 90, 105–6, 107, 109, 113
'restraint with equity', 80

separatism, 10
sexism, 23, 24
sexual discrimination, 5, 37, 41, 42, 47, 99, 115, 119, 126, 134–5, 139, 140, 141, 142–3, 144–6, 147–8, 155, 157
 institutional, 42, 43
sexual division of labour,
 home, xiii–xiv, 8, 10, 15–17, 23, 36, 37, 43, 46, 47–51, 96, 97, 163
 paid workforce, xii–xiii, 10, 20–1, 23–4, 37, 38, 46, 49–50, 135–6, 167
sexual inequalities,
 assumptions about, x
 in capitalist society, 8, 33, 39, 40–1, 47, 65, 66, 95, 100, 101, 127, 128–9, 149, 161, 162, 164, 165, 168–9
 in the home, xiii–xiv, 8, 10, 15–17, 23, 36, 46, 47–53, 98–9, 115, 116, 120, 125–6, 135, 163

 in the labour market, xii–xiii, 10, 14, 20, 21, 23, 26, 42, 46, 47, 49–50, 62, 73–4, 85–6, 93, 131, 132, 152–4, 157, 162, 167
sexual stereotyping, 6
skill, 23, 37, 47, 86–8, 93, 167
Smith, Adam, 33, 35
Social Security Review, 81
social reproduction (of capitalist system), 14, 17–18, 22, 24, 106, 148, 149
Social Welfare Research Centre, 81
socialism, xv, 11, 169
socialist feminists, 6, 7, 9–12, 13, 14, 15–32, 162
 dual labour theory, 22
 dual systems theory, 18
 partnership between partriarchy and capitalism, the, 10–11, 18–19, 23, 24
 reserve army of labour, 20–2, 24
stagflation, 35
state, the
 arbitration system, 3, 14, 21, 71–2, 73, 74, 131, 152–4
 an an arena of conflict, 11, 19, 29–30, 94–5, 162
 bureaucracy, 3, 6, 7, 8, 11, 30–1, 94, 168
 and capitalism, 4, 7, 8, 10–11, 12, 13, 14, 15, 17, 18, 19, 21, 22, 24, 25, 27, 28–9, 74, 94–5, 105–6, 168
 contradictions and complexities in role, 11, 19, 22, 27, 74, 162
 and education, 14, 18
 and the family, 15–20
 feminist theories of, 3–32, 161–3
 fiscal crisis of, 56, 61, 105–7, 112, 150
 male domination of, 31
 origins of capitalist, 12–13
 and patriarchy, 4, 5, 7, 8, 10–

193

11, 15, 18, 22–4, 26, 27, 28–9, 31, 32, 148, 162, 168
progressive role for women, ix, 4, 10–11, 14, 16, 18–19, 25, 27, 28, 30–1, 32, 43, 47, 55, 61, 94–5, 97, 127–9, 161–3, 166–9
relative autonomy of, 28
role, ix, 4, 7, 13, 17, 34–5, 41, 43–4, 54, 56, 95, 97, 105–6, 126, 127, 131, 144–9, 150
and welfare, 15–20, 81
and women's paid work, 20–4, 25, 47, 50–1, 62–3, 73–4, 82–7, 94, 99, 110–11, 126
and women's subordination, ix, 4, 8, 9, 10, 14, 15, 17, 18, 19, 21, 25, 26, 27, 30, 32, 55, 61, 81, 97, 99, 125–6, 161–2
Stone, John, 54, 114
superannuation, x, xii–xiii, 26, 51, 52, 108, 119
and actuarial data, 142–3, 156
annuities, 142, 156
benefits, 131, 132, 137
discriminatory nature, 134–5, 137–43, 144–6, 148, 149, 155, 157
federal government scheme, 135, 140, 144–5
and government retirement incomes policy, 139, 149, 150–2, 155, 157
history, 144–7
lump sum payments, 142–3
and male/female work patterns, xii–xiv, 46–53, 137, 139–42, 148, 156
maternity leave, 138, 140–2, 155, 156
national superannuation scheme, 144, 157–8
and occupational welfare, 131
participation rates, 132–3, 135
and part-time work, 133, 134, 135, 136, 138
portability, 139, 140, 152–3, 154–5, 156

preservation, 138–9, 140, 152–3, 154–5, 156
relationship to aged pension, 131, 136, 137, 144, 146, 147, 149, 150
and role of the state, 131, 144–9
spouse benefits, 132, 142–3, 146, 156
state government schemes, 135, 144–5, 146
and taxation concessions, 130, 131, 143, 147, 148, 151, 152, 157
and trade unions, 130, 131, 147, 148, 154, 157–8
vesting, 138, 139–40, 152–3, 154–5, 156

taxation, x, 20–1, 25, 26, 27, 31, 36–7, 51, 52, 53, 56, 62, 64, 67, 68, 72, 73, 77, 96–129, 130, 131, 143, 147, 148, 150, 151, 152
average rate of, 110–11, 115
avoidance, 101, 107–8, 109, 118–19, 120–1, 122, 128
capital gains, 107, 118, 121, 128
company, 97, 101, 104, 105, 106, 108, 113, 120, 122, 128
concessions, 97, 98, 128
consumption, 104, 113, 114, 116
dependent spouse rebate, 22, 27, 31, 51, 52, 98–9, 108, 112, 119, 120, 124
effective marginal rates of, 99, 110–12, 120
evasion, 101, 107–8, 109, 118–19, 122, 128
federal government, 100, 104–5
flat rate proposals, 104, 113, 114–15, 124
fringe benefits tax, 118, 121
on goods and services, 97, 100, 102–4
income splitting (joint husband and wife), 98, 113, 124, 126
indirect, 97, 104
marginal rates of, 99, 101, 103,

107, 110–11, 116–17, 122, 127
New Right proposals, 56, 104, 110–11, 112–15, 116, 122, 124
on non PAYE incomes, 97, 101, 108, 121, 122, 128
Pay As You Earn (PAYE), 97, 100, 102–4, 109–12, 122, 128
personal income, 97, 100, 102–4, 106, 108, 109–12, 113, 116–17
and poverty traps, 111–12, 119
progressive, 98, 99, 100–2, 103–4, 105, 113, 118, 119, 128
regressive, 98, 100–2, 104, 108, 114–15, 128
state government, 104–5
wealth, 97, 99, 101–2, 126, 128
terms of trade, 65
Thatcher, Margaret, 53, 113
trade unions,
and the Accord, 71–2
male domination, 23, 72–3, 75, 168
New Right attack on, 56
progressive role for women, 30, 75, 93, 95, 105, 163, 168–9
and superannuation, 130, 131, 147, 154, 157–8
women's role in, 3, 11, 73, 75, 93, 105, 154, 163, 168–9
transnational corporations, 90
Treasury (Federal), 54, 61, 70, 114
'trickle-down' theory,
assumptions of, 38, 40, 50, 114
strategy, 63–5, 79, 83, 114
Trilogy, the, 68

unemployment, xii, xiii, 37, 46, 47, 54, 55, 63, 76, 82, 85–6, 106, 126, 134
hidden, xiii, 35, 50, 82
United Kingdom, 53–4, 56, 61, 166
United States, 48, 52–4, 56, 61

Vietnam War, 141

wage indexation, 67, 72, 73, 153, 154
Walsh, Senator Peter, 87
wealth distribution, x–xii, 100, 101–2, 128, 165
welfare state, 14, 15–20, 56, 81, 106, 127, 167
Whitlam government (1972–1975), 61, 76, 150
Women's Budget, 62–3, 75
women's dependency, xiii–xiv, 8, 10, 15–17, 23, 36, 46, 47–53, 55, 96, 99, 120, 128–9, 141–2, 143, 146, 157, 162
women's movement,
attacks on Hawke government, 62, 72–3, 80
involvement with the state, 3, 30
liberal feminists in, 5–6
liberal perspective of, 6
radical feminsts in, 8
socialist feminists in, 10–11
and superannuation debates, 130, 148
and the tax debate, 36–7, 96, 105, 115, 119, 127
women's shelters, 3

Author Index

Aarons, Laurie 101
Albon, Robert 147
Amsden, Alice 33, 41, 43
Anand, Anita 38
Apps, Patricia 33, 37, 111, 114, 115, 122, 124, 126
Arrow, Kenneth 42

Baldock, Cora 4
Barker, Diana Leonard 8
Barrett, Michele 4, 9, 11, 16, 20, 21, 23, 24, 28, 31, 170
Bascand, G.M. 111
Becker, Gary 42, 49
Beechey, Veronica 19, 20, 171
Blackman, Danny 62, 72, 73
Blaug, Mark 43, 44, 172
Boserup, Ester 38
Botsman, Peter 56
Brain, Peter 88
Brennan, Deborah 62, 87
Brennan, Theresa 37
Broomhill, Ray 54
Brown, Carol 18, 19
Bryson, Lois xiv, 17, 19, 37
Buechler, Steve 16, 22
Burton, Clare 11, 24

Cass, Bettina xi, xii
Chapman, Bruce 176
Cockburn, Cynthia 37
Cohen, Marjorie 49
Cronin, James 113
Curthoys, Ann 8, 27

Dale, Jennifer 7, 24
Delphy, Christine 8
Dex, Shirley 37
Dixson, Daryl 119, 151, 175
Dolan, Edwin 48

Donald, Owen 151
Dowse, Sara 6, 8, 24, 28, 31, 161, 171
Duhs, Allan 126

Eccles, Sandra xii, 37
Edwards, Meredith xii, xiv, 33, 37, 52, 53, 98, 122, 124, 125
Eisenstein, Zillah 18
Elliot, Anthony 80

Fell, Liz 121
Ferguson, Kathy 7, 8
Ford, John 150
Franzway, Suzanne 4, 6, 24, 30, 31
Freebairn, John 110
Fusfeld, Daniel 39, 54, 172

Galbraith, John 48, 49, 57
Game, Ann xiv
George, Vic 126
Gilman, Charlotte Perkins 36
Gough, Ian 171
Grant, Wyn 171
Groenewegen, Peter 174
Gruen, Fred 155

Hall, Phillipa 62, 72, 88
Harding, Ann 37, 100, 110, 112, 116, 127
Hartmann, Heidi 11, 18, 21, 23
Henderson, Ronald 52
Hicks, A. 19
Holmstrom, Nancy 22
Hughes, Barry 54
Humphries, Jane 23

Indecs Economics 64, 70, 103, 105

AUTHOR INDEX

Ingles, David   153

Jackson, John   45
Jackson, Sue   62
Jones, Glenn   37, 111, 124
Jones, Michael   146
Jones, Suzie   93

Kakwani, Nanak   127
Karl, Marilee   38
Karmel, T.   173
Katouzian, Homa   44, 172
Keens, Carol   26, 37, 108
Keynes, John Maynard   164
Kirby, Peter   106
Knox, David   144
Kramer, Robin   37
Krever, Rick   147
Kronemann, Michaela   9
Kuttner, Robert   113

Lamaro, Ana   62
Land, Hilary   19
Laurent, André   142
Lawrence, Geoffrey   42, 43
Lewis, D.E.   173
Lipsey, Richard   49
Lovenduski, Joni   30, 85

MaCallum, John   134, 145, 146
McClelland, Alison   43, 172
McIntosh, Mary   10, 14, 16, 17, 18, 21, 29, 171
MacKinnon, Catherine   4, 8
Mathews, Russell   101, 104, 110, 175
Miliband, Ralph   7, 13, 127, 171
Mincer, Jacob   49, 50
Moore, Des   104

Nolan, David   155
Norman, Neville   137

O'Connor, James   106
O'Donnell, Carol   37
Owen, Mary   142

Pala, Achola   38

Palmer, Ingrid   38
Paris, Chris   79
Peattie, Lisa   48
Peetz, David   79
Phelps, Edmund   42
Phillips, Anne   9, 33, 37, 46, 166, 167
Piggott, John   xi, 102
Pocock, Barbara   37
Poulantzas, Nicos   171
Power, Margaret   33, 37, 38, 50, 55, 62, 72, 86, 88, 164
Power, Marilyn   10, 22
Prendergast, Helen   73

Randall, Vicki   4, 8, 11, 30, 105
Raskall, Phil   xi, 102, 175
Robinson, Joan   40, 44
Rogers, Barbara   38
Rose, Hilary   19
Rosenman, Linda   134, 136, 143, 157
Rossiter, Chris   78
Rowbotham, Sheila   29
Rubery, Jill   37

Saunders, Peter   81
Savage, Elizabeth   33, 62, 112, 120, 122, 124, 126, 174
Sawer, Marian   171
Sawhill, Isabel   42, 49, 50
Schultz, Theodore   49
Scott, Hilda   xv
Sharp, Rhonda   xii, 83, 141
Shaver, Sheila   19, 127, 174
Short, Christine   37, 74
Simms, Marian   9, 10
Smith, David   171
Stigler, G.   42
Stilwell, Frank   68, 70, 72, 80, 89, 166
Summers, Anne   31

Tamburi, Giovanni   144, 154
Taylor, Debbie   38
Titmuss, Richard   26

Vipond, Joan   78

Wajcman, Judy 82
Warren, Neil 100
Weaven, Gary 153
Wettenhall, Gib 173
Whitwell, Greg 54, 171

Williams, Ross xi
Wilson, Elizabeth 7, 10, 16, 17

Yanz, Lynda 22